W9-AFH-316

Anthropology of Contemporary Issues

A SERIES EDITED BY

ROGER SANJEK

Children of Circumstances

ISRAELI EMIGRANTS IN NEW YORK

Moshe Shokeid

Cornell University Press

Ithaca and London

First published 1988 by Cornell University Press.

International Standard Book Number (cloth) 0-8014-2078-4
International Standard Book Number (paper) 0-8014-9489-3
Library of Congress Catalog Card Number 87-23934
Printed in the United States of America
Librarians: Library of Congress cataloging information
appears on the last page of the book.

The paper in this book is acid-free and meets the guidelines for
permanence and durability of the Committee on Production Guidelines
for Book Longevity of the Council on Library Resources.

To Ora, Nadav, and Noam

Contents

Patriots and expatriates are alike—the children of circumstances.
Quarterly Review, 1818

Preface

The creation of the state of Israel in 1948 was the culmination of the force and achievements of the Zionist movement, a movement that had set out to replace both the traditional Orthodox messianic beliefs and the unfulfilled hopes that the European and Jewish Enlightenment nurtured for the integration of Jews into their host societies. Furthermore, the creation of Israel served as a tremendous consolation in the wake of the holocaust, the worst calamity in Jewish history. The return of the Jewish exiles to Zion, the revival of the Hebrew language, the establishment of a modern state, and the recurring battles between the Israelis and their Arab neighbors are undoubtedly among the most fascinating events in modern history.

How then has it happened that only a few decades after the establishment of the state, a growing number of young Israelis have chosen to return to the Jewish Diaspora? Israel cannot be compared to most other countries whose citizens have flocked to America ever since the crossing of the *Mayflower*. Its citizens enjoy political freedom and many social services, the standard of living is relatively high, and its institutions of higher education are among the best in the world. Why do people leave Israel, a country that has made real the dreams of so many generations and that has provided them with political freedom, professional skills, social security, and considerable affluence? Do the migrant Israelis manifest a characteristic of a nation of people who have become conditioned to a minority position? Do they reflect the fate of political and social ideologies that, having reached their goals, reveal their shortcomings? Or is this a manifestation of the impact of American economy and culture, which attracts not only the desperate but also the prosperous and enterprising who, rather than remain on a provincial stage, prefer to join the major theater?

Israeli emigrants carry a revealing message about our era, which has witnessed tempestuous expressions of nationalism and ethnicity. The Israeli case illuminates the individual's struggle to reconcile the contradictions between the pressing commitments to a national history, a society, and a revolution and the striving for immediate personal rewards. These conflicts, which prompt some individuals to opt for the Land of Promise and others to stay on in the Promised Land, make them all masters of their destiny. But they are to some extent tragic masters, rarely fully reconciled with their choices. The following chapters describe the emotional cost and the pain endured by those Israelis who have chosen to leave Israel—a place and an ideal—for the American alternative.

I was brought up on the ethos that one should take active part in the making of history. This educational imprint was perhaps a logical reaction to the perceived passivity of Jews for nearly two thousand years, which has had such disastrous consequences. I was growing up at the time when the echoes of momentous events in Jewish history could still be heard. The 1920s and 1930s had witnessed the major pioneering expansion of Jewish settlements in Palestine, and the holocaust took place during the first ten years of my life. In 1948, although still far too young to participate in the Israeli War of Independence, I was old enough to understand its historical impact. The great influx of immigrants from Europe, the Middle East, and North Africa followed soon after. When, on reaching my eighteenth year in the mid 1950s, I was drafted into the army, Israel's destiny was already shaped for many years to come. I was thus brought up as close witness to the major dramas of modern Jewish experience. My generation of Sabras (Jews born in Palestine) was looked upon by my parents' generation as the promising fruit of Jewish rejuvenation. For my part, I felt that I had been granted the less heroic role of an observer. I was born too late to participate actively in and share the experiences of those who had actually made history.

I therefore chose to become a professional observer. My first observations, during the late 1960s, were of the consequences of the mass immigration of North African Jewry. In keeping with anthropological tradition, I selected what seemed to be an exotic Jewish society—immigrants from the Atlas Mountains of Morocco who had been settled in a Negev village (Shokeid 1971; Deshen and Shokeid 1974). A few years later my role of observer led me to orient myself toward another situation, crucial to the development of Israeli society, that of the growing presence of the Arab minority. I selected for research the Arab population of an Israeli city (Shokeid and Deshen 1982).

Toward the late 1970s I became aware of a new phenomenon that seemed to me the most paradoxical in contemporary Jewish and Israeli experience—the growing wave of emigration from Israel to the United States. In the span of one generation I thus witnessed, first, the massive flow into Israel of Jews from all corners of the world wishing to participate in the renewal of Jewish independent nationhood, and then a turnabout, when many participants in this revolution took the boats and planes leading back to the Diaspora. I was now no less intrigued than at my first meeting with the Atlas Mountain Jews, who had exchanged their homes of many generations among the Moroccan Berber tribes for new homes in the semiarid Negev. Not yet knowing when and how, I aimed to do my next fieldwork in New York, which seemed to have become a major attraction for the new exodus.

When I tried to arouse the interest of the Ministry of Absorption in my plans, the embarrassed reaction I encountered was surprising. I was told that the ministry did not wish in any way to call attention to this delicate subject. No doubt Israeli emigrants evoked profound ideological dilemmas, and official circles at that time preferred to evade an issue that might shatter the basic tenets of Zionism abroad and at home. I therefore made my own arrangements to spend a sabbatical leave in New York and took up the offer of a two-year fellowship at the Center for Jewish Studies at Queens College of the City University of New York (September 1982– August 1984).

I am grateful to Samuel Heilman, chairman of the Center; Ernest Schwarcz, dean of the School of General Studies; and Saul Cohen, the president of Queens College during my stay. Without their generous invitation and continuing interest, this book would not have been written. I am also grateful for the grants awarded to me by the Memorial Foundation of Jewish Culture in New York and the Golda Meir Institute for Social and Labour Research. The Faculty of Social Sciences at Tel Aviv University assisted me in preparing the manuscript for publication. I am indebted to Moshe Granit and Mott K. Yaron, who helped me unveil Israeli life in New York, and to my colleagues Yinon Cohen, Shlomo Deshen, Samuel Heilman, and Sasha Weitman for their helpful comments. I thank Deborah Golden for editing the manuscript and Roslyn Langbart's office at Tel Aviv University for the typing and retyping. I also thank Claire Semel at Queens College and Yehuda Jacobson at Tel Aviv University, who assisted me during my work. I owe a special debt of gratitude to Roger Sanjek, editor of the Anthropology of Contemporary Issues series, who read the manuscript with incisive thoroughness and made many valuable comments and suggestions. I also thank Lois Krieger for her careful editing for Cornell University Press and for preparing the manuscript for publication.

Most anthropologists are strangers among the people they study, and the relatives who accompany them to the "field" are even more extraneous to their host society. My case was different. We were not strangers among the people I observed, and my family played an indispensable role in my entering into and taking part in the "field." My wife, Ora, was also the first reader of and commentator on this book, which she copied from my scribblings in order to enable the typists to carry out an otherwise impossible task. She has earned the dedication of this book through hard work.

We made many close Israeli friends during our stay in New York. I regret that I cannot name and thank them personally for their help and warm friendship. Some are introduced in the book and may therefore be easily identified. Although I have tried to conceal their identities through pseudonyms and other changes in their life histories, I assume that they will recognize themselves. They may not always agree with my descriptions and interpretations of events and behavior involving them or other mutual acquaintances, but I hope they will not bear me any grudge.

My use of the term *yordim* ("those who go down") in addressing Israeli immigrants does not imply a moral evaluation. I use it mainly in order to facilitate descriptions and discussions involving three groups that often negotiate their separate or shared identities— American Jews, Israeli citizens on a mission or visit to the United States, and Israeli immigrants (who have been nicknamed *yordim*).

Our stay in New York in the company of Israelis, the majority of whom seemed to have made a successful adjustment outside the borders of Israel, was a permanent test of our own loyalties. New York, the contemporary Rome of Western civilization, a colossal stage for both the elevated and the vulgar, the individual's Land of Promise, is indeed antithetical to its remote, tiny relation by the Mediterranean. Although the boroughs of Queens and Brooklyn alone host more people than all those holding Israeli citizenship, Israel has been for many years the center of international conflict, the stage of continuing wars, home of a faltering economy increasingly dependent on American support, and a nation divided between bitterly opposed ideologies and cultures. For whatever the yearnings (to a people, views, a climate, and a way of life, to the notion of duty, the imprint of a sentimental education, and to self-punishment) that made me return, I do not hold anything against those Israelis who have chosen to stay away and whose experiences I describe in this book. As much as I observed them I was observing myself. Perhaps that was the authentic drive behind my choice of fieldwork in New York.

MOSHE SHOKEID

Tel Aviv, Israel

Children of
Circumstances

Introduction

Recent years have seen the revitalization of both the circumstances and the myth that proclaim the United States, and New York in particular, a paradise on earth created by immigrants for immigrants. The gates, shut fast during the 1920s, have gradually been reopened,[1] and the new wave of immigration has again brought large groups of immigrants to the shores of New York. Among the recent immigrants particularly noticeable are the arrivals from the Caribbean, South America, and Asia; less noticeable are the renewed streams of European immigrants such as the Greeks.[2]

The expanding wave of recent immigration includes a growing stream of immigrants from Israel. This group, however, has received very little attention in the vast literature devoted to the new ethnics. The Israelis were first mentioned in a passage by Glazer and Moynihan (1963) in their discussion of the 2.5 million immigrants who arrived in the United States during the 1950s, most of whom settled in the New York area: "Buried in this vast population of the city are new groups (such as 18,000 Israelis) that in any other city would be marked and receive attention" (1963:9). Nearly twenty years later the *Harvard Encyclopedia of American Ethnic*

[1]Particularly effective was the Immigration Law of 1965; see, e.g., Bryce-Laporte 1979.
[2]See "Modern Greek Odyssey," in Kessner and Caroli 1981:261–81.

[1]

Groups (1980) devoted two paragraphs to Israeli immigrants, considered part of the category of Jews. This same source (p. 597) estimated that 300,000 Israelis have immigrated to America since the founding of the state of Israel in 1948, half of whom have settled in New York, with another large contingent in the Los Angeles area.

These references, in two of the most reputable publications on American ethnic groups, reveal the rapid growth of Israeli immigration to the United States. Their numbers are comparable to those of other recently arrived groups. During the late 1970s, for example, the newly emerging Asian Indian group comprised about 250,000 people,[3] the Dominicans 350,000,[4] and the Koreans 300,000.[5] Furthermore, the Israelis are not significantly different from most other recent groups of immigrants in terms of their major socioeconomic pattern characteristics.[6] They too represent various social strata, including a large population of professionals and members of the middle class. Nevertheless, most writers on trends of contemporary immigration to the United States have not paid any attention to Israeli immigrants. They are not mentioned in Bryce-Laporte's *Sourcebook on the New Immigration* (1980), or in Caroli's "Recent Immigration to the United States" (1982), and they were not included among the portraits of new immigrants presented by Kessner and Caroli (1981), who, however, did discuss a Russian Jew.[7] A special issue of *Time* Magazine featuring the "Newest Americans" indicated the presence of Israeli immigrants in Queens and Brooklyn (July 8, 1985: map, pp. 36–37) but referred to them in the text by mentioning only the presence of eight thousand Israeli engineers in the United States (p. 35). The same issue, however, devoted a full-page feature to portraits of newly arrived Russian Jews (p. 71).

Furthermore, the little research on Israeli immigrants has not succeeded in drawing the attention of researchers into the wider context of immigration to the United States. These studies, carried

---

[3]Varma 1980.
[4]Ugalde, Bean, and Cardenas 1979.
[5]Kessner and Caroli 1981:124.
[6]See Glazer and Moynihan 1975:23.
[7]"To Leave Russia as a Jew," in Kessner and Caroli 1981:160–84.

[2]

out mainly by Israeli students, were particularly concerned with the prospects of the immigrants' return to Israel (Ritterband 1969; Fein 1978; Elizur 1980). Korazim (1983) raised the question of the Israelis' adjustment in the United States by studying their use of social services. Kass and Lipset's (1982) survey addressed itself to wider issues and emphasized in particular the Israelis' sense of guilt about their departure from Israel and their self-presentation as sojourners. Sobel (1986), who interviewed applicants for immigrant visas in Israel, searched for the reasons for their planned immigration.[8] A number of research reports were also prepared for concerned Israeli official bodies anxious to learn about the socioeconomic characteristics of Israeli immigrants and the prospects of recruiting them back.[9] None of these studies, however, has yet produced a description that proffers a clear picture of the economic, social, and cultural features of this population nicknamed *yordim*. The phenomenon of Israeli emigration has come to be known in Israel as *yerida* ("descent") and its participants as *yordim* ("those who go down"). These terms introduce the opposite of *aliya* and *olim* ("those who go up") to Israel.[10]

The *Harvard Enyclopedia of American Ethnic Groups,* in its short reference to the Israelis, pinpointed two important factors that I believe have greatly influenced the particular sociological characteristics of Israeli ethnicity in the United States. First: "The Israeli immigrants pose a problem for the Jewish community: they have chosen to leave the land that every Jewish American has learned to regard as a haven, the guardian of Jewish survival, and the center of Hebraic culture. The ambiguity toward the *yordim . . .* has expressed itself in the absence of formal recognition of

[8]Only a small minority of Israeli immigrants in the United States actually start their immigrant careers with immigrant visas (see Chapter 1, n. 19).

[9]E. Cohen 1959; Elizur and Elizur 1974; Lahis 1980; Achiram, Danziger, and Libman 1984.

[10]The term *yerida* has a biblical source. Abraham, founder of the Jewish nation, was forced by pressing hunger to leave for Egypt. His departure was described in the following archaic form: "*Vayered*—he descended—*Abraham Mitzraima*—to Egypt" (Gen. 12:10). The term *yerida* used in contrast to *aliya* first appeared when Jacob (Abraham's grandson) was encouraged by God to go to Egypt under the promise: "*Ered—aa'lkha gam alo*" [I shall go down—and I shall also bring you up] (Gen. 46:4).

the Israelis as a Jewish immigrant group" (p. 597). And second: "Among themselves, the Israelis have almost no formal organization, though they have a lively informal social life" (p. 597).

The first factor relates to the alien status of Jews throughout centuries and the intended transformation of this status with the establishment of the state of Israel. The Jews have often been regarded as the best example of a Diaspora society—an "archetypal Diaspora" (Armstrong 1976:394)—and of other definitions of aliens such as the "stranger" (Simmel 1950:403) or the "sojourner" (Siu 1952:43). Zionism strived to radically transform the status of Jews from their membership in a Diaspora society into a nation-state identity.

The first disappointment confronting Israelis soon after the achievement of statehood was the realization that the Jewish Diaspora in Western societies remained unimpressed by the new Jewish national situation. After the dramatic arrival in Israel of hundreds of thousands of immigrants, including the survivors of the European holocaust and most communities of Jews from the Middle East and North Africa, it became clear that the larger and better-off Jewish communities in Europe and America had no plans whatsoever to pack up and move to the Jewish state.

Ben-Gurion in particular was uncompromising with the Zionists abroad who assumed they could remain committed to Zionism without fulfilling its major tenet—settlement in Zion. In a conference of American Zionists in New York in 1951 he told his listeners: "In order to be a Zionist we must live an all-embracing Jewish life in our homeland surrounded by the Hebrew language and Hebrew culture. We must take part in the everyday building of our country, educate our children to live and build there, to defend our homeland and fully identify with it" (1953:150–51). But Ben-Gurion's rhetoric moved neither the leaders nor the rank and file among American Zionists. The sentiments and admiration of American Jews toward the state of Israel and its people continued to be expressed in other forms of support.[11]

A new ad hoc ideological accommodation, as well as a consensual division of labor, soon developed between Israelis and Zionists in

---

[11]See, e.g., Waxman 1976.

the Jewish Diaspora: Israelis were to remain guardians of the Jewish state who would offer shelter to Jews whenever they were forced out of their Diaspora; Zionists would continue to stay on abroad and provide political and financial support. For the first time it became clear that the Diaspora situation was no longer forced upon Jews.

That Jews preferred the Diaspora to self-determination in an independent country was a painful realization for Israelis. There was one major soothing interpretation for this unwelcome phenomenon: those born abroad had become so conditioned to material comfort as to be unable to grasp the loss of authentic personal freedom denied Jews under the hegemony of Christian cultures. Many Israelis actually refuse to be designated as Jews, a definition that seems to them to imply submission to the superior status of the gentile host societies. The Canaanite movement demonstrated an extreme expression of this attitude.[12]

This conception of the basic cleavage differentiating Israelis and Diaspora Jews has recently been shattered by a development that has gained momentum since 1967: the departure of Israeli citizens from Israel, mainly for the United States.[13] Increasing numbers of those born and raised in Israel, or those who for a shorter or longer period have had the opportunity to live in Israel, are choosing to commit themselves to Diaspora life. Moreover, there is nothing in common between the contemporary emigration of Israelis and the mass emigration of Jews to America at the turn of the century. The latter entailed the exodus of about two million impoverished, persecuted, second-rate citizens from Eastern Europe.[14] In contrast, the Israelis who leave their country nowadays are often equipped with professional skills and considerable financial resources. They willingly surrender their status as members of the dominant majority in exchange for the status of hopeful immigrants.

[12]The Canaanites believed that the life of Jews in Israel bears no relationship to Jewish life in the Diaspora. They claimed instead a closer association with the ancient peoples who occupied the land (including the biblical Hebrews). See Yonathan Ratosh (1974) for the movement's ideological elaboration.

[13]The victory of 1967, which eased the sense of danger to Israel's survival, might also have freed inner forces and social pressures of obligation and solidarity which had hitherto inhibited individuals from emigrating.

[14]See, e.g., Rischin 1962; Howe 1976.

[5]

Since the mid-1970s Israeli newspapers and periodicals have continuously dealt with the issue of *yerida*. Although the writers often pinpoint the economic and social problems at home, they usually describe the *yordim* most disparagingly.[15] These frequent expressions of moral indignation manifest an ideological conviction that in turn reinforces the stigma of *yordim*.[16] This was most strongly demonstrated in 1976 by Prime Minister Yitzhak Rabin, who, during a television interview on the Day of Independence, called *yordim* "the leftovers of weaklings" (*nefolet shel nemushot*). His statement shocked Israelis abroad and the term remained implanted in the memory of a generation.

Various interpretations have been suggested by Israeli intellectuals and scientists for the apparent anomaly introduced by the phenomenon of *yerida*.[17] One major theme considers this mode of

---

[15]I quote only a few citations from this enormous corpus of writing: "The great majority of *yordim* went to New York during 1967–1973 in search of the American dream. They went there because they were haunted by the greedy dream of a quick fortune to be made, a dream nourished in Israel during the years of prosperity" (Avineri, *Maariv*, January 30, 1976:17); "*Yerida* is not much different from the cowardly flight from the battlefield. If *yordim* are not completely deprived of human and national feelings they will suffer for the rest of their life from a sense of guilt and from an inferiority complex. They shall be cast out by their children and friends" (Gothalf, *Davar*, January 16, 1976:19); "The *yored* is a miserable figure, a one-dimensional man or even less, oriented toward one goal—material gain. He is a caricature of a person, uprooted from everything that binds a human being to his geographical, social, and cultural environment" (Bar-Yosef, *Moznaim*, no. 2 [1976]:84); "I suppose that you just got fed up with it all. I can't really blame you—I too am often weary, bitter and filled with doubts. . . . But you have given up a dream, a most beautiful dream, not only of the Jewish people but of the entire human race. . . . You are, in fact, a deserter. Of course you have a right to desert, to try to replace one destiny by another. In your choice you have surrendered your superiority over all other animals. Just like them you have chosen life. You are a handsome, skilled, and well-behaved animal and I have no doubt as to your future success. But I don't envy you" (Keinan, *Yedioth Ahronoth*, April 14, 1976:5).

[16]From the other side, Nahshon (1976) expressed a lone reaction: "The uniqueness of the Israeli newcomer really is to be found in his emotional background—the United States has become a psychological safety-valve for Israeli society. People are tired—they want to relax, to slacken the reins" (p. 47). "On the surface, of course, it is very easy to find feelings of animosity and hate toward the run-away Israelis. The Israeli leaders and their half-controlled opinion-making machine constantly stimulate these feelings" (p. 48).

[17]I am not considering here the theme of *yerida* as referred to in contemporary Israeli fiction; see Zerubavel 1986.

behavior in terms of personal instrumental motivation. B. Zvi Sobel (1983), a sociologist, suggests economic aspirations and the blocked mobility in a small society as the major cause of recent emigration.[18] Far less accommodating is the second theme, which considers *yerida* mainly in terms of a Diaspora syndrome deeply implanted in the Jewish mind and personality. The most forceful propagator of this idea is A. B. Yehoshua, a leading Israeli author, who rejects instrumental considerations as an explanation for both the survival of the Diaspora and the phenomenon of *yerida:*

> The Golah [Diaspora] as a situation and possibility is one of the most fundamental components of the essence of the Jewish people. It is found in the atoms and molecules that make our national and existential identity. [1981:41]

> What reveals itself here is a behavior of a clearly neurotic sort: the nation hates the Golah and dreams of Eretz Israel . . . but at the same time all its historical activity is preoccupied with one end: how to endure Exile, how to continue to maintain this hated existence. [1981:38–39]

This approach is supported by an analysis of Jewish existence and identity as deeply rooted in "a feeling of a nebulous longing" or an "inner sense of exile" (Gaber 1983:63, 64). A. B. Yehoshua condemns the *yordim,* who reaffirm the survival of the "virus" and "neurosis" of Jewish Diaspora existence: "Our denunciation of the *yordim* and refusal to grant them work in Jewish institutions will have moral validity, because we denounce and reject the Golah experience as a whole" (1981:72).

A third theme relates *yerida* to ideological shifts and social changes in Israeli society, such as the decline of the pioneering spirit and the growing ideals of a consumption society. In this context *yerida* also has been explained as a consequence of an identity crisis among Israeli citizens who have lost the particular ingredients of traditional Jewish culture (e.g., Segre 1980; Freedman 1983). A recent sociological examination, employing a Durkheimian approach, discussed the connection between emigration

[18]This issue was also discussed by Israeli economists; see, e.g., Lamdani 1983.

rates (conceptualized as individual deviant behavior, like suicide) and the level of concensus in Israeli society as related to the Israeli-Arab conflict (Y. Cohen 1986). But whatever the interpretation suggested, Israeli public opinion remains hostile toward *yerida* and deeply disturbed by its moral and practical implications for Israeli society.

For the first time in two thousand years of exile, "wandering Jews" constitute a section separated from a compact majority in a territorial base. Regardless of the ideological problem this may entail for Israelis at home or Jews abroad, Israeli emigrants are indeed comparable to emigrants arriving at the shores of America from many other countries. They display some of the major characteristics of the "sojourner" as observed and defined by Paul Siu in his research into Chinese immigrants:

> The essential characteristic of the sojourner is that he clings to the culture of his own ethnic group. . . . Apparently he knows why he migrates. It may be a religious mission, a commercial interest, an economic adventure, a military campaign, an academic degree, a journalist assignment, a political refuge, or what not. . . . the intrinsic purpose of the sojourn is to do a job and do it in the shortest possible time. . . . In due time the sojourner becomes vague and uncertain about the termination of his sojourn because of the fact that he has already made some adjustments to his new environment and acquired an old-timer's attitudes.

> On the basis of common interests and cultural heritage the sojourner tends to associate with people of his own ethnic group. He and his countrymen, if there are enough of them, very likely live together in a racial colony or cultural area. "Little Tokyo," "Little Sicily," "Greek Town," and "Chinatown" in this country, for example, are their ghettos. [Siu 1952:34, 35, 36]

As often reported by researchers and other observers, Israelis in the United States sincerely believe that their stay abroad is temporary, pending the accomplishment of specific goals. At the same time they have not developed the major characteristic of the sojourner as suggested by Siu. Although their numbers in Queens and Brooklyn have greatly increased within a short period, and although some shops carry Israeli names, they have not set up a Little Tel Aviv or an Israel Town. The image of a lively ethnic community, as a common characteristic of both early and more recent waves of immigration to New York, certainly cannot be applied to Israelis. Recent Israeli immigrants do, however, demonstrate consistent attitudes and modes of behavior: they don't consider their stay in the United States permanent, and they don't evolve a substitute Israeli environment.

Not all immigrants to the United States have established "ethnic towns"; nevertheless they have usually evolved easily identifiable marks of an ethnic presence and exhibited a proliferation of ethnic voluntary professional and communal associations. Pertinent examples include the recent concentration of Koreans in Queens and the Bronx,[19] or the less visible but closely knit Philippine communities.[20] The Israelis, in contrast, keep a remarkably low profile (avoiding both conspicuous symbolic manifestations and the operation of active communal organs), although they have tended to concentrate in New York's boroughs, Queens in particular.[21]

Furthermore, unlike the great waves of Jewish immigration in the last decades of the nineteenth century and the new ethnics who have arrived since the late 1960s, the Israelis have not developed easily identifiable economic enclaves. While the Koreans, for example, rapidly took over a considerable portion of the fresh produce market in New York,[22] the Israelis do not seem to have evolved an economic basis of ethnic solidarity.[23]

This phenomenon of "submerged ethnicity" must relate to the Israelis' deep layers of existential experiences. Harold Isaacs (1975:34) suggests that "the function of basic group identity has to do most crucially with two key ingredients in every individual's personality and life experience: his sense of belongingness and the quality of his self-esteem." From a somewhat different orientation,

[19]Kessner and Caroli 1981:123–43.

[20]Caroli 1982:52.

[21]The borough of Queens emerged as one of the most attractive neighborhoods for immigrants in New York City; see, e.g., Greeley 1974:24.

[22]Kessner and Caroli 1981:131.

[23]See Bonachich and Modell 1980.

Daniel Bell suggests: "Ethnicity has become more salient because it can combine an interest with an affective tie" (1975:169). The Israelis, who neither attach themselves to the vast and prestigious network of American Jews' national and communal institutions nor express a separate ethnic presence, seem to be out of tune with the mainstream of ethnic behavior in America.

While immigrants may bring about change in the social and cultural status quo in their country of destination, they also undermine the self-confidence and communal moral integrity of those in the home society.[24] Their adventurous departure and willingness to take risks point to an alternative to a social environment and a way of life that most members of that society perceive as the only legitimate reality.[25] That *yordim* exemplify this threat is indicated by the revulsion their behavior provokes. The derogative designation *yored* is rarely, if ever, denied by the Israeli immigrants themselves. It remains a source of status and identity incongruity, similar to that experienced by other social minorities who would also appear to impinge on societal definitions and expectations.[26]

The Israelis, denied recognition by American Jews as well as by Israelis at home and their official representatives in the United States, have avoided an obtrusive presence. The absence of Israeli organizations and the failure of most attempts to initiate communal activities among Israeli residents are most evident. The studies of Israelis mentioned above, mainly concerned with specific instrumental issues, have in themselves also adhered to this status quo of "low profiled ethnicity." Indeed, on the whole, the phenomenon of Israeli immigration has remained an almost unknown territory of behavior in a city that offers shelter to both more and less advertised ethnic groups and social minorities.

In the chapters that follow I first describe the personal and collective characteristics of Israelis in New York, depicting the exis-

[24]Stark (1967) discussed the opposition raised to migration in both the departure and reception countries, but mainly in terms of economic considerations.

[25]My thinking here has been influenced by Lyman and Scott's (1975) analysis of adventures: "One may study adventure not only as a phenomenon of all societies but also as a structure of social life that illuminates the peculiar alienation characteristic of a particular society" (p. 147).

[26]See Newton's (1979:106–9) discussion of the incongruous position experienced by gays.

tential dilemmas involved, the strategies employed, and the paradoxes revealed in their management and negotiation of an Israeli ethnic reality and cultural identity. Second, I suggest the relevance of *yordim* society to contemporary theories of ethnic and nonethnic minorities. The latter in particular are often defined in terms of deviance or stigma management. I hope to expand our understanding of ethnicity in terms of an affective behavior that regulates social sentiments and expresses problematic identities of various minorities.

I come now to the specific chapters that make up this book. In Chapter 1, I present the circumstances of my research in Queens, the data and major characteristics of the population under study. In Chapter 2, I discuss the deep mutual resentment between Israeli immigrants and American Jews. This resentment introduces a partial explanation for the Israelis' disassociation from American Jews' national and communal institutions. Chapter 3 probes into the relationships of *yordim* among themselves. The Israelis seem to harbor little sympathy toward their compatriots, whom they often perceive in derogatory terms. Chapter 4 presents my observations of an Israeli club over a period of two years. In spite of the many attempts to offer attractive programs of cultural and recreational activities and to create an Israeli ambience, the club failed to recruit a stable membership and to initiate close social relationships between the participants. Chapter 5 looks into the contexts and forms that foster the expression of "Israeliness" by describing the passionate gatherings of Israelis for *shira betzibur*—the singing together of Israeli folk songs. The issue of Israeli identity is further researched in Chapter 6 through the analysis of the Israelis' struggle with their putative Jewish identity and their position vis-à-vis Jewish heritage. The discussion in this chapter further expands our understanding of the observations introduced in Chapter 2 concerning the relationships between *yordim* and American Jews. Chapter 7 describes the only field of a congenial encounter between *yordim* and American Jews. The efforts of the Chabad Chassidic movement at proselytizing the Israelis appear to be somewhat successful, particularly among *yordim* of Sephardi extraction. This chapter also offers a closer look into the growing presence of emigrants of Sephardi extraction. Chapter 8 presents the life stories of twelve Israeli couples and singles. This more intimate observation into the process of emigration from Israel and patterns of accommodation in the United States offers a closer penetration into the life of *yordim* as fully active dramatis personae. Chapter 9 concludes the major findings of my research and considers its relevance to the issues of immigration and ethnicity. One might have expected a separate chapter dealing with the country of origin of the emigrants. But in view of the continuing exposure of Israeli issues in the media, and the vast corpus of sociological and anthropological studies on that subject,[27] I considered this superfluous.

The mode of presentation employed in this book demonstrates the field situation of my research. The study of Israelis in Queens bears little resemblance to the usual anthropological field circumstances. I did not carry out my observations among a clearly defined population concentrated in a close neighborhood or in an institutional setting. Although some individuals and families were observed in various settings, on the whole the population shifted kaleidoscopically during my work. As a result I do not apply a monographic approach but address myself to various interrelated issues and facets of life that together divulge the existential conditions of Israeli immigrants. The chapters of the book are therefore to some extent self-contained. This method of presentation is indicative of the field situation encountered by a growing number of anthropologists on entry into less structured, amorphous organizational settings and social groups, particularly in the complex urban environment.

[27]See, e.g., Eisenstadt 1985; Shokeid and Deshen 1982; Smooha 1978.

[1]

The Israelis in Queens

The decision to carry out an anthropological study among an Israeli population in New York City was accompanied by considerable doubts as to the feasibility of such a project. Studies in complex urban societies have usually been less favored by anthropologists,[1] and few leading anthropologists have made their career in metropolitan studies. Such studies pose enormous difficulties, in particular the definition of the unit of research and the subjects of observation, and the implementation of the method of participant observation.[2] More specifically, researchers have reported Israelis in New York as reluctant to cooperate (Grant: 1981).

In any event, the field situation I met was even more difficult than I had anticipated. For the first time in my professional experience the society I came to study was not immediately accessible for research. Committed to the anthropological method of participant observation, I at first attempted to identify settings frequented by Israelis in which I could observe their social interaction. But there did not seem to be an Israeli "street corner society" or a "Tally's corner," the famous observation units employed by urban an-

[1]See Epstein's (1981) reflections on the difficulties encountered by an anthropologist carrying out research in an urban environment.
[2]See, e.g., Sanjek's (1978) comments on the methodological issues involved: "In evaluating urban ethnography one must always ask: on what basis, whether explicit or not, has this selection been made? Where is the ethnographer, and how does she or he trace their behavior" (p 257).

thropologists. Nevertheless, I soon reconciled myself to this situation, which had not been designed to satisfy the comfort and preferred tradition of anthropologists, and in spite of the uncertainties I persisted in my method of gradual involvement in Israeli activities and the slow expansion of a network of Israeli acquaintances.

Among my first informants about the Israeli population in New York was the Israeli official emissary (under the auspices of the Jewish Agency) working among *yordim* in Queens. Ami Shaham,[3] from a village in the Negev, was very popular among the Israelis because of his consistently warm and friendly attitude, which contrasted sharply with the stereotype of an indifferent Israeli bureaucrat, contemptuous toward *yordim*. On my arrival in New York he offered me both hospitality and clues about the population involved.

As he and other experienced observers reported, the Israelis in Queens tended to concentrate in the neighborhoods of Rego Park, Forest Hills, Flushing, and Kew Gardens (nearby residential areas in the center of the borough; see Map 1). This observation is supported by the data available in the Immigration and Naturalization Service's (INS') "Legally Registered Aliens by Zips" (1977, 1979).[4] Although the Israelis have little contact with New York's Jews and their institutions, they tend to settle in "Jewish neighborhoods."[5]

Prior to my departure from Israel, a neighbor told me about an Israeli couple in Queens who were planning to leave their apartment. As it turned out, the apartment had already been let, but the occupants knew of another family, also returning to Israel. We subsequently rented their apartment in Kew Gardens. Another apartment in the same building was also rented to an Israeli family. The departing Israelis informed us about yet another Israeli family residing two blocks away who could advise us on schools for our children. We ended up registering our boys at a Jewish school with their children. We gradually struck up a friendship with them and

---

[3]Ami Shaham is among the few individuals I mention without a change of identity. Most other names of the Israelis observed are pseudonyms.

[4]As shown by Grant 1981:16, and Korazim 1983:199–200.

[5]Glazer and Moynihan (1963:162) considered Forest Hills and Rego Park as "one of the areas of densest Jewish concentration in the city today [during the 1950s]."

Map 1. Residential concentration of Israelis in Queens

1 Rego Park

2 Forest Hills

3 Flushing

4 Kew Gardens

Queens Zip Code Map

[15]

with a few other Israeli families scattered within walking distance whose children were enrolled with ours at school. In time I identified a few more Israeli families and singles who lived around our block. Some were easily identifiable, but others, particularly the singles and young couples without children, were more difficult to distinguish. Couples with young children, for example, could more often be heard communicating loudly in Hebrew, and Israeli-made sandals were another clear mark of identity during the summer season. But it was only when my car was stuck in deep snow in front of another car in a similar predicament that a neighbor and I started to talk and discovered our shared nationality. Although I had often seen him and his roommate, it had never occurred to me that he might be an Israeli. Similarly, one evening while seated in my car, a young man whom I had always considered a "true American" asked me if I was leaving my parking lot. The shared accent revealed our nationality. On the whole, in sneakers, jeans, sweat-shirt, or suit, the Israelis were indistinguishable from other New Yorkers.

In time I identified most Israelis on our block, as we too must have been identified by them. But this knowledge did not involve much sociability, since shared neighborhood did not appear to be a sufficient stimulus for friendship. Neighborhood did, however, encourage social ties when other common elements sustained relationships, such as professional interests, children at the same school, or acquaintance carried over from Israel. Our stay in what seemed to be an "Israeli neighborhood" was important, since it allowed for many acquaintances and offered insights into the Israelis' life-style. But it soon became clear that close neighborhood ties and institutions alone could not be the major base of research, as often reported in classical urban studies.[6]

Another strategy I tried was to approach Israeli-owned businesses and services in various parts of Queens. Of particular value was the garage where I bought my car and where I remained a client throughout my stay in New York. I established friendly relations with the proprietors (Shlomo and his wife, Shula) and became acquainted with a few of their friends and clients. Shlomo was

[6]See, e.g., W. F. Whyte 1955; Liebow 1967; Hannerz 1969.

considered an extremely talented mechanic, dedicated and helpful. But since the garage was disorganized I often waited for hours for my car to be ready. On these occasions I had ample opportunity to observe the ongoing activities and to communicate with clients, garage employees, business partners, and other visitors. Shlomo also invited me to attend a Chabad lecture at his home and from then on I expanded my observations into this type of activity in other homes in Queens and became acquainted with the hosts and their guests (see Chapter 7). My contacts with owners and clients of other services were usually less gratifying, as for example my occasional visits to an Israeli pediatrician and an Israeli travel agent. I often visited a nearby Israeli pizzeria, which, though it offered Israeli food, on the whole served as a fast food cafeteria for a mixed clientele.

A major source of both casual and close acquaintances was the Israeli Club at the Central Queens YM & YWHA in Forest Hills. At that time the club was the only institution of its kind. I became one of its devoted "regulars" for the two seasons 1982–84. The club offered Israeli dancing on Tuesday evenings, Hebrew classes for children, and other specialized activities for smaller groups. A "social club" met once a week on Wednesday evenings, usually for lectures. It also offered parties at the major festivals and a monthly Israeli film on Saturday evenings. I mainly attended the meetings of the social club, whose participants were almost exclusively Israeli *yordim* and with whom I could more easily communicate (see Chapter 4).

A visitor to the Israeli Club introduced me to an Israeli chapter of Benei-Zion, where I got to know a few of its members.[7] Queens College was another place where I met Israelis among the faculty, administration, and student body. I also initiated contacts with a few Israelis about whom I had heard from mutual acquaintances. They usually reacted positively to my phone calls and in a few cases

---

[7]The "Israeli chapter" of Benei-Zion represented an unusual phenomenon. The membership was composed of mixed couples and mostly Israeli men married to American Jewish women. The group's activities consisted mainly of the monthly informal meetings at home and the festival celebrations open to the public. The revenue collected at these parties was dedicated to the support of a communal center in Israel.

this more "aggressive" strategy of approach initiated friendly relationships. Every new acquaintance had a potential snowballing effect—I often got to know his or her Israeli friends, relatives, and
other acquaintances.

Opportunities to meet Israelis often emerged in odd circumstances. Stuck for a few hours at the Miami airport waiting with my
family for a delayed flight to Orlando, we started to talk to an Israeli
family. We had already noticed them at JFK in New York, but only
while sharing the stress of the delay did we come together and
spend the time discussing various aspects of life in Israel and New
York. But as often happens with Israelis in New York, in spite of the
friendly conversation, we did not see them again after that brief
encounter. Similarly, on our visit to Quebec City, only one other
family joined us on the English-language tour of the Parliament
House. It turned out to be an Israeli family from Montreal and we
had a friendly chat during and immediately after the tour.

New York City offered many occasions for brief meetings with
yordim at the various "Israeli" gatherings sponsored by American
Jewish organizations or Israeli official agencies, such as the Israeli
Film Festival and the annual Israeli Parade on Fifth Avenue. Performances by Israeli artists and entertainers, Israeli restaurants and
nightclubs, offered similar opportunities. These events were, however, frequented by more American Jews than Israelis. I also often
encountered Israelis in public places, such as the subway, department stores (the Alexander's in Rego Park seemed to be particularly
attractive to Israelis), Lower East Side shops, and Central Park.

Thus the field situation I encountered was an amorphous, urban
"suburb," the population of which almost equaled that of the total
Jewish population in Israel and where even small geographical
units, in which many Israelis were concentrated, bore little resemblance to the traditional perception of community and communal life.

Selecting the Research Population

I did not design my research with the intention of introducing a
statistically valid sample, nor of presenting the distribution of spe-

cific attitudes and other characteristics among *yordim.* My network of Israeli acquaintances expanded gradually through the various directions that became available to me, and the data at my disposal were accumulated mainly through the method of participant observation. Nevertheless, the information collected at the shorter or longer encounters with a few hundred Israelis does entail a statistical dimension. In this chapter I present some of the computable data as an additional source of information and as a background to the rest of the book.

In the final count, the Israelis I met during our two-year stay in Queens (September 1982–August 1984) can be divided into three categories. First, those observed through nonverbal communication when no opportunity for conversation emerged, particularly in public places. Second, those with whom my meetings were casual and brief, such as at airports and museums, as well as at brief meetings at the Israeli Club, parties, and the like. Third, those with whom my acquaintance was developed enough in order to learn sufficient details about their life histories in Israel and New York. This last category included both those with whom the relationship was continuous and intensive and those with whom the relationship was more sporadic and neutral. Had I counted the total number of Israelis I observed for some time, talked with, or learned about from acquaintances and who are described in my notes, the research population would have reached at least five hundred and possibly many more.

The population making up the research core was drawn from the third category. It included 116 research units, each composed of either a family or a single man or woman, all of whom left Israel on their own initiative. To this group were added another 10 individuals who left Israel with their parents as children or teen-agers. Thus the research core population actually amounted to 174 Israeli adult men and women if the spouses are also included in our list of 48 Israeli couples. I introduce here only those families and individuals about whom I had sufficient basic data and, for many of them, the detailed information that resembled the anthropological data collected in more closely knit social settings.

As noted above, I do not consider the population introduced in this study a representative sample of the Israeli population either in

New York or in the United States. No research to date has produced a representative sample of this population, and it is doubtful
whether the standard procedures of sampling are feasible in this
case. The use of the telephone directory as a source,[8] for example,
may be misleading, since there is no common standard style of
names among Israelis, who have as many Eastern European and
Middle Eastern surnames as noticeably Israeli names. Moreover,
transliteration often obscures the origin of Israeli names. The definition of who is an Israeli may also vary greatly.[9] Thus, for example,
apart from those born and raised in Israel, there are immigrants
who, though not born in Israel, lived there for many years, or
others who lived there only for a short period.[10] Most estimates of
the number of Israelis abroad include as Israelis not only the house-
holder who was born or had lived in Israel for a year or more, but
also the American-born spouse and their children. There is, in fact,
no agreement as to the number of Israelis in New York and the
United States. Estimates of the Israeli population in the United
States vary from 100,000 to 500,000 and in New York from 50,000
to 250,000. These contrasting figures have been produced by the
Israeli Central Bureau of Statistics (Rabi, 1976, 1978, 1986),[11] the
Jewish Agency (Lahis 1980), the Federation of Jewish Philanthropies of New York (Shapiro 1978), and independent researchers.[12] The wide disparity in the estimates of the Israeli immigrant population is indicative of among other things, the obscurity
of the position of Israeli ethnicity in the United States.

Examining the various estimates it appears, however, that Israeli
demographers assume there are about 250,000 Israeli immigrants
in the United States (including a considerable number of Israeli
citizens born elsewhere). Lower estimates are suggested by those
researchers who rely on American official sources. Israeli politi-

[8]This is a method recently employed in Jewish population studies in New York
City by Ritterband and Cohen 1984.

[9]See Ritterband's (1986) discussion of some of the complexities of identification
and enumeration of the Israelis residing abroad.

[10]See Sabatello 1978.

[11]The most recent figures produced by the Israeli Central Bureau of Statistics
reveal that 346,000 Israelis have left Israel since 1948, of whom 190,000 apparently
reside in the United States and Canada (*Haretz* 31/3/87).

[12]See, e.g., Korazim 1983:18–22; Ritterband 1986.

cians, concerned officials, and the Israeli media tend to put forward alarming estimates of the rapidly growing population of Israeli emigrants. These estimates should be viewed in relation to the total Jewish population in Israel, which, by the end of 1984, was estimated at about 3.5 million.[13] Thus, for example, the Israeli demographers' moderate number represents a 12 percent loss of population through emigration.

It is commonly assumed that the great majority of Israelis in New York City reside in Queens and Brooklyn. The most recent comparison of social characteristics of Israelis in the two boroughs, carried out by Korazim (1983), estimated that 40 percent reside in Queens and 60 percent in Brooklyn (p. 22).[14] Korazim also concluded that the socioeconomic status of Israeli residents of Brooklyn in his survey (forty-three families for each borough) was somewhat lower in comparison with that of the Queens residents. Considering the various estimates of the Israeli immigrant population in the United States and in New York in particular, the Queens Israeli population may range from 30,000 to 45,000.

The population of the present study represents to some extent a totality, since it was largely the outcome of the natural development of a social network and of the occasional contacts of an Israeli resident in New York. My occupational life as an academic associated with a local university was not unusual in the Queens environment. My family life was in no way different from that of many other Israelis, although I did have more time to look around and pursue my interest in Israelis. My contacts were mostly with Queens residents and covered a wide spectrum of its Israeli residents' occupational and social characteristics. From this viewpoint my research core is probably more representative than most previous studies, which have concentrated on specific populations. Some researchers have concentrated on students and professionals (Ritterband 1969; Fein 1978; Elizur 1980); Kass and Lipset did not clarify the method of their sampling; and Korazim selected Israeli families according to the criteria relevant to the problem of service

[13]*Statistical Abstract of Israel 1985*, p. 32.

[14]Korazim calculated this figure using, among other things, a computer output of the INS "Legally Registered Aliens by Zips" (1979).

[21]

utilization.[15] In contrast, I did not screen my research population through any formal criteria and endeavored to disregard any pre-conceived view of the "typical" Israeli immigrant. In spite of my hesitation concerning the representativeness of my data, some of its major characteristics do, nevertheless, correspond with those sug-gested by demographers (e.g., Paltiel 1986).

Marital Status

The core group of 116 research units (excluding the 10 adult sons and daughters of *yordim*) was composed of 48 Israeli couples, most of whom (42) were already married in Israel; 25 men married to American Jewish women; 8 single men; 13 male divorcees (7 from American spouses) and 1 widower; 8 single women, 5 women mar-ried to Americans, 7 divorcees (4 from American spouses), and 1 widow (see Table 1).

Upon first arrival in America, the marital status of our partici-pants had been somewhat different (see Table 2). The main phe-nomenon subsequent to migration was the tendency of Israeli men to marry American women. The position of young Israeli men on the local Jewish scene of mate selection seemed to be much superi-or to that of Israeli women. The latter were at a serious disadvan-tage in competing with American women over either Israeli or American men. Unless endowed with particular personal assets, Israeli women were a poor match for equally or even less endowed American women, who could offer the male immigrant self-as-surance, security, and the comforts of daily life in an alien society. In fact, of the six girls who married Israeli men in America, three couples had already met in Israel and the girls were joining their boyfriends, who had already made the move. This situation may partly explain my observation of three single women who tried to return to Israel after more than five years of residence in New York (two of whom seem to have made the move permanently). None of the single men met during my stay made similar attempts to return to Israel.

[15]That survey included, e.g., only married Israeli couples.

Table 1. Distribution of Israeli men and women* by marital status and ethnic extraction (1982–1984)

Marital status	Ethnic group			
	Ashkenazi	Sephardi	Mixed couples	
Men				
Single	4	4		8
Married to an Israeli spouse, wed in Israel	26	9	7	42
Married to an Israeli spouse, wed in America	2	2	2	6
Married to an American spouse	12	13		25
Divorced an American spouse	3	4		7
Divorced an Israeli spouse	5	1		6
Widowed (an American spouse)	1	—		1
Women				
Single	6	2		8
Married to an American spouse	4	1		5
Divorced an American spouse	4	—		4
Divorced an Israeli spouse	2	1		3
Widowed	1	—		1
TOTAL	70	37	9	116

*The figures in our tables on women relate only to single women or to those married to American men.

Table 2. Distribution of Israeli men and women upon arrival in the United States, by marital status and ethnic extraction

Marital status	Ethnic group			
	Ashkenazi	Sephardi	Mixed couples	
Men				
Single	20	20		40
Divorced	3	—		3
Married to an Israeli spouse	29	11	7	47
Married to an American spouse	3	4		7
Women				
Single	9	3		12
Divorced	1	—		1
Widowed	1	—		1
Married to an American spouse	5			5
TOTAL	71	38	7	116

None of my Queens acquaintances were married to non-Jewish spouses. I assume that most Israelis who did marry into gentile society became disassociated from the company of other Israelis.

Ethnic Origin

The large majority of Israelis in our research (nearly 80 percent) were born in Israel; the rest arrived in Israel as young children or teen-agers from Eastern Europe or the Middle East. Nearly two-thirds were of Ashkenazi extraction and about one-third of Sephardi extraction. Our population included nine Israeli couples of mixed ethnic origin.

The division between Ashkenazim and Sephardim (the latter often referred to as Middle Eastern or Oriental Jews) has become one of the most noticeable features of contemporary Israeli society. The continuing social, cultural, economic, and political disparities between these two major categories (which are also often differentiated as "old-timers" versus "newcomers") are the subject of many sociological and anthropological studies, whose researchers employ various methodological, theoretical, and ideological perspectives.[16] It has often been assumed that the phenomenon of *yerida* involves mainly Israelis of Ashkenazi extraction who are drawn to the countries that originally attracted the majority of Jewish immigrants from Eastern Europe. Furthermore, research into *yordim* has often concentrated on students and professionals, thereby supporting the perception of *yordim* as represented mainly by Israelis of Ashkenazi extraction.

There can be no doubt, however, that Israelis of Middle Eastern extraction have gradually become a considerable segment of the *yordim* population. There are some indications of a greater concentration of Israeli Sephardim in Brooklyn,[17] but the overall figures and estimates are not conclusive. As already emphasized, my own selection of the population under study was not affected by a

---

[16]See, e.g., Eisenstadt 1954; Deshen and Shokeid 1974; Smooha 1978.
[17]See particularly Dahbany Miraglia 1983; Korazim 1983.

decision to represent an estimated population of certain groups in the total Israeli population. The final inclusion of about a third of Sephardim represents, I believe, the actual distribution of the Israelis I came across during my stay in New York.

Among those identified as Sephardim were represented, in particular, descendants of Yemenite, Moroccan, and Iraqi parentage. My acquaintances also included *yordim* whose families had immigrated to Israel, before or after 1948, from Iran, Bukhara, Kurdistan, Syria, and other countries in the Middle East. Nearly half of the Ashkenazi men and women migrants were unmarried when they arrived in the United States, compared with nearly two-thirds of Sephardi immigrants; and a considerably higher proportion of Sephardi men married American women.

While all ages were represented, the large majority of emigrants were relatively young (see Table 3): more than two-thirds were in the age group between twenty and forty and more than half of the population were under thirty-six. Ashkenazi immigrants greatly outnumbered Sephardi immigrants in the older age groups, while Sephardi men tended to be concentrated in the younger age groups (see Table 3), a phenomenon related to the later arrival of Sephardi Israelis in America.

Length of Stay in the United States

While two-thirds of our population of *yordim* had already been living in the United States for more than four years, only 20 percent

Table 3. Distribution of Israeli men and women by age and ethnic extraction

Age group	Men		Women		Total
	Ashkenazi	Sephardi	Ashkenazi	Sephardi	
20–30	12	12	3	1	28
31–35	18	15	4	1	38
36–40	7	6	3	1	17
41–50	5	5	4	1	15
51+	14	1	3		18
TOTAL	56	39	17	4	116

[25]

had lived in the United States for more than fifteen years (see Table 4). The majority, however, had been in the United States for less than fifteen years. In any case, the growing stream of Israeli immigrants has gained momentum since 1967. This date, paradoxically, coincided with a period of economic prosperity and national euphoria that followed the 1967 war.[18]

Most, if not all, of those living in the United States for more than four years had already obtained a Green Card and many had also acquired American citizenship. Among those who had been in the United States less than five years, some had already obtained a Green Card and most others were involved in the legal process of acquiring it. Only very few were not yet actively engaged in a search for legal status of residence and work in the United States. There is little doubt that the majority of Israeli immigrants applied for a change of status shortly after their entry on temporary visas.[19]

Occupational Status

The majority of our research population was economically comfortable. A third of the male population and close to half of the female population (not taking into account women married to Israelis) were employed in professional, scientific, and academic occupations (engineering, computer sciences, accountancy, medicine, psychology); 20 percent of the male population were engaged in business and commerce (garment boutiques, diamond and jewelry dealers, electronic retailers and wholesalers); 11 percent were small industrial entrepreneurs and craftsmen who had set up shops for mechanical works, carpentry, clothing; and 7 percent were self-employed taxicab medallion owners. Thus, altogether more than two-thirds of the male population were either well-paid salaried professionals, established in a privately owned business or self-

[18]See Introduction, n. 13.

[19]According to the information from the American consulate in Tel Aviv, only a small minority of Israeli citizens enter the United States with immigration visas. As many as 25 percent of the applicants for tourist visas have their requests denied on the assumption that they may stay on in the United States. More than 80,000 visas are issued every year at the Tel Aviv consulate (see also Paltiel 1986:74).

Table 4. Distribution of Israeli men and women by duration of stay in the United States and ethnic extraction

Duration of stay	Men		Women		Total
	Ashkenazi	Sephardi	Ashkenazi	Sephardi	
Less than 2 years	4	3	1	2	10
2–4 years	14	10	2	1	27
5–9 years	11	13	3		27
10–14 years	13	10	6		29
15–19 years	4	2	2	1	9
20+ years	10	1	3		14
TOTAL	56	39	17	4	116

employed in a craft or service. If we add to these figures those engaged in the performing arts, managerial and bureaucratic jobs, and students (see Table 5), we find only a minority of males (13 percent) employed in lower-status positions as shop assistants, mechanics, cabdrivers. Most of these considered their present jobs as a first step.

A comparison of the *yordim*'s occupational and economic position with their former positions in Israel demonstrates a dramatic

Table 5. Distribution of Israeli men and women before and after immigration, by occupation (absolute numbers and percentages)

Occupation	Men				Women			
	Israel		U.S.		Israel		U.S.	
Professionals	8	8.4	30	31.6	3	14.3	9	42.9
Business, commerce, and diamonds	8	8.4	19	20.0			1	4.7
Self-employed in crafts	8	8.4	11	11.6			1	4.7
Taxicab medallion owners		—	7	7.3				
Administrators, managers, and teachers	6	6.3	3	3.2	9	42.9	3	14.3
Skilled workers	25	26.3	5	5.2				
Sales workers		—	5	5.2			2	9.2
Arts and entertainment performers	4	4.2	3	3.2	1	4.7		
Military men	3	3.2		—				
Unskilled workers	2	2.1	3	3.2			2	9.5
Students	11	11.6	8	8.4	4	19.0	1	4.7
Completed compulsory army service	17	17.9		—	2	9.5		
Housewife					2	9.5	2	9.5
Other	3	3.2	1	1.10				
TOTAL	95	100.0	95	99.9	21	99.9	21	99.8

[27]

change (Table 5). This comparison, however, is somewhat mislead-ing. At the time of immigration most newcomers were young; many had just completed their compulsory army service or graduated from college. Nevertheless, the rate of their mobility since immi-gration was very impressive. Upward occupational and economic mobility proved to be easier in America; for example, many Israeli technicians who had been rejected by the only major school of engineering in Israel (the Haifa Technion) successfully completed their academic degrees in American colleges and universities and were now employed in various American industries as highly paid engineers.

The starting up of new businesses also appeared much easier in the apparently limitless American market of consumers. Further-more, government agencies interfered little with private enter-preneurship compared with Israel, where the tightly supervised economy is handicapped by acute problems of foreign currency exchange and the powerful influence of the Israeli labor unions. Even without much capital, but well equipped with technical skills and ambition, many Israelis dared to undertake business projects they would not have considered in Israel. Freedman and Korazim (1986) have suggested the attraction of self-employment among Is-raeli immigrants in New York City. Only eight men among those studied had been employed as professionals in Israel in contrast with thirty in New York; eight men had been engaged in business in Israel and commerce in contrast with nineteen in New York; twenty-five men had been employed as salaried skilled workers (technicians, mechanics, craftsmen) in Israel, but only five still remained in this status in America.

Comparing the occupational status of *yordim* of Ashkenazi ex-traction with the occupational status of those of Sephardi extraction, we find some differences (Table 6). There were considerably more Ashkenazim in the professions. Ashkenazi men were also more often engaged in professional studies. But there were more Sephar-dim engaged in business and small industries. There were also more Sephardim among medallion owners and cabdrivers, and they were more often engaged in technical and blue-collar occupations.

The considerable departure of Ashkenazi *yordim* from their for-mer positions in crafts and technical jobs was mainly influenced by

Table 6. Distribution of Israeli men before and after immigration, by occupation and ethnic extraction (absolute numbers and percentages)

Occupation	Israel Ashkenazi		Israel Sephardi		United States Ashkenazi		United States Sephardi	
Professionals	8	14.3	—		22	39.3	8	20.5
Business, commerce, and diamonds	2	3.6	6	15.4	10	17.9	9	23.1
Self-employed in crafts	2	3.6	6	15.4	4	7.1	7	17.9
Taxicab medallion owners	—		—		3	5.4	4	10.3
Administrators, managers, and teachers	4	7.1	2	5.1	2	3.6	1	2.5
Skilled workers	17	30.3	8	20.5	1	1.7	4	10.3
Sales workers	—		—		3	5.4	2	5.1
Arts and entertainment performers	3	5.3	1	2.5	2	3.6	1	2.5
Military men	3	5.3	—		—		—	
Unskilled workers	1	1.8	1	2.5	1	1.7	2	5.1
Students	5	8.9	6	15.4	7	12.5	1	2.5
Completed compulsory army service	9	16.1	8	20.5	—		—	
Other	2	3.6	1	2.5	1	1.7	—	
TOTAL	56	99.9	39	99.8	56	99.9	39	99.8

their attainment of engineering degrees. Referring to the tendency among the Sephardim to enter into business and self-employment, in contrast to the Ashkenazim's preference for the professions, an Israeli of Moroccan extraction, a contractor in the building industry, commented jokingly: "In Israel the Sephardim work and the Ashkenazim get rich. But here the Sephardim are independent and the Ashkenazim work in the service of the Americans." On the whole, however, there were no significant economic differences between the two groups. The cabdrivers, of low status in Israel, nevertheless made a comfortable living as medallion owners, comparable if not superior to that of some professionals. Ashkenazi men were also often attracted to medallion ownership, but relatively more Sephardi men seemed to be engaged in this occupation. In any case, the income and occupational position of a considerable number of both Ashkenazim and Sephardim had greatly improved since their immigration. In later chapters (Chapter 8 in particular) I shall describe the professional careers of individuals in more detail.

Among Israeli couples, the major decision to migrate was usually made in light of the men's economic opportunities, whereas the women's prospects of employment were usually of lesser consideration. The only noteworthy information with regard to the small group of women introduced in our figures (which relate only to single women or to those married to American men) was a trend toward professionalization (see Table 5). In New York many of them were employed in various professions as psychologists, computer scientists, and so on. To the extent that Israeli single women left Israel, they were mostly of Ashkenazi extraction, and the number of Sephardi women was too small to allow for a reliable comparison between their achievements and those of Ashkenazi women.

Motives for Immigration

The research core population was composed of only those men and women with whom I discussed the reasons that brought them to New York. Observing the motives or situational constraints that affected the population of all men, we find four major causes, which are presented by order of prominence (see Table 7):

1. *Economic and professional problems or temptations.* This category included those who faced economic difficulties or were dissatisfied with their work. Also included were those whose income and professional position in Israel were satisfactory but who were tempted by the opportunities offered or expected in America.
2. *An inner drive to get out and see the world.* This category included those who left Israel in the first place because they wanted a change, or were looking for new experiences and adventures: "I needed some fresh air"; "I wanted to roam and knock around." Most of them, however, had no clear plans for the future and were not considering emigration. Others in this category planned to leave Israel for a short period as part of a trip abroad or a visit to relatives and friends. Most of them delayed their return because of various developments, such as meeting and marrying an American girl, starting work or university studies.
3. *Pursuit or completion of professional and graduate studies.* Among these, the technicians who came to complete engineering studies were particularly noticeable. Students of the humanities, social sciences, and other subjects were more often enrolled in Ph.D. programs.

[30]

Table 7. Distribution of Israeli men and women, by initial cause for departure from Israel, ethnic extraction, and marital status (in percentages)

Initial cause	Men					Women	
	All men	Ashkenazi	Sephardi	Single and divorced	Married	Single and divorced	Married
Economic push and pull	29.5	26.8	33.3	23.3	34.6	57.1	28.5
Adventure	20.0	17.8	23.1	32.5	9.6	21.4	
Studies	17.9	23.2	10.3	20.9	15.4		
Family reunion	13.7	10.7	17.9		21.1		71.4
Personal issues	9.4	8.9	10.3	6.9	11.5	7.1	
Security, army service	4.2	5.4	2.5	7.0	1.9		
Emissaries	3.2	5.4		2.3	3.8	14.3	
Political issues	1.0	1.8			1.9		
Other			2.5	2.3			
TOTAL	99.9	100.0	99.9	99.8	99.8	99.9	99.9

4. *Pressure or wish to join their own or their spouses' relatives.*
These either joined close relatives who had already immigrated or
succumbed to the pressure of their American spouses to return
home.

Apart from these four factors initiating the departure from Israel
of the majority of the couples and singles, there were also other
more specific reasons for particular individuals. Some left because
of "personal reasons" relating to family crises (such as matrimonial
problems) or legal entanglements at home or work. Contrary to a
common assumption, only very few left because they were fed up
or worried by Israeli security problems and the duty of service with
the reserve forces; a few first arrived as officials (*shlichim*) of Israeli
institutions, while only one of my acquaintances emphasized political reasons for his departure. The decision of some men to move
was further encouraged by secondary factors. Among these, the
offer of hospitality or other types of support by relatives was particularly important, while other considered professional studies or job
opportunities.

The order of factors described above varied among the different
groups of *yordim*. Thus, for example, professional studies were
more prominent among Ashkenazi men in initiating immigration
(second in order of major factors versus fourth among Sephardi
men); single men and women were primarily motivated by the wish
to get out and see the world; single women apparently were not
affected at all by economic factors; and married men were more
influenced than others by the desire for family reunion and particularly the pressure of American spouses (see Table 8).

Only a minority of the *yordim* were aware at the time of their
departure that they were going to stay on, acquire a new citizenship, and possibly never return to Israel for permanent residence. Even among those who wished to join their relatives in the
United States, not all grasped the finality of their move. Most
students planned to go back to Israel with a degree that would
better their chances to find a good job. These tempting opportunities were considered an excuse for a break in the routine which
would enable the men to make a small fortune, gain professional
experience, and satisfy their curiosity. In fact, most immigrants

Table 8. Distribution of Israelis by four major causes for departure from Israel, ethnic extraction, marital status, and sex (in percentages)

	Economic push and pull	Adventure	Studies	Family reunion
Ashkenazi men	26.8	17.8	23.2	10.7
Sephardi men	33.3	23.1	10.3	17.9
Single men	23.3	32.5	20.9	4.6
Married men	34.6	9.6	15.4	21.1
Single women	—	57.1	21.4	—

SOURCE: See Table 7, above.

looked back nostalgically and many regretted the circumstances that led to their leaving Israel. "We got stuck" (*nitka'nu*) was a common expression they used to describe their situation. The longer the stay, the more difficult became the possibility of going home. Not only did they themselves change, but Israel also changed—in their perception and in reality.

Children of *Yordim*

I became acquainted with ten adult children of *yordim* who still identified themselves as Israelis in spite of their long stay in the United States. Most of them left Israel in their early teens and had been in America for more than fifteen years. Two women had married Israeli men, but most other men and women were married to Americans. Although the women with Israeli husbands wished to return to Israel, only one actually did go back during my stay. One other single woman was making plans to return. Although those who arrived in their teens often felt alienated in America, unless encouraged by parents or by an Israeli spouse the prospects of *yordim*'s children returning to Israel seemed most unlikely.

Those Who Return

Among the 116 familes and singles introduced in our study, 11 went back to Israel during my stay (of whom one has since returned

[33]

to New York). Five others bought apartments in Israel as a major step toward their return. Thus, altogether about 14 percent were making serious efforts to go back. Six of those who went back and all those who bought apartments had been living in America for more than five years, while a few others had been there for more than ten years. The figures are too few to allow for further analysis. However, the majority of those who went back were of Askhkenazi extraction, and those who bought apartments were mainly of Sephardi extraction. Most returnees were married except for one single woman and two divorcees.[20]

As small as the number of *yordim* who go back to Israel may seem, they do prove that the wishes often expressed by *yordim* to return to Israel are not entirely groundless. Those who stayed behind were very interested in the others' attempts to return and their trials and experiences in Israel. As long as some Israelis do return, particularly those who have done well in America, *yerida* can still be authentically perceived by many *yordim* as only a transient stage in the life cycle of Israelis.

[20]See Toren (1976), who examined certain characteristics and motivations of Israeli return migrants.

[2]

Yordim and American Jews

Israelis consider American Jews' continuing economic support and their influence on American politics in the Middle East one of the most important external factors affecting Israel's survival. But the relationship between American Jews and Israel has never been as simple as many outsiders imagine. Although Israeli leaders have always counted on American Jewry's support, some consider it second best to the Zionist role and the responsibility American Jews should feel toward immigrating to Israel. Many Israelis perceive American Jewry's economic support as an astute way to assuage their feelings of guilt for avoiding the duty of *aliya* (immigration to Israel) and the sharing of the hardships and risks of Israeli life.

Israelis usually take for granted American Jews' admiration for Israeli society and its achievements, particularly its military superiority in the Middle East. It has also become a standard assumption in Israel that the courageous front adopted by Israeli society in the face of antagonistic neighbors has enabled world Jewry to stand tall. The prosperous and now self-assured American Jews seem to owe a special debt to Israel and its citizens, who have bestowed upon them the gift of a land they can be proud of and which makes them equal to other influential ethnics in the United States.

My observations reveal that the ambivalence toward American Jews experienced in Israel is transformed into complete separatism, if not hostility, once Israelis arrive in America for an extended stay, with the prospect of changing their citizenship.

Unwelcome Guests

Although most Israelis I observed had little, if any, contact with American Jews, they usually assumed that American Jews resented them. This perception was often expressed either by relating an actual encounter or in more abstract fashion. Most common was the following story, usually told in anger to an audience whose smiles confirmed a shared understanding: "I met a contributor to the UJA [United Jewish Appeal] who asked me: 'What are you doing here?' I answered: 'It's much easier to give away money than blood. You offer money and expect in exchange that my children and I defend the Jewish state. You should understand that Israel is yours as much as it is mine. Now I've decided to change places with you. I'm going to make money and give some of it to Israel while you and your children make *aliya* to Israel.'" (This was related by a single woman in her early thirties who had emigrated to America with her parents when she was in her late teens.) A similar version was the following answer to an indignant American Jew, as related by Dina, a woman in her early forties and mother of three children, who had arrived with her family thirteen years earlier: "I invested twenty-seven years of my life in Israel; now it's your turn. What are you going to do when Hitler arrives in America?" Another young man related how his aunt had suggested that he move from New York to Los Angeles in order to be close to her. But he thought she would have preferred that he remain an Israeli in Israel. One of his listeners, an engineer married to an American woman, said: "Your aunt would have preferred you to stay in Israel and spill your blood there." The first speaker, who rejected this interpretation, explained that he was not in a combat unit anyway, and his aunt, who loved him, would have been "proud" had he stayed in Israel. He went on to comment that Israel's attitude toward American Jewry has always been hypocritical. Even Ben-Gurion, who preached *aliya*, had a vested interest in the American Jews' money.

More humorous was an Israeli businessman in his late fifties who had first arrived in America ten years earlier as a representative of an Israeli bank. When asked by an Israeli friend about the prospects of Israelis' integration into the Jewish community, he answered: "The Israeli is arrogant and the American Jew doesn't like to see him around. He gives his money away to support the Israelis in Israel and now he finds them here." As a case in point, he related his personal experience at a golf club to which he invited an Israeli visitor. An American acquaintance at the club, on discovering that his guest had studied at the Technion (Haifa School of Engineering), commented that he had once made a contribution to the Technion. The speaker, who sensed a paternalistic and somewhat condescending tone, asked him: "Tell me, Harry, was it a hundred-dollar or a two-hundred-dollar check you gave?" When the American told him he thought it was two hundred dollars, he asked: "Tell the truth, Harry, was it a client who pressed you to make that contribution?"

David, the manager of the Israeli Club, a young man in his early thirties who had come to the United States three years earlier in order to join his wife's family and continue his studies, wished to persuade the Jewish charities to expand their services to the growing Israeli constituency. At a meeting with Jewish executives he argued: "The American Jews relate to the Israelis as symbols but not as human beings. They want to see them as heroes in the Israeli army; but if the Israelis reject this definition, they don't relate to them anymore. Although the Israelis constitute 10 percent of the Jewish population in New York, they are completely neglected, as if they don't exist at all." On another occasion he told me the story of his two cousins, both holocaust survivors; one was sent to the United States and the other to Israel. Some years later the Israeli cousin also migrated to America. His relatives were surprised to see the Israeli cousin joining them. He ended his story with the exclamation: "It's all right for American Jews to live in America, but not for the Israelis." He was thus suggesting that chance or fate, rather than free will or ideology, took one child to America and the other to Israel. Various versions of this story were related to me by other *yordim*.

Although most Israelis had not personally experienced rejection by American Jews, they were sensitive to the anomaly that their presence in America presented vis-à-vis the ideology, myth, and reality entailed in their claim for Israeli identity. This anomaly was succinctly expressed by a Jewish intellectual deeply committed to Zionism with whom I often discussed the issue of *yerida:* "American Jews have donated money and supported the establishment of a state in order for the Israelis to be there. The presence of *yordim* in the United States is antithetical to the principle of Israel for Israelis."

The alienation of the Israelis from American Jews was also expressed in a lecture given at the Israeli Club by Rachel Eitan, an Israeli author married to an American, who claimed that important representatives of Israeli literature are often neglected by American teachers of Hebrew literature because the descriptions of Israeli life in their books are considered by supporters of Zionism to be evidence of disloyalty. I thought she implied that Israeli authors, although resident in Israel, raise doubts in their work about the moral stature of Israel. The other listeners' interpretations of the author's claim were somewhat different. Most of those who participated in the discussion argued that American Jews avoid Israeli literature because of the guilt it evokes among American readers over their betrayal of the Zionist duty of *aliya*. The descriptions of life in Israel, good or bad, are a reminder of their major deficiency. Another opinion, also raised on other occasions, held that American Jews neglect Israeli literature because they envy the Israelis who are portrayed as proud and self-assured, something they too strived for once they left the Eastern European *shtetl* but failed to achieve. Thus, according to the participants' perception, the problem was not related to American Jews' dilemma concerning the implementation of the Zionist ideal in Israel and its public image. Instead, it expressed their own conflicts, interests, and aversions, which concur with their resentment of *yordim* in America who are not performing the role designated for them by American Jews.

The sense of deep antipathy provoked by American Jews was angrily manifested by Yaffa, who otherwise seemed to be well integrated into the American milieu in which she had lived with her family for more than twenty years, during which time she had held office in one of the major Jewish establishments: "I can't stand the Americans and I don't believe them. They want to see you fail. I can only rely on Israelis." As proof she related a recent encounter with a Jewish neighbor who was in the habit of asking her for favors. On the one occasion when Yaffa phoned the neighbor and asked to borrow a jack, the other woman replied that she was too busy to look for it right away. Next day the neighbor called and suggested that she come over and pick up the jack. Yaffa retorted sharply: "When you're stuck on a highway you can't wait for tomorrow." With that she abruptly hung up and never spoke to her neighbor again. Since Yaffa does not drive, the details of the actual encounter may have been somewhat different, but whether real or concocted, the story and its images expressed her feelings of bitter estrangement from American Jews. Her husband, Eli, presented a less hostile attitude when he explained: "When I first left Israel I didn't imagine I would spend so many years here. I didn't stand in line at the American embassy for an immigration visa. So I don't consider myself either cut off from Israel or an American." Indeed, Eli's friends were exclusively Israelis (see Chapter 8, Profile 2). A similar position was emphatically presented at a meeting of a group of Israelis, most of whom had lived in the United States for many years and who met regularly at monthly gatherings dedicated to cultural affairs. Rina, a woman in her early forties, exclaimed emotionally: "Everyone in this room got stuck [*nitke'u*] in the United States. We consider Israel our home and ourselves different from the Americans." She and her husband were employed at a prestigious Jewish organization, but their wide network of friends consisted almost exclusively of Israelis (see Chapter 8, Profile 4).

Hostile descriptions of American Jews were often expressed by those who had business ties with them; for example, Arik, an engineer who did extra jobs after his daily work: "If you tell a black client that he owes you twenty-five dollars, he offers you five dollars extra, but the Jews try to get you to work for cheap" (see Chapter 8, Profile 10).

My own closer relationships with American Jews were mainly confined to colleagues on the various New York campuses. They informed me of the little love their acquaintances felt toward *yordim*. I was told, for example, about the term "fish" applied to Israelis, meaning "fucking Israeli shithead."

Only once did I meet an American Jew who openly defended the *yordim*. Himself a holocaust survivor who had made a fortune in America, he rejected the use of the term *yordim*, which I had used during a lecture, and added: "We have to make sure that they stay Jewish. I was also hassled when I tried to get into American society. Every Jew has the right to live wherever he chooses!"

Are Israelis Jewish?

The major arena of conflict, though rarely expressed explicitly, is in the field of personal and national identity. In Israel, secular Israelis consider themselves Jewish regardless of their alienation from any form of Orthodoxy. They are usually unaware of American Jewry's attachment to Jewish religious traditions that are often very different from those represented by Israeli Orthodoxy. Although every Israeli has heard about the enclaves of extreme Jewish Orthodoxy in Brooklyn, only a small minority is informed about the American style of modern Orthodoxy as well as the Conservative and Reform movements, which bring together the majority of organized American Jewry. These forms of Jewish life, which fit in with American mainstream culture of denominational and communal association (Glazer 1957), are alien to Israelis' perception of Jewish identity, which is an elementary component in the Israeli definition of citizenship and nationality (see Chapter 6). Arriving in America, they immediately find a wide disparity between American Jews and their Israeli brethren. The Israelis discover the central role of the synagogue (or temple) in the life of American Jews,[1] and the American Jews are stunned by the ignorance and complete withdrawal of Israelis from Jewish tradition and from Jewish organizations. At a lecture I gave in a modern Orthodox synagogue in a prosperous Long Island suburb, a prominent physician asked me in astonishment: "How is it that Israeli-born young men who speak Hebrew have no elementary knowledge of Judaism, have no idea what to do in the synagogue or during the festivals?" He told me about an Israeli who planned to open a falafel restaurant and was told about the necessity of a kosher kitchen for a successful business in New York: "He didn't know the first thing about *kashrut* [Hebrew dietary laws]."

[1]See Glazer 1957.

Separated from Israeli family gatherings, which are held among secular Israelis during Jewish festivals, and cut off from the national seasonal holidays dictated in Israel by the Jewish calendar, the disassociation of the Israelis from Jewish tradition and the disparity between American Jews and the *yordim* seem even more profound. During lectures and debates (particularly at the Israeli Club) when the issue of Jewish identity was raised, participants usually mentioned spontaneously as its major characteristics service in the Israeli army, residence in Israel (without specifying length of time), and the speaking of Hebrew. They were frequently rebuffed by the American Jewish lecturers, who denied the prospects of Jewish survival in the United States without any religious commitment. Some Israelis presented an arrogant stand, such as that expressed by a student who claimed: "I am an Israeli; I don't perceive of myself as Jewish. It is only by chance that I was born to Jewish parents." But at the same gathering an emphatic reaction to her statement was voiced by Dani, an outspoken young man who had been living in New York for three years: "I have a blind spot two thousand years wide." In other words, he felt that his Jewishness was lacking entirely in the traditions developed in the Diaspora since the destruction of the Temple. Dani was indeed searching, albeit unsuccessfully, for ways to fill this vacuum (see Chapter 8, Profile 12). Aware of this disparity, Dina often expressed her anger at American Jews who "do not consider the Israelis as Jews but perceive them as a separate group." The spectrum of the Israelis' reactions also included Ruth's exclamation that since leaving Israel three years before she had become emotionally Jewish. She explained that it was possibly easier in her case because she had spent her childhood in Eastern Europe and only immigrated to Israel in her early teens. As a symbol of this change she mentioned that she now took her son to the synagogue on "Yom Kipper" (Yiddish intonation) since those who look for "Yom Kippur" (the Israeli intonation) are in the wrong place here. There were also Israelis who occasionally would have wished to go to a synagogue but refrained from taking this step because they thought that they would not be welcome or would be looked down upon as guests who did not pay regular membership fees.

While the religious disparity between "Jews" and "Israelis"

seemed unbreachable, particularly with regard to secular Israelis of Ashkenazi extraction (see Chapter 6), both sides viewed the related field of Jewish education as a matter of great importance and urgency. Both *yordim* and American Jews became gradually aware that the chances of the *yordim*'s children remaining either "Israelis" or "Jews" depended a great deal on their exposure to some kind of parochial education. There is no definitive data on the extent of the enrollment of Israeli children in Jewish educational programs. Representatives of the Federation of Jewish Philanthropies and the Jewish Board of Education claim that the rate of enrollment is very low, 25 percent at most.[2] In contrast, Korazim (1983) states that about 80 percent of Israeli children are enrolled in Jewish schools. According to my estimate, the actual registration of *yordim*'s children in Jewish schools is higher than that assumed by the official sources of American Jewry, yet considerably lower than that suggested by Korazim, whose sample was highly selective (see Chapter 8).

The low estimate of federation officials fits the common perception among American Jews of the Israelis as far removed from Jewish tradition and reluctant to join Jewish organizations or form their own. I believe, however, that the federation's low estimates were also influenced by other factors: in most mixed couples, for example, the American spouse is the major family agent at school; and some schools are not affiliated with the Jewish Board of Education.

Israeli parents were extremely uncertain about making the right choice concerning their children's education. Many expressed their wish for an Israeli-style secular school. But this option seemed to be the least likely possibility. The Israeli authorities were reluctant to support a service that would make life easier for the *yordim*. The Jewish organizations were doubtful about the value and substance of a "religion-free" education, which, they argued, would not be much different from a school whose curriculum is taught in Italian or Spanish. The *yordim* themselves were neither able nor willing to finance the establishment of their own schools. Moreover, some *yordim* doubted whether many Israeli parents would register their

[2]See Cohen and Levi 1983:9; Levi 1986:173.

children at an Israeli school were this alternative available. As evidence they pointed out that the Israeli-style Sunday school at the Central Queens YM & YWHA in Forest Hills, a neighborhood heavily populated by Israelis, was unable to recruit more than a dozen children in spite of extensive advertising.

Many *yordim* enrolled their children, albeit reluctantly, at the various Jewish schools. My own children were registered in preschool classes of a Jewish school whose population of students of all grades included at least 50 percent of Israeli parentage. The school was unknown to the Jewish Board of Education, but was supported by the network of an orthodox movement. The fees at this school were lower than those paid at the more prestigious Jewish day schools. In spite of the orthodoxy of their children's school, none of the Israeli parents of my children's classmates was associated with a synagogue. Moreover, a few of my acquaintances enrolled their children at Orthodox schools reputed to have a more rigorous curriculum in general studies, although other Jewish schools (such as Solomon Shechter in Queens) better suited their secular style of life.

I am not implying that the Jewish organizations are wrong about the reluctance of *yordim* to enroll their children in Jewish schools. This reluctance was often articulated, particularly by Israelis on official visits and by the better educated among *yordim*. An Israeli woman whose husband was sent to New York for four years and who was instrumental in establishing an afternoon Hebrew school, declared at a meeting of a search committee of services for Israelis set up by the Federation of Jewish Philanthropies: "In my school we teach the Bible as a cultural source and not as a document of religion. I shall not send my children to a Jewish or an Israeli day school. I don't want my children to be segregated. When they go back to Israel they'll become Israelis again within two weeks!" She did, however, enroll her children at the afternoon Israeli school when she discovered that they were losing their proficiency in Hebrew. She believed that the afternoon "cultural" school was a solution to the problem of the preservation of Israeli culture among Israelis in America. Her position was supported by other Israelis and *yordim* also attending the meeting in the capacity of experts on *yordim* society. They all argued that Israelis avoid Jewish day

[43]

schools because the association with these schools might confirm the permanence of their stay in America and therefore their stigmatized identity as *yordim*. The Israelis and the researchers of *yordim* thus supported the beliefs held by the Jewish establishment concerning the *yordim*'s attitudes toward Jewish culture and Jewish education.

Unaffiliated *Yordim* versus Organized Jewry

The issue of synagogue and school affiliation relates to a major structural difference between American Jews and the *yordim* population, namely, the establishment of community and nationwide organizations. American Jewry, probably more than any other ethnic group in America, has proved unique in the proliferation of viable communal and national institutions. In striking contrast, Israeli immigrants in New York, while disassociating themselves from active participation in Jewish communal and national organizations available to them, have not initiated even one viable institution of their own. "Israelis in New York," the only committee organized during the early 1980s in order to promote cultural activities among New York's population of *yordim*, survived for a very short time and was restricted to the organization of a few parties associated with Jewish festivals. It was first initiated by the manager of the Israeli Club in Forest Hills with the support of the Federation of Jewish Philanthropies. However, the leading participants of the committee rejected the federation's supervision, and their attempts at independence resulted in a continuing limbo. During the two years of my stay the committee did not function at all.

Both sides were well aware of this striking difference. An American friend once told me: "You don't need more than two American Jews in Israel to immediately set up an association of some sort. This is the way of life in America. But Israelis, even in greater numbers, wouldn't do that—they are used to depending on governmental agencies." The manager of the Israeli Club in Forest Hills, however, suggested defensively that Israelis were not used to association building in the American Jewish style because in Israel "unity and communal action are attained through the shared security problems and the solidarity of family and neighborhood."

A third possible reason for the reluctance of *yordim* to join American Jewish organizations, as well as to establish their own ethnic associations, was similar to the explanation of *yordim's* attitudes toward education—namely, their behavior is rooted in their reluctance to confirm the finality of their departure from Israel. Thus, for example, an Israeli official delegate involved in issues of Hebrew education in the various Jewish agencies argued during a meeting of the Federation of Jewish Philanthropies: "A contribution to the UJA made by an Israeli would add the last nail in the coffin of *yerida,* reaffirming his position as an outside observer of Israel instead of his self-image of a sojourner." A researcher employed by the federation stated the related view that the Israelis still consider themselves at the receiving end of the exchange relationship between Israel and world Jewry.

But the Israelis' disassociation from American Jewish organizations was also rooted in their sense of being rejected and discriminated against, in comparison to other groups of newcomers to the Jewish constituency, such as Russian Jews. In the eyes of the Israelis American Jews felt that they had already given sufficient support to the Israeli government. The intricacies of the exchange relationship between "Israelis and Jews" was expressed during the first conference on the phenomenon of Israeli immigrants in the United States, held in Manhattan in November 1983. In view of the fact that the conference, convened by the City University of New York, was widely advertised in Israeli circles, I expected a large Israeli turnout. But, in fact, there were very few Israelis and the conference was mainly attended by American Jews. Moreover, the discussion that followed the formal presentations was completely dominated by the American attendants. The Israelis, who were the subject of the conference, remained incognito.

On the way home to Queens only three of us were left to carry on a heated debate about the conference. Dani complained about the planning of the conference, which, in his view, should have contained a confrontation between the Israelis and American Jews: "This would have convinced the Jews to stop offering us services which suit them now that their number is in decline. We need an Israeli school to make sure that our children will be able to go back to Israel." His stand was completely rejected by Eli, whose longer stay in America and association with American Jews at work made him an expert on American Jews. With the growing immigration of Israelis he also seemed more inclined to comply with American Jews' perceptions of the Israelis. He thus presented the American Jews' viewpoint: "A Russian Jew arriving in America has no place to go back to and so American Jews offer him support. Why should they help an Israeli who sold his apartment and came over with considerable means to start a business, but failed? American Jews offer support to Jewish communities and groups, but some time later they come back to them and ask for their contribution. The Israelis don't contribute to the UJA. We are ready to take but not to give and when asked to contribute we react, 'How come?' [*Ma pit'om?*]" Although Eli represented the American Jews' point of view at this encounter, on other occasions he appeared to consider the Israelis of superior status and therefore entitled to special allowances: "The Israeli *yored* is still a better Zionist than the American. The American Zionist has never made *aliya*. The *yored* is an Israeli and whenever something happens in Israel he packs his suitcases and boards the first available flight, while the American Jew stays behind." In a more conciliatory mood on another occasion he pointed out: "The American Jew assumes that the Israeli is more Jewish than himself, while the Israeli assumes that the American is more Jewish." Thus both sides seemed to acknowledge their deficiency—the Israeli who is estranged from Judaism, and the American Jew, who has never experienced life in Israel.

It is impossible to pinpoint the "true" source or interpretation of either the *yordim*'s reluctance to join Jewish organizations (including those whose main aim is the support of Israel) or of the absence of their own initiated ethnic organizations. Whatever the roots of this phenomenon, which is indeed surprising when compared with other new waves of immigrants in New York, it serves to enhance their invisibility and at the same time exerts little pressure on the American Jewish establishment to consider more seriously the largest group of Jewish immigrants to have arrived at America's shores since the aftermath of World War II.

The Sealed-off Homes of American Jews

The cultural and organizational disparity between Israelis and American Jews was most painfully experienced by the Israelis in their attempts to socialize with American Jews. Most Israelis I met from various socioeconomic strata complained about or pointed out the impossibility of penetrating into American society, Jewish society included. Dani, among my closest friends, an extremely outgoing, gentle, and helpful man, told me when we first met that I was the second Israeli he had talked to after two years in America. He had finally decided to look for Israeli company after giving up hopes of developing a network of American friends: "I wanted to make friends with Americans and integrate into a new society and culture. I did everything in my power. At one stage I decided to try the singles bars, but couldn't stand it after two visits. As a last resort I decided to get into American homes through the back door: I advertised my technical skills in the newspapers and thus had the chance to meet Americans through my trade. It was very tiring doing those jobs after a long day's work and led to nothing in my craving for American company. All and all I made two friends in two years, a Jewish girl and a non-Jewish immigrant from Europe. With this achievement in hand I finally admitted my failure." Since then, his growing network of friends was exclusively composed of Israelis.

A successful Israeli financial consultant, a single man in his late thirties, told me: "Socially I have not integrated in spite of my fourteen years in America. I am a stranger to my American friends." Arik, married to an American Jewish woman, often commented: "You can't develop a friendship with Americans; they usually stay at home and watch television. Today is my father-in-law's birthday. I will pop in, say hello, and go on to the swimming pool. In America it's enough to say hello in order to be a friend."

A diamond dealer in his mid-thirties who had arrived in America three years earlier said: "Here everyone carries on his life in splendid isolation. You can't get close to American Jews either. It works like this: Mr. Smith calls on Mr. Jones and invites him to dinner after telling him, 'It's such a long time since we last met.' They have a very friendly evening together and then don't see each other for another six months. If you meet an Israeli who tells you that he has made American friends I don't believe him. I miss my friends in Israel so much."

Sarah, an academic married to an American Jewish man, had been living in America for twenty-seven years. She commented

[47]

painfully: "It is all only a substitute here. In Israel you go to the theater, you meet strangers and start talking to them. You wind up the evening drinking coffee at their home. There is nothing here beyond the specific context of the meeting. The best time I ever had was when the kids went to a Jewish summer camp and I accompanied them as teacher. The atmosphere there was cozy and informal for a change. I spent ten months out of every year waiting for those two months in spite of the strain of a full year of teaching [in the company of many Jewish colleagues]. I know there is an explanation for this alienation: the distances, patterns of work, etc. True, the Americans have their friends, but these bonds are very shallow." Another Israeli intellectual, also married to an American Jewish man, concluded: "The Americans lack warmth and are difficult to get to know. They are intimidated by strangers but are also reserved among themselves." In a more positive tone, Dani stated the difference that makes an Israeli: "An Israeli is a person who is 'open' and whom you can easily approach and befriend." On second thought, by way of explanation for the above characteristics, he added: "An Israeli is a person who shares my experiences in the army, the youth movement and speaks my language." Carol, the American wife of an Israeli (see Chapter 8, Profile 10), commented: "Israelis are outgoing and that is what I love about them, in contrast to Americans, who are reserved and selfish." She made the same observation as Dani when she added: "The Israelis have shared experiences which most Americans don't have."

An Israeli professional married to an American Jew often commented that he could not attune himself to the American style of entertainment: "They either sit around drinking or go out for dinner. In Israel when people meet they talk, sing, and dance." An Israeli woman married to a prominent Jewish intellectual, commented: "It's true, the Americans are more formal and their sociability is centered around meals. The Israelis are ill at ease with that and they are also too aggressive for American taste. The Israelis are a tribe, they need the company of each other every Friday night [the Israeli weekly occasion for hospitality at home]. They are also much more politically minded than the Americans. When you get into a taxicab in Israel, the driver immediately starts talking pol-

[48]

itics. So the meeting between unacquainted Israelis is much easier than meeting Americans."

Only one of my acquaintances considered American Jews to be no less warm and hospitable than Israelis. He had left Israel twenty-five years ago; as a holocaust survivor with no relatives in Israel, he had felt painfully lonely in the small and family-oriented Israeli society of the 1950s and had often been looked upon with pity. In New York he met another survivor and a family friend who offered him help, and he eventually got married and set himself up in business. His case was indeed very unusual among the Israelis, whose major sense of loss was usually related to the absence of Israeli informality and a close network of relatives and friends. Even those *yordim* who found the American style of sociability more congenial pointed to the sporadic nature of their social ties. An engineer married to an American Jewish woman, living in the United States for five years, said: "It takes months until you meet a friend and a lot of planning. But when you finally meet, the meal is excellent and the occasion serious."

As noted by many Israelis, not only did American Jews make no effort to facilitate the Israelis' entry into American society, but they themselves appeared to be no less reserved and unapproachable than gentile Americans. This same observation was made by two of my Israeli acquaintances on sabbatical leave. One of them, who regularly attended an Orthodox synagogue, was deeply offended because no one in the congregation had ever invited him for an informal visit at home. The second academic, who was more sensitive and took the blame on himself, decided to shorten his sabbatical because his family lacked "the social protective cover" necessary for a comfortable stay. He felt, as did many *yordim*, that he had failed to penetrate American society. The two academics felt that the reception by their colleagues on campus and in other circles, among whom were many Jews, was much cooler than that offered to American visitors in Israel. Politeness and friendliness that did not lead to an invitation home was interpreted as a refusal to allow entry into the more intimate territory of social relationships. In terms of Israeli norms of sociability, the partners to these relationships remained strangers.

[49]

Eliminating a Social Anomaly

American Jews and Israeli *yordim* regard each other with little sympathy. Each reminds the other of what they would wish to be, and of the fact that they cannot reconcile themselves to the price involved in the attainment of these goals. The *yordim*, striving to achieve the economic and social position gained by their American brethren, are, nevertheless, inhibited by their inherent disdain of Diaspora Jews and their aversion to being identified as such. Israelis' contempt of Diaspora life has most recently been expressed by A. B. Yehoshua in his collection of essays *For the Sake of Normality* (1980).[3] As expressed in these essays, the Jews' continuing existence in the Diaspora, which entailed much suffering and humiliation, represents the most acute symptom of a national neurosis. Israelis are brought up to believe, as A. B. Yehoshua does, that the Jews could have escaped the Diaspora much earlier had they had the courage to break their chains of bondage, which were at least partly forced on them by Jewish religious beliefs of redemption by the Messiah. Religious passivity and the priority of economic security are to blame for the Jews' endurance of Diaspora existence.

Reaching out for American Jews by joining their synagogues and other organizations demands the transformation of a crucial part of the *yordim*'s identity and self-perception as compared to that of Diaspora Jews. Their sense of real or assumed rejection by American Jews supports the self-image of *yordim* as closer to the Israeli axis of identity in spite of their present status as Diaspora Jews.

American Jews are bewildered by the presence of Israelis in their midst (S. M. Cohen 1986). For many of them, Israel has become a new symbol of Jewish identification, particularly among the less Orthodox. They have, however, in effect refuted the prospects of their own emigration to Israel. Instead they have adopted the role of guardians and supporters of Israel, while preserving a slim hope of a move to Israel in the unspecified future. In the meantime, many have made Israel a site for pilgrimage and visits, which usually confirm their beliefs about life in the Promised Land. But the

---

[3]The English title of the book *Between Right and Right* (1981) does not convey the tone of the Hebrew title.

arrival of the skilled and often affluent Israeli immigrants who have left the Jewish homeland raises doubts as to the raison d'être of Zionism and, at the same time, appears to threaten the viability and security of Israel. The Israelis in Queens tend to concentrate in "Jewish neighborhoods" and their presence cannot be avoided. These Israelis, attracted to the safety and congeniality of a Jewish environment, thus give rise to a continuing confrontation with their inhospitable brethren.

Israeli citizens wishing to settle in America introduce an anomaly with which it is difficult to come to terms. For many generations Jewish communities everywhere have extended help to their brothers in bondage or at physical risk. American Jews have been particularly generous. Russian Jews are the most recent group to have received such support, although they are the least "Jewish" in their education and religious outlook. The *yordim,* on the other hand, introduce a total revision in the definition and categories of Jews in the Diaspora. They indeed have a most peculiar identity. On the one hand, they openly repudiate Jewish tradition, assuming instead a superior Hebrew culture; on the other hand, they have forsaken the Jewish homeland and cradle of the culture, which they claim to represent.

Although the comparison may seem farfetched, the *yordim* represent a social anomaly that can be perceived in terms of Douglas's (1966) analysis of the treatment of cases of anomaly and ambiguity that threaten the cultural categories of a social structure and moral order. For example, in some West African tribes, twins are killed at birth in order to eliminate a social anomaly, since it is held that two humans cannot be born from the same womb at the same time. Douglas argues that "anomalous events may be labelled dangerous. Admittedly individuals sometimes feel anxiety confronted with anomaly" (p. 39). Although American Jews do not go so far as to kill the Israelis in order to eliminate a social anomaly and an ambiguous identity, they may wish to restore the categories and definitions that constitute the order and values of Israeli, Jewish, and Zionist identities, respectively. To that purpose they employ other strategies: they ignore the *yordim,* avoid associating with them, and express their disdain and resentment to the extent that their code of civility allows them to do so. They do permit *yordim* to join their

[51]

institutions, particularly if that affiliation might be profitable. Thus, for example, Israelis have joined the YM-YWHA in Forest Hills, where they make use of the sports facilities. But the Y's management was not willing to support programs for the Israeli constituency unless funded by the Federation of Jewish Philanthropies. The federation's support of the Israeli Club, however, was never made a permanent arrangement and the club's continuing operation remained uncertain (see Chapter 4).

The dilemma confronting the federation was clearly expressed in the first recommendation concerning Israeli adults put forward in the 1983 final report prepared by the subcommittee on services to Israelis:[4] "The *delicate balance* of not losing Israelis to the Jewish community yet not creating a support system for Yerida must be maintained" (Cohen and Levi 1983:16).

The term "fish" and other degrading references applied to Israelis by some Jews remind one of another theoretical theme in Douglas's thesis, that of ritual uncleanliness—the dirt and pollution that endanger the moral order and sacred patterns of culture. The *yordim*'s presence in the United States defiles the idea of the major creation of the Jewish people in the twentieth century. Yitzhak Rabin, who called *yordim* the leftover of weaklings (*nefolet shel nemushot*),[5] seemed to designate a pariah group, synonymous with ritual uncleanliness.

Kass and Lipset (1982) define *yordim* as "sojourners" because, in their view, the *yordim* themselves perceive their stay in America as temporary. The majority of the Israelis I met did indeed claim that they would return to Israel when the time was right in the near or more remote future. Not only did they consider their stay in America temporary, but they also expressed bewilderment at the circumstances that led to their departure from Israel and their unantici-

---

[4]The subcommittee on services to Israelis was first appointed in 1977 to gather information about the characteristics and needs of the Israeli population in greater New York; see Levi 1986.

[5]Rabin made this statement during a television interview on the Day of Independence in 1976 (see Introduction). Rabin reconfirmed his position on this issue when, during a visit to New York in 1984, a few months before he was appointed minister of defense, he called *yordim* deserters: "I consider everyone who leaves Israel a deserter. He defects from the battlefield, from the building of Eretz Israel" (*Yedioth Ahronoth*, March 4, 1984, p. 2).

pated stay in the United States. Rina's exclamation—"Everyone here got stuck [*nitke'u*] in the United States"—displays a feeling of the joint forces, inner and outer, which affected their lives and carried them away from Israel. This self-designation of having gotten stuck, temporarily, at one stage of their life history, may be regarded as a strategy of liminality,[6] which maintains an orderly, integrated definition of indentity as compared with the anomalous position of *yordim* in both Jewish and Israeli society. The absence of *yordim*'s own initiated communal or national institutions also serves this state of social liminality. *Yordim* appear to be nonexistent as a separate and well-defined social category.

It is interesting to compare the Israelis with the recent wave of Indian immigrants to the United States. In 1975 there were twelve associations for less than fifty thousand Indian immigrants in greater New York. The monthly meetings and an annual picnic organized by these associations attracted participants from far away (Saran and Eames 1980; Fisher 1980; Saran and Leonhard-Spark 1980). The growing proliferation of Indian associations has brought together participants of varied education and occupations who meet at political, religious, professional, and recreational activities. There are also indications of the development of national Indian organizations, which will include the various groups of immigrants from different regional, linguistic, and caste enclaves of Indian society. For a similar or possibly larger population of *yordim*, concentrated in smaller areas, there was not even one active voluntary association in New York during the years 1982–84. And this despite the fact that Israelis are not divided by anything comparable to the regional, linguistic, and caste divisions common to Indian society. I also doubt the soundness of the assumption that Israelis are disinclined to initiate voluntary associations because they are accustomed to depending on governmental agencies. There is enough evidence from Israel to challenge this sociological claim,[7] which has

[6]I employ Victor Turner's (1967) elaboration on the liminal stage during rites of passage. During this stage, the novices are separated from the status of youth but are not yet bestowed with the status of adults. They are, therefore, structurally nonexistent.

[7]This was first suggested by Eisenstadt (1956), who commented on social processes immediately following statehood.

been echoed uncritically for many years. The recent proliferation of political associations in Israel is one example. Israelis in New York have the talents, resources, and initiative necessary to set up various associations. They also often express a need for ethnic gatherings and corporate action. Nevertheless, they appear completely incompetent in this sphere of action.

It seems that both the American Jews and the *yordim* themselves prefer to deny the permanency of *yerida*. This denial reinforces the state of ethnic invisibility. Seemingly on a temporary voyage, the Israelis refrain from joining American Jewish organizations, as well as from setting up their own institutions. American Jews are therefore justified in withholding the helping hand of their various services from a population of tourists on an extended visit. By adopting the status of Israelis on a "long vacation," unattached to local communal organizations, the immigrants seem to avoid both the designation of *yerida* and the predicament of identity as Diaspora Jews. At the same time, American Jews eliminate the social anomaly represented by *yordim* and thus maintain the ideological status quo through which American Zionists adhere to their faith and expectations, as well as to their role and existential position as they relate to Israel and the Israelis.

The alienation of Israelis from American Jews represents only one dimension of the social relations of the *yordim* in their new world. We shall now turn to another dimension—their relations with their own compatriots.

[3]

Yordim among Themselves

The American ethos introduces a dual myth and accommodates a dual reality of ethnicity: the melting pot on the one hand and cultural pluralism on the other.[1] Ethnic cultural traditions persist in spite of the striving for a homogeneous American identity. This survival of ethnic presentation has been made possible, partly at least, through the immigrants' geographical concentrations, as well as through the voluntary establishment of ethnic communal institutions and national organizations. The *landsmanschaften* of Eastern European Jews are only one example of this tendency.[2] Such organizations could not have come into being had the individuals concerned not been willing to meet regularly, to communicate, and to negotiate with their brethren not only within the intimate circles of relatives and close friends, but also within the wider contexts that bring together casual acquaintances and strangers.

Israeli immigrants, although concentrated in a few residential areas in Queens, have proved reluctant to initiate their own ethnic organizations. It is difficult to introduce observations that reveal the forces responsible for the absence of communal institutions. But we

[1]See Gleason 1982.

[2]The number of *landsmanschaften* (communal or national organizations) increased rapidly after the 1880s, particularly during World War I, eventually representing most of the cities and towns of Eastern Europe. By 1914, New York City alone had 534 such organizations, with membership ranging from 50 to 500 (*Encyclopeadia Judaica* 10:1414–15).

[55]

can show how expressions of attraction and rejection characterize relationships between members of the group and how they influence the phenomenon under consideration. In this chapter we shall discuss the negative terms in which Israelis perceive their countrymen in America. Only a few Israelis whom I met did not view other *yordim* in derogatory or derisive terms.

Yordim as Hypocrites

A frequent comment by *yordim* on *yordim* was the reference to a claim apparently made by all Israelis regarding their imminent return to Israel. At our first meeting Shlomo, a mechanic, said: "Have you noticed something interesting? Every Israeli around tells you that he is preparing for his trip back home. I know one who has been here for twenty years already, but he never stops telling me that. But let me tell you something else; they don't know why they came here in the first place." Shlomo, who was much influenced by Chabad's missionary activities (see Chapter 7), argued on another occasion: "We have been banished from our country because of sins we must have committed. Every Israeli in New York feels that he is in exile." To that, his friend, a car dealer, responded by telling a story made popular by the Gashashim (a well-known troupe of Israeli comedians); a *yored*, whose suitcases are ready for the trip home to Israel, is only waiting for his son to graduate from college. When asked how old the boy is, he answers laconically: "He is already three years old." This joke, created in Israel for an Israeli audience, was often related in the company of *yordim*. But while expressing their amusement at the common pretension of the forthcoming return to Israel, many of the more recent arrivals continued to assume that their own return was imminent. During 1982–84 Shlomo and Shula made a few trips home to look into the possibility of setting up a garage in Israel. Although they usually returned swearing that their life in America was totally wasted, they could not resolve the economic difficulties and fears that the move involved. Serious as Shlomo and Shula were about their wish to go back, they did in fact seem to fit the Gashashim joke (Shlomo had already been in the United States for ten years).

Arik, whose American wife had made him leave Israel seven years earlier, often joked about the hypocrisy of the Israelis in New York. He always repeated the story of his own departure: "I left Israel in broad daylight after throwing a big party for my friends [implying the sneaky departure of others] and when I decide to go back I won't talk about it. I'll just pack and leave." But Arik himself, although he always emphasized his preference for Israel, never complained about his life there, and openly blamed his wife for their immigration, became the object of laughter among his Israeli acquaintances when, on his way to a family visit in Israel, he was observed at Kennedy Airport in his best American office attire of suit and tie (in sharp contrast with the informal style of Israel), his American passport prominently displayed in his front pocket.

Of all my acquaintances Dani was the most anxious to return to Israel. He painfully missed his close relatives and friends, as well as the Israeli climate and way of life. He preserved and emphasized Israeli habits of behavior, dress, and speech to the extent of symbolic exaggeration if not grotesqueness. He could conceive of his stay in America only as a temporary phase and he believed that most of his Israeli acquaintances were also seriously considering going back. Yet he too realized the obstacles that stood in the way of his return and often changed the date of his return to a more remote future, though never more than five years away (see Chapter 8, Profile 12). He told me several times: "Those who came here hoped to make good within a short time and earn enough money in order to return under improved conditions to Israel. I also thought so. But now it seems almost impossible." On another occasion he was more cynical and amused about Israelis who put down roots in America yet continue to express their longing for Israel as, for example, during the sing-along gatherings (see Chapter 5). Like many others, Dani was continuously searching for "authentic Israelis" (*Israelim amitiim*) who resembled his ideal of "pure" Israeliness, which included an unfaltering attachment to Israel. But even Dani did not escape a sarcastic observation by Nathan, himself suspected of presenting a false front about his plans to return to Israel (see Chapter 8, Profile 9), who told me: "Dani looks as if he's going back to Israel tomorrow, but he's actually striking deep roots here!"

[57]

The older Israelis, who had been in the United States longer, did not joke about the Israelis' claim of imminent return. Eli had been in America for more than twenty years and his return to Israel seemed most unlikely, particularly since his wife and sons were unwilling to leave. We were on close friendly terms and well acquainted with the life histories of many regulars of the Israeli Club (see Chapter 4). Nevertheless, when I expressed my doubts about the prospects of their return to Israel, he said: "In contrast to other immigrants, all Israelis constantly think about their return, they hold on to their apartment in Israel [which Eli did], fly El-Al, and spend a month or more every year in Israel [which he very rarely did himself]." When Eli was asked in my presence by a young female acquaintance who had lived in America for seven years if he was planning to return to Israel, he ignored her question and exclaimed instead: "Everyone makes plans for returning. Here we remain Israelis as long as we haven't got to the point when it becomes important for us to vote for the presidency and when we perceive the American army as our own." But his claim was not as false as some might have thought. Eli had never reconciled himself to the finality of his departure from Israel. His wife jokingly expressed his predicament, exclaiming that once she was dead Eli would not remarry but would instead immediately return to Israel. Since she was younger than Eli, her uncharitable remark seemed to emphasize the futility of his presentation of self.

The continual watch over each other's presentation of self did not ease relationships among *yordim*. Moreover, in the company of their compatriots they often felt compelled to pretend that their own return to Israel was imminent.

Yordim as Unreliable

Most Israelis in industry and business claimed that they did not employ other Israelis because the newcomers wished to establish their own businesses as soon as possible and thus could not be trusted. Ron, a contractor of electric systems who had left Israel nine years earlier, often repeated the story of his experience with an Israeli employee: "A few years ago I decided to employ an Israeli worker. I informed the proprietor of an Israeli restaurant that I was looking for an electrician and told him that I would help out a good candidate to settle in America. A young man arrived. He looked at my home and the business and asked me, 'How much money do you make a week?' I answered him sharply, 'In America you don't ask such questions.' I paid him forty dollars net per day, plus expenses for lunch. I didn't want him to complain that I was exploiting him. But he disappeared after three days. Since then I prefer not to work with Israelis." Ron's friend, who had left Israel fifteen years earlier and who owned a large electric appliances store, also refused to employ Israelis. Once he had employed an Israeli who had immediately asked for a raise. He concluded: "An Israeli who sees that you make money immediately wants to be your partner." Ron added jokingly: "When two Israelis meet, they greet each other with the question 'How much do you earn?'"

Ron and his friend were reacting to a phenomenon that would not have surprised them in Israel, where the casual inquiries of friends and strangers about income (or about the price paid for various items they have recently purchased) is not unusual. But the same manifestation of familiarity irritated them upon meeting their countrymen in New York.

Dani was keen to employ Israelis, just as he was continuously looking for Israeli company. Nevertheless, his experience was not very encouraging. Those who suited his definition of congenial Israelis (who shared his experiences in the army and youth movement and who seemed honest and friendly) lacked the qualifications he needed in his business, whereas those who might have been better qualified fit the negative stereotype expressed by other employers. Instead, he employed skilled newcomers mainly from Yugoslavia, none of whom were Jewish. He was deeply involved with the daily affairs of his employees, who came from the country he had left in his childhood.

Some *yordim*, however, did employ Israelis, as for example, Reuben, a boutique owner, whose sales assistants were mainly recruited from among Israeli newcomers. Reuben did not express dissatisfaction with his employees, who were usually unskilled and who often arrived in America as tourists (and who were thus very dependent on his goodwill). The more competent and ambitious

[59]

among them did indeed aspire to open their own businesses. Once during a discussion at the Israeli Club someone mentioned that in the factory where he worked in a managerial position all shop-floor employees were blacks and Puerto Ricans. His listeners were greatly amused when somebody reacted: "Of course, you can't expect an Israeli to be somebody else's employee."

At the same meeting a young student expressed his astonishment and dismay at the lack of mutual support among Israelis once they reach New York: "The Greeks in my Brooklyn college were always helping newcomers whose proficiency in English was poor. But among the hundreds of Israeli students, nobody cared about anyone except himself."

Israelis tend to perceive their own society as altruistic. It is often said, for example: "If you have to break a leg, make sure it happens in the streets of Tel Aviv." In New York, however, the Israelis we observed conceived of their own compatriots as extremely competitive and selfish.

Yordim as Ugly Israelis

Many *yordim* were unhappy with the growing numbers of Israelis in New York. Reuben once exclaimed: "How did it happen to us! This landslide started only after 1973. Before that we were here in small numbers." Reuben himself had arrived in New York a few years *after* 1973. An Israeli who sold out a successful business and returned to Israel after fourteen years in New York told me during a visit to New York: "When we arrived here fifteen years ago, there were not many Israelis around. Everyone who came at that time had a special personal reason for leaving Israel [he himself had left because of a matrimonial dispute]. But the second generation of *yordim* are completely different. They come over because they've heard about the prospects of success in America. Whenever I used to see an Israeli I escaped immediately to the other side of the street. Among our friends here was only one Israeli couple who we knew from Israel. Luckily a few of our friends in Israel came to New York in various official capacities. We also had some close relatives here who came from Europe many years ago." On another occasion he told me: "I'm anti-Semitic; 95 percent of all *yordim* should stay on in the United States."

Sarah, who came to New York during the 1950s after marrying an American student she had met at the Hebrew University, told me: "When I myself left, Israelis were leaving for other reasons than those which motivate them today, such as economic or security pressures. At that time people left in order to broaden their intellectual horizons and see the world."

The old-timers in particular emphasized the deteriorating image of Israelis in the United States, who are often associated with bad manners, drug trafficking, bankruptcies, setting fire to their businesses in order to get insurance compensation, and other illegal activities. A woman in her mid-thirties confessed in the company of unacquainted Israelis how offended she was when Americans would often comment in surprise, "Are you an Israeli? You don't look like one." She went on in an assured tone: "Don't you try to keep your distance from other Israelis?" An Israeli woman married to an American told my wife that when she first saw me at the Israeli Club she thought: "What is a nice man like this doing here; he can't be a *yored!*" Aware of this unwelcoming attitude, Eli commented: "When somebody comes from Warsaw, everybody comes out to greet him; but with us it is different. When an Israeli arrives everybody exclaims in astonishment: 'You too? What on earth are you doing here?'" The speakers quoted thus expressed the deep resentment many *yordim* share with their compatriots in Israel and with American Jews of the expanding Israeli population in New York.

While the old-timers were often sensitive to the worsening image of Israeli immigrants, the more recent arrivals seemed less worried by the growing number of their compatriots and sometimes described the newcomers in more positive terms, which naturally reflected on their own position. Their view of the old-timers was, however, less favorable. Thus, for example, a divorcee who had arrived seven years earlier with an American spouse claimed that up to 1973 the Israeli arrivals were those who had not been able to find a place in Israel and were ashamed to acknowledge the fact. But since then Israelis have been leaving because Israel cannot offer them the opportunities they are looking for. These Israelis are not ashamed of their *yerida*. Dina, whose husband was pressing for

[61]

a move back to Israel, was very hesitant about the prospect of returning. She often commented: "Why do so many leave Israel now? Years ago only ordinary people left, but now you see many better-educated Israelis around, even those who were in the army and in party politics!"

The apparent demarcation between the attitudes of old-timers and newcomers was often blurred by observations that contradicted a generational differentiation. For example, the Israeli "returnee" mentioned above, who claimed great differences between the first and second generation of *yordim,* also emphasized his continuing avoidance of all *yordim,* old-timers included. A similar attitude was held by a newcomer, an entertainer who, when not performing, drove a taxicab. While waiting for his turn to perform at a party he commented on his surroundings: "Look at the Bronx Zoo! Can you see the hawkers from the Carmel market [Tel Aviv's biggest open-air market for food and clothing]? Although they are well disguised under masks, you can smell them out." The party was being held at a Queens hotel and the participants looked quite prosperous. On the same occasion I met Hanan, an engineer married to an American woman who came to the party with two other mixed couples. He also seemed unhappy with the surrounding company, whom he considered noisy and vulgar. Actually I could not differentiate between his own appearance of prosperity in a three-piece suit and that of most of the other guests. An Israeli woman at his table said to me: "Israelis from higher strata don't look for other Israelis, but prefer the company of Americans. The lower strata Israelis are those who prefer Israeli company." She was thus distancing herself from the surrounding participants.

A similar attitude was expressed by Eli, although his social life was completely confined to Israelis. He told me that he had stopped attending performances of Israeli entertainers because "I get depressed on these occasions. I love the sensation of Israel as experienced in Israel, but I hate the presentation of Israel in New York. I enjoy observing an Israeli crowd in Tel Aviv where people come in groups from various walks of life. Here you watch a vulgar crowd of Israelis who talk Hebrew in high-pitched voices and get excited at meeting acquaintances they haven't seen for a long time." Nevertheless, during my stay Eli did go once more to an

Israeli evening of entertainment that brought together a few popular performers; it turned into a scandal, with the audience noisily demonstrating its dissatisfaction (see Chapter 4). Eli regretted the temptation that had made him attend this event against his better judgment (his wife was visiting her ailing parents in Israel at the time and he might have felt some loneliness and a growing nostalgia for Israeli culture). "When I looked at the crowd I subconsciously saw myself in the mirror. When you see other Israelis screaming in Hebrew you realize that you may possibly look the same. Unfortunately, I rediscovered the ugly Israeli."

The Israelis also considered their countrymen arrogant know-it-alls. At a Saturday evening gathering that brought together five couples (including Israeli students who had been in New York for nearly four years), the assembled referred to the "Israeli cancer." All agreed to the assessment made by one participant: "Every Israeli who arrives at Kennedy Airport believes that he already knows everything and better than anyone else." A similar mood dominated another Saturday evening meeting. Excluding their close friends, our hosts, Joseph and Rina, described the Israelis in New York in unflattering terms: although not very knowledgeable, they are self-assured about their capabilities, which they assume surpass those of everybody else. Moreover, the Israelis were described as exploiting the American environment to which they brought poor standards of discipline and loyalty at work. In addition, they accused their compatriots of taking advantage of the sheer size of the American population to evade the law.

Most of those quoted were deeply attached to Israel and to Israeli company, so their vehement criticism of their compatriots in New York was neither a way to distance themselves from Israel or to legitimize their own departure. They did, however, distance themselves from other *yordim*, who were seen to represent the worst of Israeli society. Those looking for new acquaintances who seemed to represent "nice Israelis" were often rebuffed. Attending a Purim party at the Israeli Club, I met an Israeli in his late twenties who reminded Hanan of a kibbutz member or a combat officer. My new acquaintance actually turned out to be a graduate of the Israeli College of Sports and Athletics. According to his story, he soon became bored with his teaching job and set out to look for new opportunities in America. He started as a shop assistant in electronics and eventually established his own business importing records and video films from Israel. Hanan was very disappointed to discover the transformation of an athlete into a "trader like anyone else." He lamented the Israeli reality in New York, commenting: "Whatever we do, even if born péasants [*falachim*], we'll end up back with the old Jewish tradition of business and trade."

On one snowy evening, Arik was too bored to stay at home and watch television. In this sort of weather he missed Israel more than ever and he suggested that we go to the Israeli Club. Since the building was closed, we decided to visit Dani, who lived a few blocks away. We were discussing the family and business affairs of some close acquaintances when Dani exclaimed: "Looking around I suddenly see strange faces. Had I painted a picture of all this [implying his Israeli acquaintances in New York], it would have turned out to be a frightening Kafka painting. Had someone hung the painting in his living room, whoever came in would have run away as quickly as his feet could carry him." On our way home, Arik asked me if I intended to write a book about the Israelis and their life in America. Noticing my hesitant reaction, he told me that I should write in order to tell the truth about Israeli reality in New York.

Although Hanan, Eli, Joseph, Rina, Dani, and Arik all sought out Israeli company, they could not be satisfied. The Israelis with whom they came into contact seemed to represent a selection of undesirable *yordim*. They themselves were often similarly perceived by their own acquaintances.

Shlichim—*Yordim* in Disguise

The colony of *shlichim*—Israeli official delegates—included the staff of the Jewish Agency, the Israeli consulate, and representatives of various ministries, political parties, and financial institutions. The *shlichim* made up a category of Israelis that many *yordim* considered in more contemptuous terms than those used about other *yordim*. The chief target of resentment were the *shlichim* from the Jewish Agency and the Israeli consulate. For many years the major task of the Jewish Agency had been the recruitment of *olim* (immigrants to

Israel), whose numbers in Western countries had long ago dwindled drastically, but not so the number of *shlichim*. Although the consulate's main task was the granting of various bureaucratic services to applicants, it was perceived as the major national representative in New York.

The Israeli bureaucracy is held in little esteem by its clients in Israel due to its reputation for inefficiency and discourtesy. This deeply embedded resentment toward Israeli officials was even greater in New York because of the contempt and disrespect the consulate staff was assumed to feel toward *yordim*. This assumption was not groundless, considering the official attitude of the Israeli authorities. For example, *yordim* are not eligible for employment in Israeli official agencies and American Jews and gentiles are given priority for these positions regardless of the qualifications of *yordim* candidates. Many Israeli residents are obliged to contact the consulate in order to validate or renew their Israeli passports, and they tend to interpret any show of discourtesy as a clear sign of disrespect and aversion toward themselves.

The *shlichim*, who are the closest representatives of Israeli society in the United States, were perceived as demonstrating a fraudulent identity. Although only a minority of the *shlichim* and their children stayed on in the United States after the termination of their official post, those who did served as proof of the assumption that the *shlichim*, whose expenses are generously paid by the state of Israel, are actually *yordim* in disguise. Only a few *shlichim*, whose motives and civil demeanor seemed beyond suspicion, such as Ami Shaham (who served between 1981 and 1983), were spared the mistrust and contempt shared by many *yordim*. The following observations reveal the bitter feeling between *yordim* and official Israeli representatives.

At my first meeting with Shlomo, the mechanic, when he told me about *yordim*'s assumption of their eventual return to Israel, he also argued, though with no bitterness, that *shlichim* as well as *yordim* come to America because there is something in their personality and inner motives which forces them out of Israel. Less philosophical, but coming to a similar conclusion, was a popular joke often related as a true story: at the Jewish Agency's headquarters on Park Avenue a *yored* is waiting for an elevator on the second floor. When

[65]

the door opens and he sees an Israeli acquaintance inside, he asks him: "Are you going down? [*Ata yored?*]" He gets a nervous reply: "No, no, I am a *shaliach,* only here for another two years!" Thus the linguistic ambiguity created by the same terms used for the simple activity of "going down" and the designation of an Israeli immigrant appears to represent the fine line that distinguishes between the prestigious status of a *shaliach* and the despised status of a *yored.* When David, the manager of the Israeli Club, phoned the Israeli information attaché and invited him to present a lecture at the club, the attaché asked him in a resentful tone: "Is this for an audience of *yordim?*" David replied: "You well know that every *shaliach* is a potential *yored!*" I could not check David's story, but he did succeed in recruiting the attaché, who appeared in formal attire and spoke in a very impersonal style.

Among our close neighbors was a representative of an Israeli financial institution. His wife was deeply offended when at a casual encounter a *yored* asked: "Are you here too?" She answered in surprise: "What do you mean?" Amused, he responded: "Although you are *shlichim,* you too will stay on." When the same *shaliach* and his wife met other friends of ours, the atmosphere was heavy with tension. Our friends, who were among the few we met who returned to Israel a year later (see Chapter 8, Profile 5), accused *shlichim* of taking advantage of their position and claimed that they are unjustly overpaid in comparison with American standards of professional rewards. They also said that *shlichim* are relieved of the risks and insecurity they would have to endure in America without the protection provided by their official status.

The resentment toward *shlichim* seemed to emerge at the very first stages of immigration. An Israeli who had recently arrived with his family in order to complete his engineering studies, whom I met at a furniture sale advertised by a *shaliach* residing at the Parker Towers (a prestigious and comfortable apartment complex in Forest Hills), told us ironically: "I've rented an apartment somewhere close to Main Street, no doubt unsuitable for a *shaliach.*" An Israeli woman employed at the Israel Discount Bank in Manhattan exclaimed in astonishment: "I've been here for only five years but am considered a *yoredet.* But among Discount's *shlichim* there is one man who has been here for sixteen years, yet he despises *yordim.*"

Less restrained was Nira (see Chapter 8, Profile 8), who vehemently exclaimed: "We emigrated [*yaradnu*] to America under no false pretensions and at our own expense. But the *shlichim*, who first come here for two years and whose official posts are extended for another few years, are *yordim* deluxe. They are shipped, housed, salaried, and given free air tickets to visit Israel, all of which is paid for by our parents and brothers. But they have the impertinence [*chuzpah*] to view us in a superior manner. Who needs them anyhow? If we wish to go back we'll do it without their advice. It's corrupt!"

The official attitude of ostracism was somewhat shaken when Abie Nathan arrived in the summer of 1983 on a private mission to call back the *yordim*. In the past Nathan, an Israeli pilot, had made other spectacular gestures that gained much publicity, such as a one-man flight on a peace mission to Egypt, a private delivery of aid to the refugees in Cambodia, and an appearance among the hungry and dying children in Ethiopian camps with a gift of medicines and lollipops. On this occasion, in September 1983 Nathan chartered a passenger plane that he hoped would carry home a few hundred *yordim* granted cheap one-way tickets on a specially scheduled flight. The Jewish Agency and Israeli authorities joined, possibly unwillingly, in the project initiated by this charming and optimistic master of public relations. Very few, if any, *yordim* were actually persuaded to take up the offer. This bizarre event served, however, as a symbol of a possible change in attitude of the Israeli authorities toward *yordim*, who until then had been given the status of a polluting entity.

A few months later (March 1984) the Jewish Agency's newly appointed *shaliach* to the Israeli constituency (replacing Ami Shaham), who had accompanied Abie Nathan on his American tour, came to deliver a lecture at the Israeli Club. He talked about the security of Israel as projected through the war in Lebanon. He was wearing a three-piece suit and tie (in stark contrast to the casually dressed audience) and mentioned neither his official post in New York nor the constituency he had been entrusted to take care of. An astonished participant told him that his lecture had not offered any information not already available in the newspapers and that he would have preferred to learn about his approach to his special task in New York. The *shaliach* answered that he had been advised by David (the club's manager) to avoid any sensitive subject that might upset his listeners. He went on to explain that anyone needing help should contact him at his office. He also mentioned that he was not in the pay of the Israeli government, but of the World Zionist Organization.

This meeting of a *shaliach* with his constituency was strange in several ways. Although he may have had valid reasons for wearing formal attire, he did in fact project something less than the typical comfortable Israeli ambience. Avoiding "touchy subjects" left both sides observers of a calculated truce. The information he offered about the source of his income indicated his awareness of the grudge *yordim* hold against *shlichim*. David later denied the *shaliach*'s claim that he had advised him to steer away from "touchy subjects." I can only assume that the *shaliach* interpreted David's worries about the official disrespect toward *yordim* in a manner that suited his own wish to avoid a confrontation that might provoke unrestrained emotional reactions from both sides. By now Abie Nathan's visit, which had offered *yordim* a kind understanding, seemed a fairy tale from ancient times. Although low-key and calm, this meeting between *shaliach* and *yordim* highlighted the mutual suspicions and tensions that charge their relations.

A few sensitive *shlichim* did raise doubts about their task, as well as about their moral standing as compared with that of *yordim*. The wife of an Israeli bank's *shaliach*, who was the only member of the community of *shlichim* who participated in activities at the Israeli Club, told me that her husband could not tolerate *yordim*, but that she herself had some doubts about this position: "Are we really any different from most *yordim*? We have been here for five years on official business, while they came here at their own expense." Another bank representative, who stayed on at the end of his contract, told me in an amused tone: "As long as I worked in the Israeli bank I was a *shaliach*, but when I stayed on in the same apartment and had a similar job in another company, I was considered a *yored*." Rina, wife of a *shaliach* who stayed on after his contract was terminated, blamed the Israeli institution of *shlichut* for the increase in *yerida*: "Those who can afford to travel on public money [*shlichut*] can go back to Israel. But those who try to imitate them and travel at their own expense may decide to stay on."

The fact that I was on sabbatical leave granted me an ambiguous status in the Israeli community. I never denied the possibility that we might stay on, and the extension of our stay for an additional year was proof of that possibility. I still remember very clearly the day I declined the offer to stay on in New York for a third year. I sensed that the line between my status as a visitor and that of a permanent resident in America had begun to fade. Since it was not my home university that suggested I stay on, my extended leave of absence would no longer have been supported and legitimized by an institutional definition. For a shorter or longer duration I would have become a *yored*. Since neither Israelis nor American Jewry tolerate Israeliness that is separated from active citizenship, *shlichim* are granted the liminal status denied *yordim*.

Acting Out a Stigmatized Identity

As shown earlier in this chapter, *yordim* often view other *yordim* in unsympathetic or derisive terms. In their verbal descriptions and through their active avoidance of Israeli associations they seem to adopt and confirm some of the common attitudes and stigmatized perception of *yordim* as expressed by the Israeli media and by Israelis in Israel. This identity ambivalence and some of its expressions, reminiscent of Goffman's seminal analysis of the behavior of stigmatized individuals, were succintly expressed by, for example, Eli's experience at an Israeli show, where he observed "the ugly Israeli"; Dani, who described the "frightening Kafka painting" he saw before his eyes; the entertainer who encountered "the Bronx Zoo and the hawkers from the Carmel market"; Ron, who said that Israelis' first greeting to each other was "How much do you earn?"; and the discussions on the "Israeli cancer."

The following observation by Goffman seems pertinent: "Whether closely allied with his own kind or not, the stigmatized individual may exhibit identity ambivalence when he obtains a close sight of his own kind behaving in a stereotyped way, flamboyantly or pitifully acting out the negative attributes imputed to them" (1963:131). But Goffman goes on to suggest a counterreaction: "The sight may repel him [the stigmatized individual], since after all he supports the norms of the wider society, but his social and psychological identification with these offenders holds him to what repels him, transforming ashamedness itself into something of which he is ashamed. In brief, he can neither embrace his group nor let it go" (pp. 131–32). A clear indication of this reaction was given by the woman who related being told by casual American acquaintances, "You don't look like one of them [Israelis]," as well as her own question: "Don't you try to keep a distance from other Israelis?"

The stigma of *yordim* was even more closely and painfully experienced through the attitude of ostracism of Israel's official agencies and their officers, the *shlichim*. But the *shlichim* who lived abroad for extended periods, some of whom actually became *yordim*, also offered a target for hitting back at the source of *yordim*'s stigma. Although most *yordim* usually manifested a deep concern about Israel's affairs and exhibited an uncritical position toward its national policies, they were unrestrained in expressing contempt and irreverence toward Israel's official delegates in America. We may interpret this apparently paradoxical behavior in terms of stigma management and as an expression of *yordim*'s dilemma of perception and distinction between *yerida* as a type of collective behavior of which they disapprove and *yerida* as a private action taken by individuals confronting particular existential problems. The *shlichim* seem to have been allowed to get away unstigmatized while using national resources and goals for their own ends. The blurring of borders between the categories of privileged *shlichim* and the stigmatized *yordim* as expressed in vehement contempt toward *shlichim* had a profoundly soothing effect on the public and self-image of *yordim*. At the same time, however, *yordim* who disapproved of *yerida* as a type of collective behavior found it difficult to embrace the company of other Israelis in national or local ethnic associations. The story of the Israeli Club in Forest Hills, described in the next chapter, demonstrates the reluctance of *yordim* to interact regularly with their compatriots in America.

[4]

Impersonal Sociability
at an Israeli Club

The growing Israeli community in the city of New York and its
suburbs has led to the establishment of restaurants and coffee bars
that advertise Israeli food (mainly Middle Eastern favorites such as
falafel, humus, and techina, but also more specialized dishes such
as the Yemenite malauha).[1] These establishments have become
meeting places for Israelis where, apart from the "ethnic cuisine,"
they can also seek out information or advertise apartments, furniture, cars, baby-sitters, or jobs. Among these, Naomi's Pizza in
Queens on Flushing's Main Street is a good example. The place
carries the name of the lady of the house, who is of Yemenite
extraction and who runs the restaurant with her husband, other
family members, and hired workers, all of whom speak Hebrew. Its
strategic location, the spicy food and its variety, the cozy atmosphere, and the convenience of a spacious additional dining room
make Naomi's Pizza attractive at all hours of the day. (It is closed on
Friday evenings through the Sabbath.) Although many Israelis visit
the restaurant, it lacks the stereotypical characteristics of an ethnic
club and caters both to an Israeli and an American clientele.

Some restaurants also offer Israeli entertainment, for example, at
the Shalom Bar in Queens an Israeli musician performs on Saturday
nights. A few Israeli nightclubs (Hafeenjan, for example) operate in

---

[1]Falafel—a spiced Oriental pastry; humus—an Oriental dish of chickpeas; techina—an Oriental dish of thick sesame oil.

Manhattan. For a few years the Federation of Jewish Philanthropies of New York supported an Israeli cultural establishment, B'Tsavta, also located in Manhattan. (The name B'Tsavta is reminiscent of a successful cultural institution in Tel Aviv named Tsavta.) B'Tsavta in New York offered professional performances, lectures, and conferences on various issues related to Israel. More impressive in recent years has been the growing number of popular Israeli troupes, performers, and entertainers who have discovered the commercial potential of New York's Israeli community. These performers often come to the United States for only a few shows, sometimes even one. They have thus changed the major pattern of Israeli show business in New York, which, until the late 1970s, involved performers on contract with specific nightclubs or agents who remained on in America indefinitely (see Chapter 8, Profile 2). These Israeli artists make their debut at hotels and other halls that can accommodate a large audience. The shows are widely publicized in the local Israeli and non-Israeli media. In 1983 many celebrated Israeli perfomers and entertainers came to New York, including lyricist-composer-singer Naomi Shemer, singer Yehoram Gaon, writer-entertainer Dan Ben-Amotz, and Meni Peer, host of a popular Friday night Israeli television program.

The Israeli Club at the Central Queens YM-YWHA in Forest Hills is a completely different type of institution. It was designed to offer a more stable and intimate environment for continuing social and cultural activities. Its geographical location made it easily accessible to the residents of some of the more populous Israeli neighborhoods in Queens, particularly Forest Hills, Rego Park, Flushing, and Kew Gardens. The club, which was launched in June 1982 with the financial support of the Federation of Jewish Philanthropies of New York, was open to both members and nonmembers of the Y. Its activities included a weekly Wednesday program (the social club), Jewish festival celebrations, and an Israeli film one Saturday night a month. Later, a weekly Monday program for singles was introduced. The new club became associated with the Y's weekly Tuesday program of Israeli folk dances. The social club met in a large room on the Y's top floor. On most Wednesday evenings, there were no other activities on this floor and a sense of seclusion lent support to the sense of occupying a no-man's-land. I observed activities at the social club for nearly two years, starting shortly after its inception in the fall of 1982 and continuing through the 1984 spring season (the club did not operate during the summer recess from August to September).

The manager of the club, David, was recruited and employed specifically for this purpose by the Y. A young man in his early thirties, David had come to the United States a few years earlier with his wife to pursue graduate studies. He was born in Eastern Europe and had immigrated to Israel with his parents at an early age. His wife's parents lived in New York, where they had immigrated from Israel some years before. The prospects of David's return to Israel or continued stay in the United States appeared as ambiguous as those of many other Israelis in New York. He was always meticulously dressed, polite, and mild mannered. He was liked by some participants for his unobtrusive behavior and civility, but also somewhat resented by others for not showing "the colors and signals of the tribe," namely "typically Israeli" appearance and behavior. He did not, for example, wear sandals during summer, nor was he casually dressed in winter; furthermore, he was reserved about expressing his feelings.

David spared no efforts to produce the monthly program, which offered a wide variety of lectures and other activities, all in Hebrew. In spite of a small budget, a limited source of suitable Hebrew speakers, and the hostile attitude demonstrated by the Israeli official establishment toward the local community of *yordim*, he managed to recruit academics, professionals, artists, politicians, and even Israeli officials to address the club's weekly Wednesday meetings. The lectures and discussions were usually well presented by the speakers, who were often well known for their professional skills and personal reputation. The speakers were either Israeli residents in America or Israelis on official appointments or on temporary, semiofficial visits, such as a university sabbatical. The December 1982 program, for example, included a lecture on the fish of the Red Sea by an Israeli scientist on a visiting research fellowship, a lecture by a distinguished Israeli author who had been a resident of the United States for more than ten years, a meeting with Israeli

[73]

Chabad Chassidim on a visit to their rabbi's headquarters in Brooklyn, and a sing-along evening of Israeli folk songs led by a former army troupe member who had arrived in New York a few years earlier as representative of a family business.

The lecturers at these meetings never remarked on the residential and citizenship status of their audience and, even when provoked by the listeners, never went on the offensive. The club did not have an interest in recruiting Israelis back to Israel and, in order to avoid offending the various types of Israeli residents in Queens, declared its noncommitment to any ideological message except to that of the comfort of Israeli company that could be found at cultural activities associated with Israel. This was often stated in the club's monthly program fliers, for example: "The activities of our club aim to create a place where Israelis can come for a few hours and feel at home." The same flier (of December 1982) quoted an anonymous female participant who claimed: "No exciting entertainment in this bustling American metropolis can replace the Israeli corner at the Y." Another flier quoted a male participant who made a more pointed confession: "When I came to New York I tried to forget that I am an Israeli, I went to bars and nightclubs, I tried to be an all round American. It took me some time before I started to look for Israeli company."

The club's activities were often advertised on the Hebrew radio program "Kan Israel" (Here Israel; 98 FM, WEVD, broadcast every weeknight from 9:30 to 11:00), as well as in the New York weekly Hebrew newspaper *Israel Shelanu* (Our Israel). The program fliers were sent out to a mailing list of one thousand Israeli families and singles in Queens and were also distributed in places where Israelis were known to shop, such as the Carmel delicatessen in Forest Hills. During the fall of 1982, a few participants volunteered to telephone nearly two thousand Israelis in order to encourage them to attend the club. Although they soon became tired of the task, a considerable number of Israelis were contacted. With these various methods of advertisement, the club's existence was made known to a wide population of Israelis in New York, far beyond the borders of Queens. Among the regular participants were a few residents of Long Island, and the festival celebrations in particular recruited residents from far away, notably from Brooklyn.

Attendance and Participation

In spite of the efforts invested in advertising the club's programs and its accessibility to a major concentration of Israelis, the attendance at the club often did not satisfy the sponsors' expectations. Moreover, after two years of operation it had not developed a strong core group supporting its activities. Attendance was erratic: one week fifty participants might show up, the next two weeks no more than twenty people would attend, and a festival celebration might recruit nearly two hundred old and new faces.

During the 1982 fall season, the three-dollar entrance fee charged to nonmembers of the Y was considered a possible reason for the poor attendance, although coffee, tea, and cake were offered free to all visitors and a variety of Israeli newspapers were available. David and the advisory committee, which he appointed from among the regular participants, assumed that Israelis were not accustomed to paying for social facilities. They therefore decided to initiate free entrance but to charge fifty cents for coffee and fifty cents for cake. With this change of policy at the opening of the spring season attendance improved, but David's continuous reminders to the audience to pay for refreshments was in vain. A visitor at the club who attended the new program for singles, which required a three-dollar entrance fee, complained: "It's not fair to make us pay in order to meet *chevre* [one's close network of friends]."

The Israelis' reluctance to contribute toward the expenses of the services the Y extended to them was a constant embarrassment for David. Consequently, a minimal fee of two dollars for nonmembers was reinstated at the opening of the 1983 fall season. Whatever the reason, attendance at the club was often lower than during the previous season. The possible correlation between attendance rate and entrance fee, which was often remarked on by the participants themselves, seems puzzling when we consider the economic status of the population involved. Most participants were not poor, and they did not hesitate to spend considerably more on other types of entertainment. Moreover, the five-dollar entrance fee at festival celebrations did not seem to affect attendance. These celebrations, which included Israeli entertainers, musical troupes, and dancing, permitted anonymity and were "less demanding," in David's

Jacket of the May 1984 club flier inviting Israelis to the Israeli Independence Day celebration. The picture was taken at the 1983 indoor candle *kumzitz* party. Courtesy Central Queens YM & YWHA, 67-09 108th Street, Forest Hills, N.Y.

words, than the club's weekly activities, which might involve more of a commitment to the club. Compliance with the entrance fee to the weekly programs would suggest an intentional act of association and an explicit acknowledgment of the desire for Israeli company.

Only a few participants challenged their compatriots' reluctance to support the club's activities. Most others remained unconcerned by the club's financial difficulties, even when informed by David that the Federation of Jewish Philanthropies was seriously considering the curtailment of its support, which might cause the club to close down. His listeners assumed that these matters would be solved somehow without their intervention. At this stage of the club's precarious existence only two participants bothered to send letters of praise to the Y's director in support of the club and its devoted manager. One of the two was the only American male participant and the other was the only participant whose American wife was an enthusiastic club visitor.

Assuming that the entrance fee had an impact on the turnover of participants, the fact remains that even during the long period of free admittance, attendance was unstable and only specific activities attracted a larger audience. Moreover, the Israeli Y membership, which was considerable (estimated at about 10 percent of the Y's total membership), did not prove to be an important source of club participants. Nevertheless, the overall yearly attendance at the club included a large crowd of Israelis. The nine months of weekly Wednesday meetings, attended by approximately 1,750 participants, saw no less than 1,000 Israelis who showed up for one activity or more. The Chanukkah, Purim, spring, and Independence Day parties added a few hundred new faces. The monthly Israeli film and the Monday club for singles, which was in operation for a few months, recruited additional participants. Thus about 2,000 Israelis might have participated in one or more activities during a single year. This estimate does not include the program of Israeli folk dances whose participants included American Jews and the families of Israeli officials.

The main phenomenon characterizing attendance at the club was the slow development of a group of "regulars" and the overwhelming frequency of "one-night-stand" participants, some of whom might appear again at a later date for a second one-night-stand. There were

Jacket of the June 1984 club flier inviting Israelis to the spring festival. The picture shows the club's choir. Courtesy Central Queens YM & YWHA.

also those who participated regularly for a few weeks or months and then disappeared altogether, although few had changed their address or personal status.

Throughout nearly two full seasons of the club's operation (from fall 1982 to spring 1984) I counted thirty-seven visitors as regulars. They included one American female spouse and one American single man. Twenty-five on this list (including the two Americans) frequented the club's Wednesday meetings at least once a month. The other twelve visited less frequently. Most regulars also attended the holiday celebrations. Two-thirds of the regulars were in their late twenties to late thirties. The rest were in their forties, fifties, and early sixties. The regulars included seven couples who usually came together. The others were either married participants who rarely, if ever, brought along their spouses (seven men and three women)[2] or divorced and single participants (five men and nine women). The ratio of men to women was almost equal. Two-thirds of the men and women were of Ashkenazi and one-third of Sephardi extraction. Two-thirds of all participants were born in Israel and one-third in Eastern Europe or the Middle East. Only a few of the younger regulars had been living in the United States less than five years or more than fifteen years (the latter had all arrived as teen-agers with their parents). Of the older participants, most had been in the United States for more than fifteen years.

On the whole, the group of regulars seemed to be composed of an educated, skilled, and economically comfortable population.[3] I

[2]All those who attended the club with their spouses, except for one couple, were Israeli men and women. All the younger men who came without their wives were married to American women.

[3]Concerning the regulars' modes of employment, it is easier to discern a pattern of occupations among the younger participants. Among the younger men, the majority (nine out of fourteen, including the American) were professionals, mainly engaged in engineering and computer sciences. Three were engaged in blue-collar occupations (a self-employed craftsman and two medallion-owner cabdrivers), two were engaged in business. The older men were mainly engaged in business and crafts. The women's occupations were more diverse, but of a somewhat lower income level since they also included secretarial and service jobs (store clerks and shop assistants). The majority of the married men and women were homeowners. The majority of the single and divorced lived in rented apartments. Both homeowners and tenants were residents of what are considered safe and comfortable neighborhoods of Queens, particularly Forest Hills, Flushing, Kew Gardens, and Rego Park. A few regulars came from more distant neighborhoods of Queens, and one couple came from Long Island.

do not have the statistical data necessary to confirm the extent to which the socioeconomic characteristics of the regulars also represented the one-night-stand visitors. Nevertheless, my short communications with the one-night-standers and the reports of other participants support my impression that both groups were drawn mainly from the same category of Israelis.

The club appeared to make a breakthrough in its appeal to a larger audience and in the consolidation of social ties among the participants with the performance of a Hebrew play, *Immediate Occupancy*, written, directed, and performed by the club's participants. Although based on an American play (*6 rms riv vu* by Bob Randall), the Hebrew version was adapted to a Tel Aviv setting and Israeli characters. The actors, who met frequently for rehearsals at the director's home, developed close social ties. A large audience (about eighty people) showed up at the club one cold February night, although it was only a few days after an unusually heavy snowstorm and driving and parking were hazardous. Although the Hebrew version of the play did not conceal a number of elements incongruous to daily life in Israel—for example, the search for apartments is completely alien to Israelis, most of whom own their own dwellings, and the "super" does not exist in Israeli apartment buildings—the play and its performers were enthusiastically received by the audience. But after a few parties thrown by members of the cast, the group dispersed and only a few dyadic relationships survived for a longer duration. So, as it turned out, the play had no enduring impact on the club's activities. Another project involving the performance of a choir at the spring festival had similar consequences. Both the play and the choir, in spite of their remarkable success, did not sustain an active group that might have initiated or supported new projects. Nor did they long sustain the apparently close relationships that evolved among the participants of these activities.

When the club's new program for singles was launched, seventy men and women showed up for its inauguration party one Saturday night, including large numbers from Brooklyn. The few volunteers from among the club's regular participants, who had helped out with the preparations for the party, were greatly disappointed with what seemed to them a small attendance, from Queens in particular. These disappointing numbers were discussed at the following Wednesday meeting. A twelve-year resident of Queens whose own participation was very infrequent exclaimed: "How is it that from among the hundreds of thousands of Israelis who live in our neighborhood we can't recruit 150 participants for every meeting of our club?" A few more observations made by the participants emphasized the reluctance of their compatriots to commit themselves to communal activities. Arik, seven years in New York, commented: "You always see a small group of regulars, while all the rest are newcomers. They usually say they enjoyed the evening and promise to come back, but they never show up again. The Israelis are just looking for entertainment." Hanan, an infrequent participant, told me: "A visit to the club is a pain-relief tablet for the Israelis. I come because of the interesting lectures advertised in the programs. The Israeli institutions [implying the club, Naomi's Pizza, and so on] offer important support to the Israelis who live in America." Hanan did not, however, mention a desire to establish stable relationships with the Israelis who frequented these institutions.

Yaffa, who very rarely joined her husband on his frequent visits to the club, argued: "Only the desperate go to the club. The Israelis are afraid to be revealed as having failed to integrate into American society. They prefer to hide in their holes rather than come out and identify themselves." On another occasion she explained her own reluctance to visit the club: "The fact that people speak Hebrew isn't sufficient to make them my friends. I am entitled to select my own friends." But her husband, Eli, who was among David's few confidants, argued: "The Israelis will flock in great numbers to a Naomi Shemer show or gladly accept the invitation to a meeting with high-ranking Israeli army officers. An Israeli will discuss the latest news from the Israeli stock exchange with his close friends rather than talk about the American economy, but he won't attend the club. He prefers to keep a low profile because he feels guilty about being here." He went on: "Consequently an elephant [the club] is being fed in order to support an ant [the small attendance]." The club's activities were strongly resented by Joseph, who had been active on the now defunct Israelis in New York Committee and who would have been willing to initiate social programs for Israelis had he been granted the federation's support for an independent policy. He claimed that Israelis were unsuited for continuous activity and "need a short but intensive type of activity." He continued: "They prefer the company of small circles of friends."

During the fall of 1983, one of the most devoted of the club's couples announced their decision to discontinue their attendance because of the two-dollar entrance fee, although they were relatively affluent and very generous on other occasions. They said they would show up only at particularly interesting lectures, adding: "It is much easier to entertain our friends at home." They never showed up again at the club. Another enthusiastic participant gave up the club when the Wednesday meeting interfered with an English course she had started taking in the fall of 1983. There were other instances of dropping out as a result of new priorities. David and others among the small group of loyal participants were puzzled by the endless turnover of the club's population. The continuing fluctuations and the changing population, which made David's position precarious within the Y's bureaucracy, forced him to introduce himself and the club's activities at every weekly meeting. The regular participants would silently mouth his opening sentence: "My name is David . . ."

I myself was sometimes baffled and frustrated when a promising new friendship would turn to nothing. I would strike up a friendly conversation with a new visitor or couple who seemed impressed with the club and interested in getting better acquainted. We would depart with the clear intention of meeting again next week or the week after. But no further meeting with the person would take place, at least not at the club.

Dani, who considered the club good for Israelis in America, wished to see the club develop into an Israeli community center that would become a model for other such centers. He saw David's personal failure to represent "Israeliness" as a major obstacle to the club's success. He thought David was unable to initiate activities embodying unique Israeli characteristics, activities that would have attracted more local participants. David's pragmatic administration and Dani's obsession for Israeliness were clearly demonstrated in their respective plans for celebrating Israel's Independence Day.

Having applied too late to get the Y's main hall on Sunday night,

April 17, 1983, David decided to celebrate at the following Wednesday's meeting on April 20. The party, which took the form of an indoor candle *kumzitz* (campfire),[4] was a great success. With nearly one hundred attending, it surpassed all expectations in its joyful and intimate atmosphere. Much of the food and drink served at the party was voluntarily prepared and contributed. Communal singing went on for hours and a few participants, who emerged as natural performers, entertained the audience with their repertoire of songs and jokes. The ecstatic audience, seated in the dim candlelight, refused to turn on the electric lights in the room, so as not to dispel the illusion of another place in another country (see Chapter 5).

Dani wanted to celebrate the Day of Independence at an outdoor *kumzitz*, as many do in Israel. He held fast to his desire for "the real thing" until July, when the weather allowed an outdoor party. A few weeks before then he recruited his closer friends among the club's participants to help prepare the *kumzitz*. He made up a list of thirty to forty guests, mainly from among those of the club's visitors who in his eyes exhibited the ingredients of *Israeliyut* (Israeliness). He also requested a permit from the New York City Parks and Recreation Department to light a campfire on a Queens beach. But he faced last-minute disappointments on all fronts. The Parks and Recreation Department's officer, who had at first appeared sympathetic to Dani's request "to allow us to celebrate our national holiday according to our tradition," ultimately refused to grant permission to hold a campfire on public grounds. Dani found an alternative site for the *kumzitz*, which he thought would not attract police attention. But this time he was discouraged by his colleagues, whose enthusiasm soon dissipated. Moreover, most participants could not attend the *kumzitz* on the scheduled date. He eventually gave up the plan "because there was almost no one left worth my continuing investment of energy." Thus, while the indoor candlelight *kumzitz* organized by David for a crowd of strangers turned out to be a great success, the "real thing," organized by

---

[4]A *kumzitz* is a popular form of social gathering, particularly in youth movements and among army units. Broiled potatos and coffee add an atmosphere of intimate commensalism to the sing-along, which is the major activity of the occasion.

volunteers for selected participants supposedly embodying "true Israeliness," failed abysmally.

As we have seen, participation in club activities was characterized by the Israelis' reluctance to participate regularly and to invest effort in ethnic social activities beyond their close network of relatives and friends. Even when apparently pleased with an ethnic activity and the social bonds that evolved through it, they might easily drop out when a new priority emerged. They seemed, however, more inclined to participate in infrequent, large-scale gatherings either at the club or at commercial entertainment shows, where their role was more passive and less socially involving.

Interaction between Club Participants

Another puzzling aspect of club life was the failure of regular participants to develop enduring social ties. As already mentioned, although the play and the choir gave rise to some informal activities and a few close dyadic relationships, most of these quickly dissolved. After a short period of enthusiastic and frequent meetings, disenchantment with personal characteristics and other more technical obstacles reduced the frequency of meetings and weakened the bonds.

Many club participants and other Israelis I met in New York bitterly criticized American Jews and gentiles, whom they regarded as extremely reserved, with only a very few close friends, few of which they entertained at home. In contrast, they perceived the dominant pattern of interaction in Israeli society to be much more informal. The openness and frankness between visitors during casual meetings at the club, and the cozy and jocular atmosphere that prevailed, seemed representative of the Israeli style and ethos of easygoing informality, which generates spontaneous hospitality. Nevertheless, most participants were reluctant to establish close relationships that might involve visits to one another's home. Sarah, a middle-aged, well-dressed, pleasant, outgoing academic, once told me how she felt after more than twenty years in America: "I feel as if I'm going crazy! In America you work with the same people at the same place for years; you talk to them, you laugh together, but they never invite you home. The club is no different; at the end of the evening's program everyone goes his own way. I tried to set up ties, but it was useless. I can't stand it any longer, I must go back to Israel." When Sarah bitterly claimed during a sing-along evening that both the singing and the social meetings at the club were no more than a "substitute for the real thing," a by-stander said sarcastically: "But it's cheaper than the six-hundred-dollar air fare to Israel."

I enjoyed more enduring ties with club participants than most others. I had no inhibitions about making contacts, although I was somewhat selective: I was not particularly inclined toward the youngest and oldest visitors, and among the singles I had closer relationships with men than with women. Attired in the casual American uniform of sneakers, jeans, and sweatshirt in winter, and Israeli-made sandals, jeans, and T-shirt in summer, I must have misled some participants into thinking I was in my thirties. I was not quick to correct them, since I believed it made it easier for me to associate with the younger participants. I also enjoyed the comfortable position of an Israeli academic who had extended his stay at an American university for a second year (neither a *yored* nor a *shaliach*). There were, however, a few club participants with whom I was unable to pursue a closer bond in spite of the seemingly demonstrative, friendly mutual relationships. Thus, for example, after many meetings at the club with a professional couple, we exchanged telephone numbers. They were in their early forties and had lived in the United States since 1970. I phoned them and invited them to visit us on a Saturday evening, and they immediately agreed. When Saturday arrived, they called and apologized: they would not be able to make it because of a prior commitment that they had completely forgotten about—dining at a Yemenite restaurant with a couple they had met at a show. They suggested that we join them for the meal. Since we had made no baby-sitting arrangements we could not accommodate the change of plans. Although we frequently met at the club after the broken engagement and although they often extended an open invitation—"We live so close, you must visit us with the kids"—no specific invitation was ever made. This situation did not interfere, however, with the warm hugs with which we met each time and the frequent conversations on personal matters (in particular, on their conflicting wishes and plans to return to Israel or stay in the United States). In Israel, our mode of communication would have implied a close relationship, which probably would have led to mutual visits at home. But for nearly two years our relationship was completely confined to the borders of time and space offered by the club. (Interestingly, I discovered another club participant who had experienced a similar story of a broken engagement with the same couple.)

During a well-attended meeting in the fall of 1983, David suggested that it was time to choose a name for the club. The participants reacted with jokes. The first suggestion from the floor was: "Let's call it the *Yordim* Club." The audience roared with laughter. Someone else suggested they call it Mapai's Club, and a third said: "Let's call it the Histadrut Club." (Mapai is the veteran Labor party associated with Ben-Gurion's premiership, and the Histadrut is the labor unions' organization; in recent years both have become nicknames for old-fashioned and unattractive institutions.) The crowd was obviously enjoying itself. Although rebuffed by these reactions, David suggested naming the club Hapina Hachama (The Cozy Corner). But this was completely out of keeping with the audience's sarcastic mood. The issue of the club's name was never raised again. The participants seemed reluctant to demonstrate attachment to the club or to acknowledge its role in evolving intimacy between its regulars.

Attendance at the club manifested a paradoxical mode of behavior. On the one hand, participants were noticeably open and friendly toward new acquaintances and often expressed a desire for an Israeli social atmosphere to contrast with the more reserved norms of American interaction. On the other hand, they often refrained from taking advantage of the opportunities they appeared to be looking for and were wary about striking up close friendships. By showing up at irregular intervals, they avoided a growing commitment to the place and its visitors and made the development of intimate relationships impossible. Although at first encounters they seemed easily inclined to divulge personal information, they in fact held back much about themselves. This seemingly unrestrained Israeli type of sociability was at the same time impersonal and masked. Perhaps it was an accommodation to the American style of reserved sociability. Certainly such behavior was conducive to the management of the ambivalence and strain involved in relationships with those who shared the ambiguities of their identity and who might provoke embarrassing situations beyond the limited territory of the club.

Israeli Ambience at Expressive Performances

There were many club meetings that could be called successful by dint of large attendance, the verbal expression of satisfaction, and an outburst of emotions. These included:

1. most sessions of communal singing of Israeli folk songs;
2. most festival celebrations, which usually developed into extended sing-alongs;
3. a series of lectures dedicated to Israeli songs, entertainers, and humor;
4. a performance of a Hebrew play, *Immediate Occupancy* (*Knissa Miyadit*);
5. a lecture by former Knesset member Meir Pàil;
6. a number of discussions on Israeli society and the Palestinian problem;
7. a lecture on venereal diseases and a lecture on graphology.

Excluding the last item, which involved subjects of particular interest, most other successful meetings evolved a similar type of expressive activity on which I expand in Chapter 5. The songs sung by the participants at the monthly sing-alongs and at the festival celebrations, or listened to on records when introduced at lectures on Israeli entertainment, epitomized a symbolic journey into Israeli history and ethos, as well as into the past experiences of the singers and listeners. I include also in this mode of activity the production of and attendance at the play *Immediate Occupancy*, which, although it was hardly representative of life in Israel, nevertheless it captured the audience's imagination as encapsulating Israeli reality. The translator-adaptor of the play skillfully integrated Israeli names of people, places, and magazines into the text. He managed to incorporate daily paraphernalia, as well as ethnic stereotypes and other Israeli social, ideological, and material images. Thus, for ex-

Children of Circumstances

ample, one of the major characters, Aliza Gonen, is described as a
woman whose knowledge about fashion and society derives from
the magazines *La'isha* (For the woman) and *Ha'olam Hazeh* (This
world), which are among the most popular Israeli magazines of
social gossip and scandal. It goes on to describe her as a woman who
is anxious to be considered modern, but alas remains "a Tel Aviv
yente." When the second major female character (named after a
popular Israeli actress, Gila Almagor) describes her life history, she
mentions as a highlight of her youth a meeting with the author
Moshe Shamir, who has become a member of the Israeli Parliament. Indeed, Shamir, a renowned enigmatic figure, wrote a
number of popular Israeli novels published during the early years
of statehood and later became an ultra-right-wing Knesset member.

Looking around the apartment he wants to rent, one of the characters, David Gonen, exclaims: "What a marvelous view; if you look
out of the bathroom window you can see the Yarkon." The Yarkon is a
small river that runs through Tel Aviv to the Mediterranean and
serves as a romantic playground for many, if not most, of Tel Aviv's
youth. In another scene the same character laments the aimlessness
of his generation with the following complaint: "If we disappeared
from the face of the earth our absence wouldn't be noticed until we
were called up to do military reserve duty [*miluyim*]." When the
romantic couple, who met while hunting for apartments, leave their
spouses and children at home in order to spend an evening together,
the narrator tells his audience: "When fate calls, you obey as you
would an army reserve summons." At their nocturnal meeting David
Gonen makes a confession: "Never before [since having married]
have I flirted with another woman except once on a bus ride to Haifa
and once during military reserve duty." Thus, *miluyim*—the regular
(annual) and the irregular (during periods of tension at Israel's borders or during war) service with the military reserves—is mentioned
three times within a short span of the play's text. No doubt, *miluyim*
plays a profound part in the life of most Israelis and is a continuing
ordeal for many men and for most of their spouses and relatives. But
for many men it is also a time of comradeship, less inhibited deport-
ment, and escape from routine life. Life in *miluyim* has a major place
in Israeli folklore.

In spite of the farfetched transplantation of the American metropolitan life-style into a Tel Aviv middle-class milieu, the audience was engrossed in what was described by a frequent visitor to the club as "the best meeting we have ever had at the club. It really was an Israeli cultural event!"

A very different reception awaited another play, *Yordim* (Those who left), which, though in English, was written and produced by a young Israeli resident of New York and performed by Israeli actors at an off-Broadway theater. The play was intended to comment on the Israelis' ambivalent attitudes toward Israel and the forces of push and pull that drive them to America and back to Israel. When I saw the advertisement for the play *Yordim* with the list of Israeli actors, I assumed the play would be in Hebrew. But only a few dozen playgoers showed up at the Manhattan Lion Theatre on Forty-second Street, and the play closed within a week. When I attended its third performance, there were about twenty people in the audience, including at least ten relatives and friends of the director and actors.

Both of these plays were unknown entities. The public's information was based mainly on the title and on the advertisements. The Y's flier notified the public about an Israeli comedy in Hebrew, *Immediate Occupancy*, adapted to Israeli life from the American comedy *6 rms riv vu*. The play at the Lion Theatre, which was advertised in a flier, an attractive poster, on the radio, and in the English and Hebrew newspapers, bore the title *Yordim* in English and Hebrew letters, as well as the translation "Those Who Left" and the subtitle "The Isramerican Experience."

I assume that there was no single factor affecting the success of *Immediate Occupancy* and the failure of *Yordim*. But to the extent that Israelis considered participating in expressive modalities, they were not looking for events that involved soul searching or that tried to analyze their reasons for leaving Israel. Instead, they preferred those occasions that seemed to symbolize and lend support to a continuing association with Israel as a geographical, material, social, and cultural entity. A similar mode of affective response was again witnessed during the contrasting performances of Meir Pa'il and Dan Ben-Amotz, two well-known Israeli personalities.

Pa'il is a retired army colonel with a doctorate in history, a former Knesset member representing Shely, a small, militant, left-wing

The poster for the play *Yordim*. Design and illustration © 1983 Beery Associates & Nurit Karlin.

party. His ideology, which strongly refutes the Likud's right-wing policies, was not endorsed by many of those in the audience. Indeed, at most public discussions I attended, as well as at many informal meetings, the discussants tended to support the Likud government's political policies.[5] This support did not necessarily spring from ideological conviction, but often from a wider concern about the welfare of Israel. According to this view, the political interests of Israel would be better served by the Israeli government then in power than by the views and needs of the American government or of American Jews or Israelis who do not carry the actual burden of decision making. A public attack on the Israeli government, even if made by Jews, Israelis, and well-wishers, was condemned because it might encourage external pressure on Israel and endanger the Israeli people. Meir Pa'il, however, did not hesitate to vehemently attack the Likud government using the most offensive, degrading, sarcastic, and obscene terms and images the Hebrew language can offer. The tone of his voice, his intonations and mimicry—all compensated for the words he could not express forcefully or offensively enough. Although Pa'il's views are well known, a huge crowd packed the club's hall and many could not find a seat. This large attendance sharply contrasted with the small audience of a week earlier at a lecture on Likud policies presented by an official delegate of the Likud party.

The majority of the audience resented Pa'il's ideas, but he succeeded in charming them and there could be little doubt about their fascination with his oratory. When a regular participant attacked him for expressing his criticism of the Lebanon War in front of the American public on a television news program, Pa'il reacted: "Had I spoken like General Sharon [defense minister during the Lebanon invasion] and exclaimed that we must fuck the Arabs in their ass, you would have loved it, you would have no doubt

<hr/>

[5]My research coincided with the last two years of the Likud coalition government in Israel (1982–84). The Likud's rise to power in 1977 replaced the Labor's coalition governments, which had dominated Israeli society and its political culture since the establishment of the state in 1948 (see, e.g., Y. Shapiro 1980). Heated arguments related to social and political issues in Israel, which reflected ideological conflicts between the Likud and the Labor parties (such as those concerning the Lebanon war or the future of the West Bank), often colored meetings of Israelis in New York. I refer to these in the text without further elaboration.

reached orgasm!" Accused of friendship with Shmuel Mikunis, veteran leader of the Communist party and a Knesset member, he answered sharply: "Only a good-for-nothing [*nevela*] like yourself uses that style. You didn't understand much while you were in Israel and here in the United States you understand even less. You enjoy life here, but you don't understand the pluralistic system." Somebody added uncharitably that leaving Israel was the only good thing Pa'il's interlocutor had ever done in his life. At this the audience roared with laughter. Amid all the noise Pa'il pleaded, smiling: "Please, don't be Israelis.'" His listeners reacted with unrestrained laughter.

It was nearly midnight before the audience and speaker acquiesced to David's plea to close the meeting. It had been the longest Wednesday meeting in the club's history. Although the listeners disagreed with Pa'il's opinions, they were reluctant to let him go. The next day, an Israeli who had spent a few years in New York pursuing graduate studies and who was preparing to return to Israel phoned me and said: "I fully agree with Pa'il's opinions, but I can't accept his style. He represents the impertinent and arrogant Sabra manner [*tzabariut*], someone who knows everything and better than everybody else." Sabra derives from the word for the fruit of a cactus, densely covered with thin spikes but deliciously sweet inside. The term was given to the new generation of Israeli-born children who, adored by their parents' generation, seemed to represent a new specimen of Jews, relieved of the political dependence and personal inhibitions that traditionally characterized Diaspora Jews. The Sabra generation's characteristics and modes of behavior as described in daily parlance, Israeli literature, and folklore are supposed to indicate a prickly exterior but a tender heart. It was Pa'il's impertinent and arrogant manner, an extremely exaggerated embodiment of the stereotype of a Sabra, that made him so appealing to his audience. He laughed at himself no less than at his opponents; he was open, warm, and emotional. Although he had no doubt whatsoever that he was presenting the only possible truth, his manner was not pompous. He did not deny the audience their right to support the war in Lebanon even though they had stayed safely away. Instead, he spoke as if the debate was being held in Israel.

Pa'il did not try to change his image in America, but continued to dress and behave as if he were in Israel. Other lecturers, particularly Israeli official delegates, often arrived in their American working attire: suits and ties. They were restrained, polite, and careful to avoid discord with their audience. They had no wish to get emotionally involved. To employ a term Pa'il used often, though for other purposes, his spectators reached an emotional and cultural orgasm in the sense of collective participation in an event dominated by archetypal Israeli behavior—uninhibited, passionate, stinging, self-confident, warm, witty, and unassuming. Moreover, they were treated as equal partners in this cultural modality.

The participants' reaction to Pa'il's lecture strongly contrasted with that of another celebrated enfant terrible of Israel. Dan Ben-Amotz, renowned bohemian, author, contributor to modern Hebrew slang, and popular entertainer, arrived in New York in November of 1983 for one show (at which he was also host to other Israeli artists). He started the show by telling the audience that they should not feel guilty for staying abroad. He explained that he had always thought everybody has the right to stay wherever they prefer and no one is entitled to preach or intimidate others for their personal preferences. Moreover, sharing Pa'il's political convictions, he expressed satisfaction that the Israelis in New York were being spared the economic and political disaster in Israel brought about by the senseless and futile war in Lebanon. Toward the end of his speech, which he was prevented from completing, he told the increasingly enraged audience: "Stay on here, go on working and making a lot of money. But don't forget us. The day may come when you will offer shelter to our refugees." To his surprise, his message, which he presented using his famous eloquence, cynicism, and obscenities, provoked tremendous rage. Bewildered by this unexpected hostile reaction, Ben-Amotz told his indignant compatriots that he was being absolutely honest with them; in fact, he had already published a similar speech in an Israeli journal in which he announced his coming trip to New York and explained his reasons for doing so.

The atmosphere at the club certainly differed greatly from that of the Manhattan hotel where Ben-Amotz spoke. But regardless of the influence of their respective stages, the two speakers, although

[93]

delivering a similar message, performed in intrinsically different ways. Pa'il, without trying to woo his audience, nevertheless communicated the sense of embracing them as equals and drawing them into Israeli mainstream culture and experience, which he represented. In contrast, Ben-Amotz, who came onstage barefoot (in late November in front of a well-dressed audience), seemed an eccentric bohemian. Although he was a prominent member of the Israeli bohemian community, in New York his behavior was out of step with the acceptable perception of Israeli culture, its extremes included. Had he confined himself to the role of entertainer, he might have been enthusiastically received. This actually happened for a while when he read with an exaggerated Oriental accent from his humorous Abu Nimer stories (apparently told to him by an Arab). But when he suggested the separation of the Israelis in the United States from the fate of their brothers in Israel, this was taken as a personal assault. Pa'il's lecture, which turned into an expressive performance, was a symbolic rite of incorporation, whereas Ben-Amotz's lecture was interpreted by his sensitive audience as a symbolic act of separation.[6]

Israelis in New York have been drawn in particular to expressive representations of an Israeli reality in which they can immerse themselves while retaining a passive role. In order to take part in these experiences they need neither a community, elaborate texts, nor other preparations. They warm up quickly in the company of strangers and are transported to a brief, well-defined adventure during which social, cultural, and physical Israeli reality seem to dominate their immediate surroundings.

Rehearsing Israeli Realities

The last category of our list of successful meetings held at the club, which demonstrated an affective modality, included a number of tense and long discussions. These discussions evolved at lectures

[6]The terms "rite of incorporation" and "rite of separation" are borrowed from van Gennep (1960:11) and Peacock (1968:219–20).

that did not attract a large audience and despite the fact that the lecturers themselves were not at all provocative. On these occasions, members of the audience appeared to be performing a spontaneous "didactive play" about a number of major issues in Israeli life. At three such events the discussion concerned the influence on Israeli society of the prospect of annexation of the West Bank. At only one such meeting was the prior presentation directly related to the Palestinian "problem." On this occasion, six speakers dominated the discussion and substantiated their claims with personal experiences.

The three older speakers, who had either witnessed or participated in the 1948 war, all argued that the Arabs were to blame for the present political impasse: first, by defying the United Nations' partition plan; second, by fleeing unwarrantedly. Thus, they were to blame for the fact that the Palestinians became refugees and have remained so. A woman in her early sixties who had been in the United States for more than twenty years told the story of Jerusalem under Arab siege: "They wanted to throw us out, we defended ourselves." Her voice was filled with emotion and her face tense as she gave an eyewitness account: "An eighteen-year-old boy stopped single-handedly the tank corps which intended to crush Jewish Jerusalem. With one homemade grenade he struck at the leading tank and made them stop their assault! I saw it with my own eyes!" An academic in his early fifties who had also been living in the United States for more than twenty years added his own haunting memory from the 1948 war. He was positioned at his unit's headquarters in a Jaffa apartment building whose residents had fled from the city. With two other soldiers he opened a locked door in the apartment, where, to their great surprise, they found the furniture and other belongings of the former inhabitants. These possessions must have been stored by their owners under the assumption that they would return after forty-eight hours, as promised by the Arab leaders who encouraged the evacuation of Jaffa. This testimony was confirmed by another participant, a shopowner, who claimed that his unit, positioned on the outskirts of Jaffa, was ordered to shoot at Arab vehicles in order to stop the evacuation. The three older speakers, though representing different pragmatic or ideological convictions, all argued that Israel could not return to its pre-1967 borders. They

[95]

claimed that although Israel absorbed the Jewish refugees from the Arab states long ago, the Arab states have purposely refused to dismantle Palestinian refugee camps, which have now become a threatening force in the Arab world. In their view it was not Israel's responsibility to solve the Arabs' self-made problem.

The younger participants, all in their early thirties, expressed a very different attitude. They were not concerned with the historical sources of the conflict, but rather with its impact on contemporary Israeli society. One woman, a teacher, protested against the thesis presented by the first speakers, saying that it did not matter whether the Palestinian identity is new or old and who is to blame for the present human and political mess. "I want a solution which will confront the realities of the problem as they are at this time." Her argument was taken up by an engineer who had been in the United States for five years. He claimed emphatically that he did not care as much about the accuracy of historical details as about the injustices incurred by both sides. As he saw it, the major issue was what sort of a country Israel would become if it absorbed a growing Arab population. In a highly charged language he said: "I don't want to be a conquering power over another nation and I don't want to become a feudal landlord over Arab laborers. I want a small moral country which is mine, and where it is worth living. My parents left a big country [in Eastern Europe] where we were a minority. I don't wish to be made a member of a minority again!" At this juncture somebody interrupted pointedly: "But here you *are* in a minority!"

Before he could react to this challenge, the third young speaker joined the discussion. Alex, a cabdriver, had been in the United States for nearly fifteen years (see Chapter 8, Profile 7). A frequent club visitor, he was rarely outspoken, but he now made an impassioned speech: "I don't care whether the Arabs did or did not flee voluntarily in 1948. We have another problem today, which is a Zionist problem. Zionism is not working anymore; we can't stop *yerida* and we can't encourage *aliya*. When I read the Israeli newspapers I see that they also disparage the state. Sometimes I ask myself, Why did I leave Israel? I think it was because of the endless fights and debates, such as whether the state should be committed to the rules of the Torah or to the ethos of secularism . . ."

[96]

He was unable to complete his sentence because of the increasing noise as others tried to present their arguments, comments, and jokes. Rachel, a woman in her late forties who had arrived in New York with her family seventeen years before (see Chapter 8, Profile 3), tried to sum up the discussion and calm the audience: "I am not associated with any Israeli political party, but I can trace the voices of Mapainiks here [members of Mapai, a major faction in the Labor party]. It is our responsibility to be Jewish [nonpartisan][7] and take sides with Israel. In this room we must be united, we must identify with Israel."

If not for the occasional reminder that the discussion was taking place on American soil, one might have been listening to Israelis holding a debate anywhere in Israel. This resemblance relates to the issues and opinions raised, as well as to the patterns of debate. Whether in Forest Hills or Tel Aviv, Israelis demonstrate the same soul-searching and emotional involvement, the expansion of the debate into subjects only vaguely associated with the main topic, the interruption of speakers, the cynical and humorous comments, and the deafening noise.

The Israelis in New York were easily swept up into vibrant debates on ideological and political issues. They were not, however, easily swayed by sentimental provocation toward verbally expressed nostalgia. This was clearly demonstrated at the Wednesday meeting on May 11, 1983, dedicated to commemorate the liberation of Jerusalem, a festive day added to the Israeli calendar after the 1967 war. The program advertised two short films and a discussion. The audience quietly watched the films, which were about Jerusalem's history, archeology, views, and people. But the subsequent discussion failed to arouse the emotions for which David was aiming. In order to encourage the audience, he related his own experiences, such as the early-morning and late-afternoon walks he used to take from the Intercontinental Hotel (on top of Mount Scopus), during which he looked at the magnificent view of Har

[7]Israelis, who have often rejected the relevance of Jewish identity, did sometimes use "Jewishness" as an alternative reference to a nonpartisan Israeli national identity. The use of the term "Jewish" within the Israeli context has actually increased in Israel since 1967 with the growing number of Arabs under Israeli jurisdiction.

HaBayit (Mount of the Temple). He went on to describe his memories of the Friday afternoon atmosphere in Jerusalem, with the last-minute preparations for the Sabbath. At this point, Rachel, the saem woman who at an earlier meeting had passionately exclaimed, "In this room we must be united!" now jokingly interrupted: "It's the same in Tel Aviv, where everybody arrives home on Friday afternoon with *prachim* [flowers] and *pistukim* [a colloquial term for peanuts]." She pronounced *prachim* and *pistukim* in a singing tone that emphasized the triviality of David's romantic description and evoked wild laughter, leaving the speaker hopelessly embarrassed. Rachel said that from her point of view there was no difference between Jerusalem, Tel Aviv, and Acre. The discussion quickly died out after a futile effort to enliven it through the introduction of a political element. But it was too late and the reluctant audience simply joked and laughed more and more. This reaction demonstrated a recurrent trait of refusing to express inner experiences in a direct verbal manner. These were, however, the same people who could become ecstatically engaged in singing poetic Israeli folk songs about Jerusalem.

An attractive advertisement for a meeting devoted to a lecture (with audience participation) on psychodrama failed to draw a large audience. And the participants who did arrive were reluctant to cooperate with the therapist. The meeting was dominated by questions and jokes, which kept the bewildered therapist on the defensive. Toward the end of the session I asked the analyst whether she had an explanation for the obvious failure of the lecture. To the apparent satisfaction of some members of the audience, she retorted: "We are Israelis. We have been raised to be heroes who know everything and who are ashamed of exploring weaknesses. We are willing to exhibit aggressiveness and be jocular. We can say *hara* [shit], without difficulty, but we are unable to acknowledge that we are in pain. American participants in a similar activity would have tried to be nice; we try to prove the opposite. But this is us!"

Surprisingly, except for a few people who seemed bored or disappointed, most participants expressed satisfaction with the meeting. Moreover, they encouraged David to schedule another one. But only a few of those who had attended the first psychodrama meeting showed up at the second. This time the participants were less aggressive and more aware of their hesitation in cooperating, which they attributed to their "Israeliness." For example, when Nathan explained that he was unable to get involved without a clear understanding as to where the activity was leading, another participant said: "You see, Israelis must know everything before they get into something." The therapist noted that fantasizing was particularly difficult for the participants. Her assertion was supported by two women who explained this phenomenon as a natural consequence of life in Israel, where there is no time for "games" and where children are told that there are only serious things to be done. One of them went on to relate an incident that occurred on a trip to Europe she had made with a group of Israelis. When the group was told about a nearby nude beach, a few of the men decided to give it a try. On their return, one of the men said that he could not see himself participating in this type of leisure activity when a summons to military reserve duty might be waiting for him at home. The woman's story was proof that even at leisure the Israeli cannot "waste time" and freely indulge in fantasizing.

The participants passionately rehearsed Israeli realities at meetings not necessarily dedicated to Israeli issues and folklore. Their personal reactions and experiences were often inseparable from the "Israeliness" imprinted upon them since childhood. They enjoyed observing "archetypal" Israeli behavior by selected individuals and liked to be reminded of their Israeli characteristics when positively evaluated; they also liked to make fun of those who seemed lacking in "Israeliness." But they were embarrassed by some of these characteristics when projected onto them by Israelis not very different from themselves. The collective performance of "Israeliness" was something to seek out, but at the same time it was a source of apprehension.

A "One-Night-Stand" Ethnicity

The nickname *yordim* is a degrading national designation that assumes base motives of greed and cowardice. Those who have written about *yordim* or spoken on their behalf emphasize the stigma they carry and the feelings of guilt they themselves nourish. The notion of guilt was indeed expressed in my presence, though usually as relating to other Israelis and sometimes in a scornful manner. No doubt, the separation from Israel is often a source of pain and at certain moments a reminder of a wasted existence in an alien environment. I do not embrace, however, their identification as sojourners (Kass and Lipset 1982), an identification that suits the perception of the existential situation common to many groups of immigrants (Siu 1952). In my own experience, based on continuous ties rather than focused interviews, many Israelis were well aware that they might never return to Israel. The accommodation by *yordim* to the guilt of their breaking away from Israel recalls the guilt of members of other stigmatized groups. Although other such groups sometimes regret their deviant tastes and envy the main-stream, they are too committed or obsessed with their preferred life-style to seriously consider a major change. The attraction and response of *yordim* to Israeli company, as described in this chapter, may shed light on modes of accommodation to their identity as Israelis in America.

The Israelis in Queens avoided display of noticeable communal designations. Though many Israelis did live in close proximity, there were no visible signs of this population density. For example, there was no concentration of shops in Queens carrying Israeli merchandise or catering mainly to an Israeli clientele. Israeli residents might consult Israeli professionals (medical experts in particular) and use Israeli services, but this specific reliance had no communal significance. Most important, the neighborhood was not conducive to social interaction and friendships, a mode of interaction prevalent in the old country.

Moreover, contrary to popular stereotypes, the Israelis were not concentrated in a few specific occupations, but were dispersed in various occupational fields and economic strata. They often possessed educational and technical skills, and also financial assets, which facilitated easy integration into the American economy. The population observed at the club was mainly composed of economically comfortable men and women who were either employed by American companies or self-employed. Only a few of the participants were employed by other Israelis. They did not need, at least at this stage of their stay in the United States, an ethnic network to support their instrumental adjustment. Moreover, their proficiency in English allowed them to pursue most sorts of entertainment available in New York. Thus, on the whole, they were indistinguishable from the mainstream of New York society surrounding them at home and at work.

Most participants maintained few close social ties. They were unable to sustain the extensive close-knit networks of relatives and friends that many had had in Israel. Nevertheless, to the extent that they looked for Israeli company beyond the small circle available, they were reluctant to become involved in social ties that might entail obligation and commitment. At the club, the majority preferred the "one-night-stand" type of participation. Moreover, those who attended Israeli activities more regularly did not develop close ties with other regulars. The intimate ambience that engrossed most participants was left behind once the visitors left the building. Regulars who stopped coming and were never seen again were rarely mentioned by other regulars.

The club's visitors were attracted to those meetings that enabled them to display or observe Israeli expressive modalities. They arrived as individuals or couples who, upon entrance, appeared to leave behind their American experience and status, but who, at the end of the evening's Israeli activity, returned to their American reality. This phenomenon seems comparable to the observations concerning members of another minority who also share a problematic identity, although they do not constitute an ethnic group. In spite of the obvious differences separating these two groups, the impersonal sociability observed among the Israelis seems to resemble the phenomenon of impersonal sex as reported in studies of gay society.

Members of these two minorities appear to have a choice of three modes in dealing with a complex situation of identity and its display: they may divulge their problematic identity and associate mainly with their own kind; they may refrain altogether from any public exposure of this identity; or they may confront their concealed identity in secluded settings carefully separated from their usual fields of activity. Here they may display their hidden selves without seriously threatening their otherwise well-managed public identity. Impersonal sex at bars, baths, parks, and restrooms and the impersonal sociability at the Israeli Club, Israeli restaurants, and Israeli shows all offered similar outlets: the instant gratification of a deprived identity without the burden and risk involved in an obligation and commitment to the partners in the activity. Hanan, a "regular irregular," commented that a visit to the club or to Naomi's Pizza was a pain-relief tablet. When a visitor responded to Sarah's complaint about the club with "But it's cheaper than the six-hundred-dollar air fare to Israel," he was probably not too far from Humphreys's assertion on tearoom sex: "This encounter functions, for the sex market, as does the automat for the culinary, providing a low-cost, impersonal, democratic means of commodity distribution" (1975:154). Impersonal sociability also entails a democratizing effect in that younger and older Israelis, males and females, Ashkenazim and Sephardim, professionals, businesspeople, craftspeople, cabdrivers, secretaries, and shop assistants can all comfortably communicate about their work experiences and other personal details while enjoying the display of "Israeliness."

True, not all the participants came to the club for impersonal sociability only, and there were those who expected to strike up more lasting friendships. This attitude was also revealed by Styles (1979) in his study of a scene characterized by impersonal sex. A third of those he interviewed at a bath claimed that although they went there for sexual contact, they were also seeking a long-term relationship that would extend beyond the setting of the specific encounter.[8] In both settings the expectations for long-term relationships were often frustrated and the expectant visitor ended up with another one-night-stand.

The comparison between these two situations—entailing impersonal encounters and identity management—also relates to the ethos displayed on occasions of expressive manifestations. Newton (1979:105) argued that the "camp" ethos in the gay world plays a role analogous to "soul" in black subculture (see, for example, Keil 1966). Both soul and camp minister to the needs of problematic identities. This analogy can be expanded to include the ethos or

[8]A few of his informants reported that they regularly met with the same person, whom they saw only at the bath.

style of "Israeliness." The "Israeliness" communicated at expressive modalities as, for example, during Meir Pa'il's lecture, the play *Immediate Occupancy,* and particularly at sing-alongs contained shared elements with soul and camp: the sense of common life experiences, the partaking in a unique vocabulary of subtle meanings, the receptive emotional mood, the humor directed at the participants and their world, which often highlighted the incongruities in their lives and identities.

It is my intention to take contemporary theories and definitions of ethnicity a step further than has been done so far. Although increasingly flexible and subtle in considering factors that affect ethnicity, most researchers still perceive ethnic phenomena in terms of a unique political, cultural, or situational manifestation.[9] This approach often separates ethnicity from the sociological analysis of other social minorities whose members share the problem of identity management. The Israeli case leads me to consider ethnicity in terms of an affective dimension[10] comparable to other affective forces and forms that bear upon the life of individuals and groups.[11]

[9]For a recent review of these theories, see, e.g., van den Berghe 1981; Shokeid and Deshen 1982.

[10]See also Epstein's (1978) treatment of affect among the factors sustaining ethnicity.

[11]I employed a similar approach in my study of aggressive behavior (Shokeid 1982).

[5]

The People of the Song

The gatherings of *yordim* centered around the singing of Israeli folk songs were among the events that most puzzled and impressed me during my stay in New York.

Folk songs are a standard part of Israeli youth movement education, and I myself sang at the *kumzitz* gatherings during army service and afterward. These songs are regularly broadcast on radio programs, particularly during the annual celebrations of the Day of Independence. On this festive dày the main streets and squares of most villages and towns entertain thousands of people walking and dancing under the spell of blaring loudspeakers playing their repertoire of old and new songs. During the late 1970s and early 1980s Israeli television aired a few *shira betzibur* programs (sing-alongs). These were recorded on the grounds of a kibbutz, thus evoking nostalgia for a different Israel than that of my own urban upbringing. It was Israel as depicted on posters, untainted by the harsh realities of mounting economic, political, and social problems.

After my arrival in New York, I sang more in one year than ever before. At long last I had occasion to experience the passion associated with the kibbutz, albeit in a situation that appeared to be diametrically opposed to kibbutz ideals—in Forest Hills, Flushing, and Rego Park. I first became involved in communal singing at the Israeli Club in Forest Hills. The club's weekly Wednesday meetings, with their lectures on Israeli-related subjects, usually attracted a crowd of less than thirty participants. The crowd attending the monthly gatherings of *erev shira betzibur* (an evening of communal singing), however, rarely included less than fifty participants. Moreover, on particular occasions, such as the parties scheduled for the national holidays (Chanukkah, Independence Day, and so on), at which communal singing was a major activity, attendance reached a few hundred. The participants were neither kibbutz nor *moshav*[1] veterans, but mostly former residents of the major urban areas in Israel. In Israel these same people had rarely, if ever, participated in regular communal singing. Sometimes they spoke of being puzzled that in New York they sang ten times more than they had in Israel. This enthusiasm could not be attributed to David, the club's manager; he was not at ease with singing, dancing, and other kinds of expressive activities, and after introducing the musician who would lead the singing, he left to attend to administrative tasks.

Communal singing was an important aspect of most other gatherings of Israelis I attended in Queens. It took place whenever a crowd of Israelis met for entertainment or celebration either informally at home or at more public occasions. Other resident Israelis in New York reported the same observation to me.

Although the audiences at the sing-alongs usually included both young and old participants, the majority were in their late twenties to late thirties. Most of them had left Israel within ten years after their army service and had been living in the United States for at least five years. Many had been there for more than ten years.

Members of the Israeli community of official delegates (*shlichim*) and their families—who represent a wide variety of Israeli cultural, political, and economic institutions—participated in the weekly meetings of the Israeli folk dance program held at the Central Queens YM-YWHA, which was also attended by many American Jews. *Shlichim* also sometimes attended specific lectures held at the Israeli Club. But apart from the occasional participation of one delegate's wife, no other Israeli belonging to this community ever attended the sing-alongs. One American man attended regularly. He hoped to settle in Israel and came to the sing-alongs and other programs "in order to be exposed to the Hebrew language and to the Israeli people."

[1]A small-holders cooperative.

The majority of Israelis, either in Israel or abroad, rarely remember the lyrics of folk songs, the corpus of which is enormous.[2] Most are familiar with the chorus of some songs and only a few words or lines from others. Since they do know most of the tunes, they usually mumble words and lines as close as possible to the original text. When the sing-along is well prepared, the participants, led by a musician usually playing the accordion, are aided by songbooks or photocopies of texts of selected songs. Alternatively, they may read the lines of the songs projected onto the wall by a slide projector. The slides are sometimes illustrated with pictures relevant to specific songs, such as views of Jerusalem's monuments, farmers at work, the figure of a smiling young soldier carrying a rifle.

The texts of songs distributed at sing-alongs were usually taken from songbooks containing two hundred songs. The slides added another fifty to a hundred songs to that corpus. The sing-alongs I observed in other places included a similar repertoire of songs. During a regular sing-along about forty songs might be sung altogether.

Classification of Israeli Folk Songs

I do not classify the Israeli folk songs most often sung by Israelis in Queens according to their literary and musical structure, but rather according to the following five categories: (1) songs associated with prestate *Yishuv*[3] society (sometimes referred to jokingly as "the songs of the first *aliya*")[4]; (2) songs associated with the War of Independence (sometimes referred to as "the songs of 1948"); (3) songs associated with the post-1948 army troupes; (4) songs associated with popular professional troupes, musicals, and festivals, as well as with individual singers; and (5) the corpus of songs written and composed by Naomi Shemer.

[2]See, e.g., the collection of 600 songs (in three volumes) by Pesachzon and Eligon (1981, 1983, 1984), 250 songs by Ephi Netzer (1983), and 130 songs (in three volumes) by Naomi Shemer (1967, 1975, 1982).
[3]Prestate, twentieth-century Jewish society in Palestine.
[4]The first wave of modern Jewish immigration to Palestine.

Songs of the Yishuv

This category includes a considerable number of foreign folk songs, particularly of Russian origin, the music of which was often borrowed and dressed up with new Hebrew lyrics. Most participants in the sing-alongs regarded these songs as authentic Israeli songs. Some of the most popular songs to this day, which often open an evening of communal singing, are of Russian origin. The main themes of the early Russian songs include love, war, and the beauty of nature. The first songs usually performed in this series are "Katyushka" and "Zivonim" (Tulips). "Katyushka" is a melodious song about love and nature:

> The pear and apple have blossomed
> The mist has covered the river
> And Katyushka took a walk
> To a beautiful beach.
> The girl was longingly singing
> A song, her sweetest song
> About her most beloved one . . . [5]

"Zivonim" is probably the only joyful song about war in the Israeli song corpus:

> Mother said to Vania:
> My dear son Vania
> Stop strolling in the streets
> Looking for red girls to love.
> Vania, my dear Vania,
> Take me to the war.
> You will be a red commissar
> And I will be a devoted nurse.[6]

This group of popular songs also includes "Zoya," "Lushinka," and those less noticeably Russian, such as "Rina" and "Ruach Mevaderet" (The wind blows her skirt). The same themes appear in

[5]Hebrew lyrics by Noah Pniel, copyright © by Noah Pniel.
[6]Hebrew lyrics by Levin Kipnis, copyright © by Levin Kipnis.

many, if not most, of the songs in all categories, excluding, to some
extent, the professional performers category, in which the themes
are more varied. Many refer to Israeli battles, the love of young
soldiers, the attraction of and commitment to specific sites and
scenic views in Israel. Representative of these among the prestate
songs is "Veulay" (And perhaps), written by the young poetess
Rachel, who was struck down with tuberculosis and forced to leave
the kibbutz on the Kinneret (Lake of Galilee). From her deathbed
she expressed her tragic longing to return to work in the fields and
to the scenes of her beloved lake. The poem ends:

> My Kinneret, oh, my Kinneret,
> Were you really there, or was it a dream?

Another song in this category is "Shir Ha'emek" (Song of the
valley):

> Rest has come to the weary
> And calm to the worker.
> A pale night spreads
> Over the valley of Yizrael.
> Dew below and moon above,
> From Beit Alfa to Nahalal.
> Oh, what a night of all nights,
> Nothing stirs in the valley of Yizrael.
> Sleep, oh, valley, glorious land,
> We shall be your guards.[7]

Similar songs are "Yesh li Kinneret" (My Kinneret), "Anachnu
Sharim Lach" (We sing to you, homeland and mother), "Shir
Ha'avodah" (Song of work). This last popular song includes the lines

> Blue is the sea of water
> Lovely is Jerusalem.
> The sky sheds its light
> Over the Negev and Galilee.
> The song—stand up

[7]Hebrew lyrics by Nathan Alterman, copyright © by Nathan Alterman.

Play with hammers
Play with plows.
There is no end to the song
It starts right now.[8]

Songs of the war of 1948

The war of 1948 produced many songs that have not yet lost their popularity either in Israel or in New York. These include, for example, "Shir Hafeenjan" (Song of the coffeepot), a Russian melody based on a Hebrew poem, a song closely associated with *kumzitz* gatherings, and "Shir Hapalmach," a song of an underground organization (Palmach) during the British mandate whose recruits were mainly kibbutz members. Palmach recruits combined the ingredients of both pioneerism and heroism best represented in their dedication to the land:

Around us the storm rages
But our heads are unbowed
We are always prepared
We are the Palmach
From Metulla to the Negev
From the sea to the desert
Every man is combat-ready
Every man on guard.[9]

Another popular song of 1948, 'Lech Lamidbar" (Go to the desert), tells of the young men who conquered the Negev Desert:

Go, go to the desert
The roads will lead you,
Before nightfall
Go, my friend, to the desert.

---

[8]Hebrew lyrics by Nathan Alterman, copyright © by Mif'alei Tarbuth Vekhinuch.

[9]Hebrew lyrics by Zerubavel Gila'd, copyright © by Mif'alei Tarbuth Vekhinuch.

Barren, windy, and hostile land
The warriors have returned like a storm,
To the desert, land without water,
Oh, my land, we have returned to you.[10]

Another song, "Haamini Yom Yavo" (Believe me, the day will come), tells the story of love and war:

Today is our war, sister,
Therefore I am far away.
Celebrate our meeting
In our little kitchen.
Believe me, the day will come
I promise you I will be back
I will come and embrace you
And make you forget all thoughts of war.
And if you can't fall asleep
Sing this little song
Then you will hear the song of our land.[11]

Army Troupe Songs

Since 1948 the army troupes have become a very important institution in Israeli entertainment. Some of the most celebrated Israeli artists are graduates of these troupes, which have given rise to new songs dedicated to love, the consequences of war, and the commitment to the land, including the sites gained in the Six-Day War in 1967. Particularly popular are the songs performed by troupes of the Nachal regiment, whose volunteers combine regular army service with kibbutz life. One of their famous songs is "Mool Har Sinai" (Opposite Mount Sinai):

It is not a legend my friends
And not a passing dream,

[10]Hebrew lyrics by Hayim Hefer, copyright © by Hayim Hefer.
[11]Hebrew lyrics by Refael Klatchkin, copyright © by Nagen Publishing Company.

Here, opposite Mount Sinai
The bush is burning.
It is glowing in song
On lips of regiments of men.
This day should be recounted, my brothers, as
The day the nation returned to stand at Sinai. [12]

Another of the Nachal songs is "Shir Lashalom" (A song for peace).
Its poetry is difficult to translate, but its message is clear and
powerful:

Let the sun rise
Let the morning shed its light.
Sing a song of peace for those
Who have fallen.
Bitter tears, pure prayers, and songs of praise
Will not return them to life.
Only peace will vindicate their death. [13]

Among the army troupes' popular songs are a number of love songs
that also portray scenes of nature and army life, such as "Ma Avarech" (What shall I bless) and "Beeretz Haavati" (In the country of
my love). "Ma Avarech":

What shall I bless the boy with?
The angel asked
And he blessed him with eyes
To see all flowers and birds
And a heart to understand
All views and images.
And he blessed that his hands
Would tend the flowers and
Would learn to handle the power of steel. [14]

The songs on this list gain particular force from a lyrical style that
emphasizes polar existential conditions and personal qualities, such

[12]Hebrew lyrics by Yechiel Mohar, copyright © by Yechiel Mohar.
[13]Hebrew lyrics by Jacob Rotblit, copyright © by Jacob Rotblit.
[14]Hebrew lyrics by Rachel Shapira, copyright © by Rachel Shapira.

as peace versus violent death, softness versus toughness. Love of the land is also obvious: "tend the flowers . . . handle the power of steel."

Professional Performers' Songs

Professional troupes, musicals, films, and festivals, as well as the growing number of individual performers, have all introduced a wider variety of themes and more humor into Israeli folk singing. Their songs often contain observations of Israeli daily life which have led to the infusion of social parody into folk songs. The festivals, which originated in the annual song competition held on the Day of Independence, have produced songs that display personal, individualistic characteristics, as well as traditional national themes.

The Ayalon troupe, for example, introduced a popular folk song and parody about what has become the Israeli national food, falafel:

> Every country in the world
> Has a national dish
> We have falafel, falafel, falafel
> Once when a Jew came to Israel
> He kissed the earth and prayed.
> Today when he gets out of the plane
> He immediately buys falafel.
> The preparation of falafel is an art
> Well known to every Yemenite.
> But falafel prepared by Ashkenazim
> Carries the strange taste of gefilte fish.[15]

The various festivals and the Chassidic song competition have also produced many popular songs, such as one based on a line from the prayer book:

> He [God] will bring peace upon us
> And upon all the people of Israel.

[15]Hebrew lyrics by Dan Almagor, copyright © by Dan Almagor.

Popular songs first introduced by celebrated singers include, for example, "Simona from Dimona," about a girl with a pseudo–North African name and who resides in a new town in the Negev. The song gives a romantic aura to the Israeli melting pot and the settlement of new immigrants in remote towns. It was first introduced by Yaffa Yarkoni, who has entertained army units since 1948 and who holds the unofficial title "Singer of Wars."

> Every day on the heights of Dimona
> There she stands sorrowful.
> She is suntanned and her name is Simona
> And she is waiting for her mate.
> I shall wear a hat
> I'll drag my feet in the heat
> I'll climb eight hundred meters
> To my Simona, from Sodom.[16]

The song "Bashana Habaah" (Next year) was first introduced by Ilanit, one of the younger generation of Israeli performers:

> Next year we'll sit on the balcony
> And count migrating birds.
> Children on vacation will play hide-and-seek
> Between the house and the fields.
> You will see, you will see
> How good it is going to be
> In the coming year.[17]

A more individualistic mood is represented, for example, in "Erev Shel Shoshanim" (Evening of roses), a love song first introduced by a pair of popular singers known as Hadudayim:

> It is an evening of roses
> Let us go out to the grove.
> Myrrh, spices, and frankincense
> Are the threshold at your feet.

[16]Hebrew lyrics by Hayim Shalmoni, copyright © by Hayim Shalmoni.
[17]Hebrew lyrics by Ehud Manor, copyright © Ehud Manor.

[113]

> The night falls upon us slowly
> And a breeze of roses is blowing.
> Let me whisper a song to you
> A song of love.[18]

These last two songs, although apparently neutral in their themes, nevertheless suggest an Israeli environment: the balcony where Israeli city dwellers spend their leisure time at home during the long summer, and the fragrance of the groves on a summer evening.

Songs by Naomi Shemer

Naomi Shemer holds a unique position in Israeli folk culture. Although audiences rarely identify the lyricists and composers of folk songs, songs with lyrics and music by Naomi Shemer are usually recognizable as such. For more than twenty years, Naomi Shemer, who is still in her professional prime, has been the most prolific and popular songwriter in the country. Distinctly nationalistic in her political views, she has written two songs whose popularity has almost no precedent in Israeli folk singing: "Yerushalayim Shel Zahav" (Jerusalem of gold), which coincided with the 1967 war, and the more recent "Al Hadevash Veal Ha'oketz" (On the honey and the sting). The latter's first performance coincided with the bitter debate on the peace treaty with Egypt, which committed Israel to evacuating all Jewish settlements in the Sinai.

> On the honey and the sting
> On the bitter and the sweet
> On our baby girl
> Do guard my good God.
> Don't uproot the planted
> Don't forget the hope
> Bring me back and I will come
> To the good country.

---

[18]Hebrew lyrics by Moshe Dor, copyright © by Moshe Dor.

Preserve, my God, this house,
The garden and the wall
From sadness, from sudden fear
And from war.[19]

Another engaging love song by Naomi Shemer is set in the fields of Bethlehem on the West Bank:

The moonlight shines on the mountain,
A white night spreads over the fields of Bethlehem,
A stone lies upon my heart
Like the stones in the fields of Bethlehem.
Somewhere at the end of the road
You will be waiting until dusk.[20]

The songs sung at most sing-alongs included a selection from all five of the above categories. Together, these five categories of lyrics, melodies, and performers capture the recent history of a nation. Although some participants complained that the collection represented "old songs," closer observation revealed that while the proportion of old and new songs might vary with particular musical leaders or specific events, the repertoire usually represented all categories.

Special Interventions at Sing-alongs

A sing-along evening was not entirely controlled by its musical leader, nor was it strictly a singing event. First, the participants might request to sing particular songs not included in the list prepared by the leader. Second, particular songs often stimulated verbal commentary, jokes, or mimicry. Last, the participants might sometimes call for a "solo," the performance of one or more songs by a participant. These songs, usually of a comical-theatrical type, were often unknown to the other participants (the musical leader included).

[19]Hebrew lyrics by Naomi Shemer, copyright © by Naomi Shemer.
[20]Hebrew lyrics by Naomi Shemer, copyright © by Naomi Shemer.

Comments on the content of particular songs alluded either to the discrepancy between the message of the song and the reality of life in New York, or to that between the message and reality of life in Israel. Thus, for example, the singing of a popular prestate song revealed a paradox:

Here in the cherished ancestors' land
All hopes will be materialized.
Here we'll live and here we'll create
Life of freedom and liberty.
Here the Divinity will reside,
Here will flower the language of the Torah.[21]

While the crowd proceeded enthusiastically with the song, Dani pointed his finger downward, his face shining with mischief, and exclaimed loudly: "Here, here" [in America]. All those next to him burst out laughing. A perceptive participant told me about a similar experience he had witnessed at a sing-along elsewhere in the United States at which the musical leader was singing ecstatically "From the Summit of Mount Scopus." As he sang the last lines of the song his face and body expressed the anguish and determination of his feelings: "Jerusalem, Jerusalem, I will not move from here!" At this point his listeners collapsed into hysterical laughter, since the reference seemed to be to the spot where he was standing, which they all shared as home for the foreseeable future.

The words of the song "Shekhav Bni" (Sleep, son) are a mother's narrative; they include the stanza "You will grow up in the Land of Israel; like your father, you will be a worker." When this was being sung at the club an amused participant remarked: "The person who wrote this song was an optimist." He thus implied the growing involvement in the Israeli economy of Arab workers from the West Bank and the supposed preference of Israeli Jews for white-collar jobs. The remark evoked smiles and laughter.

Jokes that interrupted the singing often revived a repertoire of Israeli army jokes with sexual connotations. These interruptions also included jokes about the political situation in Israel, taken from

[21]Hebrew lyrics by Yisrael Dushman, copyright © by Yisrael Dushman.

Israeli newspapers or from popular Israeli comedians. No complaints were ever made about these jokes, even by those who may have favored those being ridiculed. Thus, for example, much laughter followed a stingingly anti-Likud joke told by Arik: "Why do Mr. Begin's supporters keep their fists tightly clenched when they shout in the streets, 'Begin! Begin!'? Because if they opened their fists they would fall off the trees!" The joke contained an ethnic reference to Begin's constituency, which is said to include most of the less-educated, Middle Eastern Jews.

The most effective interruption by participants occurred, though not very often, when an individual volunteered or was encouraged to entertain the audience with his own private repertoire of songs. These "natural performers" had often played a prominent role at sing-alongs in Israeli youth movements and army units. One such "natural" made a particularly successful appearance during a party held at the Israeli Club on Independence Day. The party, organized as an indoor, candlelit *kumzitz,* turned out to be an ecstatic sing-along evening. The volunteer performer was a newcomer of unusual appearance—he had a clean-shaven head and dressed in a worn T-shirt and tight jeans. He started with a well-known song about a Yemenite girl who is worried about her father's reaction to the news of her love affair. He was cheered enthusiastically and encouraged to perform another "solo." He proceeded with a song unknown to most participants, which turned out to be a parody of an Israeli tour guide who manipulates a naive American female tourist into a trip to various sites and finally to a secluded Mediterranean beach, where a sexual encounter leads to a happy ending. Greatly amused by his narrative and performing skills, the audience demanded more. The newly discovered star complied and informed his fans that his next song would be a tribute to his buddies, the paratroopers of his former army unit in Israel. He said that the song was the private anthem of his unit. The song, which borrowed the music of a popular 1948 song, "Feenjan," tells the story of a parachutist who, during action, was daydreaming about his girl friend's intimate parts. Excited by these sweet thoughts, he forgot to land properly and, alas, ended up with broken legs.

Both the participants and the musical leaders were usually reluctant to end the sing-along on time (10:45 P.M.), as requested by the club's director, who was anxious to let the janitors clean and lock up the building. Finally everyone had to be almost thrown out into the cold Forest Hills night.

Participants' Reflections

Not surprisingly, various participants and other observers commented on the love of folk singing shown by people who did not seem otherwise inclined to singing and who had not been particularly enthusiastic about it in Israel. The following remarks, made during or immediately after singing together, seem representative of such comments. A successful businessman in his late forties: "What makes Israel special is the army. People there share experiences." A taxi driver in his early thirties: "The songs remind us of the army and the *kumzitz* gatherings." A housewife in her late thirties: "The songs are the connecting thread." A nurse in her late thirties: "The songs are reminiscent of our youth." A professional in his mid-thirties: "Singing together should come from the soul. It expresses something which people cannot otherwise say." More complex was Nira's reaction: "We need this bond. Although communal singing touches on our nerve centers, it is only a small part of my life now. I need it from time to time, but no more than that. We've been brainwashed with Trumpeldor's[22] testament that 'It's good to die for our country,' but that's going too far."

Eli commented analytically: "These people, who used to be part of a majority, have become a minority here. Singing together they have a two-hour opportunity to experience being a majority again." But although he was well aware of the temporary duration and artificial nature of this activity, Eli himself was much moved by the communal singing at the Independence Day *kumzitz* mentioned above. He said that had we closed our eyes and listened to the singing, we would have thought we were at a *kumzitz* at Tanturah Beach (an attractive spot on the Mediterranean between Tel Aviv

[22]A national hero who was killed in 1920 while defending one of the first settlements in Galilee. It is commonly believed that Trumpeldor's last words were "It is good to die for our country," which has become a popular motto of Israeli national education.

and Haifa). Alex commented less excitedly: "It was one more evening of singing together," to which Eli reacted: "No, it was a state of spiritual elevation [*hitromemut ruach*]!" The only participant I met from the community of Israeli offical delegates, a woman in her mid-thirties, told me: "The songs give us strength. They were written during days of war. The songs make us forget our pain."

When I presented the material in this chapter at a conference in New York, an Israeli social scientist employed at a local university who had been living in the United States for more than twenty years confessed to me that my presentation had made her shed tears. The songs could thus arouse a flow of emotion even when translated into English and presented in a detached manner interwoven with irony and humor.

American Jews who sometimes observed the Israelis singing together were usually impressed by this flow of emotion. Partly amused, partly sympathetic, the husband of an Israeli woman once exclaimed: "Poor things, they miss home so much!" But a newcomer to the United States who represented an Israeli cultural institution, upon visiting the club, angrily exclaimed for everyone to hear: "I don't need to sing in order to feel that I'm an Israeli, I am an Israeli!" Like most other Israelis on an offical appointment, she never showed up again.

Benny, who had left Israel ten years before and was now in his early thirties, had an amused and derisive reaction: "I would rather attend an American club than listen to a Hebrew singer or sing about the Negev Desert with other Israelis." He avoided the company of Israelis, whom he called *yordim*, and in fact, two years earlier, he had purchased an apartment in Israel for which he was still repaying the debts. A year after making the above statement, he returned to Israel with his Israeli wife and two children.

My own reactions are relevant here. I usually enjoyed communal singing and often openly expressed my pleasure and displeasures with particular songs and the way they were performed. Sometimes I was amused, as, for example, when the singers enthusiastically repeated the lines of a song that begins with the command "Go, go to the desert, the roads will lead you there," while the night lights of the American metropolis could be seen through the glass windows of an overheated room. But sometimes I shuddered at the

[119]

singing of songs that alluded to the death of soldiers in war. At these moments my thoughts carried me back to Israel, reminding me of people I knew whose sons had died the summer before in Lebanon. I also thought about my own two young sons, who one day would join the Israeli army. On other occasions I remembered nostalgically my home in Israel and even recalled some neighbors I had never liked. At these moments I suddenly felt alienated from the other participants, some if not most of whom might go on for years coming to the clubs, hotels, and apartments in Queens, singing about the sacredness of Jerusalem, the beauty of the Golan Heights and the Negev Desert, and about the heroic deaths of handsome young men.

I realized, however, that I was not the only one sensitive to this incongruity. Once I attended with a few close friends a concert of Israeli songs during which the audience often joined in with the singers. I suddenly noticed that the woman seated next to me, who had lived in New York for more than ten years, remained silent while the rest of the hall, bursting with emotion, sang a famous war song. She was usually a devoted singer of Israeli songs and an enthusiastic participant on these occasions. I commented on her silence and she answered: "There are some things which are inappropriate." Had she been inhibited by my own reserved reaction or was she also disassociating herself from the audience of *yordim?*

Communal Singing as Cultural Performance

Susanne Langer (1953) has described music as a "significant form" with the characteristics of a symbol: "A highly sensuous object . . . feeling, life, motion and emotion constitute its import" (p. 32). "Music is a tonal analogue of emotional life" (p. 27). Langer also claims that when words and music come together in a song, music swallows words: "Song is not a compromise between poetry and music . . . song is music" (p. 152). There can be no doubt that even the best Israeli lyrics would not have survived without evocative melodies, but the emotional effect of most Israeli popular folk songs is produced through a striking combination of words and music. The audience is usually well aware of a song's content, which arouses various emotional moods and sometime provokes comments, mimicry, and jokes.[23]

Participants in the sing-alongs seemed to be involved in a collective experience of nostalgia in the purest sense of "a painful yearning to return home" (Davis 1979:1)[24] This could be seen, for example, by the American observer who exclaimed: "Poor things, they miss home so much!" They appeared to be using the occasion to revisit their lost youth, immutably linked, in particular, to memories of their army service. But this simplistic view of their nostalgia does not represent the full repertoire of the behavioral expressions and the symbolic contents displayed at the sing-alongs, nor does it accommodate the sociological perspective of nostalgia.

Few of the memories evoked by the songs had, in fact, been experienced by the participants. In addition, the "nostalgic content" revealed in the songs related to recent phenomena in Israeli life, including, for example, the dedication to territories regained or settlements established after many of the participants had left Israel. Moreover, the revived past was never compared to deprived and lamentable present conditions. Such a comparison is the main feature of nostalgia as defined by Davis (1979:18): "A positively toned evocation of a lived past in the context of some negative feelings toward present or impending circumstances." For most of the participants the yearning or homesickness was clearly demarcated from the pressing needs and hopeful plans of their present lives. From that vantage point, they were not so different from New York Orthodox Jews, who in their prayers express their yearning and dedication to the Temple in Jerusalem and to a code of observances prescribed for those who live there. Neither Israelis at a sing-along nor Orthodox Jews at prayer evaluate their present life in New York as particularly disadvantaged, nor do they actually try to retrieve the subject of their yearning, although it is accessible. In most other cases of personal and collective nostalgia, the subject of yearning is beyond reach.

---

[23]In the following discussion I do not analyze the participants' responses to the musical stimulus per se. See Meyer (1956) and Feld (1982) for discussions of the emotional response to music in general and to folk music in particular.

[24]See also Paz 1981:208.

There was, however, more to the sing-along evenings than the expression of nostalgia. Participants were making a cultural claim and expressing an existential predicament. They were deeply absorbed in a type of activity that Singer (1955), Geertz (1973), Heilman (1983), and others have defined as a "cultural performance." As suggested by Geertz, the participants in a cultural performance express, approve, experience, and communicate moods, motivations, and metaphysical concepts that form a perspective for a world of beliefs. Expanding on this approach, Heilman, who observed Talmud *lernen* circles,[25] argued that "listening to himself and his fellows brings to life the voice of the Talmud, the participant publicly reflects, communicates, perpetuates and develops the pattern of meanings and inherited conceptions that define traditional Jewish culture" (p. 61). Although the term "cultural performance" has usually been applied to the context of religion and rituals, Geertz himself suggests that it may also apply to nonreligious contexts.[26] The symbolic activity carried out by Israelis at sing-alongs may seem relatively simple when compared with complex Indian rituals, Balinese dramas and games, or the *lernen* of Talmudic texts. But the significance of a cultural performance cannot be properly evaluated through comparative analysis, which tends to attribute greater value to what appears to be less comprehensible in terms of the observer's own culture.

The Israelis observed singing together, either at scheduled programs of singing or on less formal occasions, formed in Goffman's terms (1961:9–10) a "focused gathering" that, in common with other observations of cultural performances, was clearly demarcated from the usual routine of daily life. Such gatherings, though often consisting of a crowd of strangers, stimulated communication through a particular language of signs. This form of communication informed close situational familiarity. For a few hours participants became united through the flow of sentiment, bursts of laughter, the winks and mimicry that communicated shared understanding of the imagery and moods expressed by the songs' Hebrew texts and

---

[25]*Lernen* is a Yiddish word for the Ashkenazi Jews' pattern of study of the Talmud.
[26]Geertz 1973:113.

their melodies, as well as those evoked by the comments and jokes. During the singing encounter, not only did the participants free up suppressed emotions and their longing or "nostalgia," which is probably the most obvious interpretation, but, as suggested by Geertz (1973:444), they "displayed" these emotions and the plethora of imageries and sensations lying at their roots.

The absence of members of the official Israeli community at these gatherings is important in assessing the symbolic significance of the sentiments evoked. The songs introduced a world of Israeli history as taught, told, mythicized, and experienced, as well as a core of intimate bonds with sites, landscapes, and a way of life (its ironies included).[27] Israelis on a "legitimate visit" to the United States, or those *yordim* whose return to Israel was imminent, found it emotionally difficult to recreate and display this world in the company of those who, in their eyes, had voluntarily given up the commitment to share the reality, the responsibilities, and the dangers of daily life in Israel. An Orthodox Jew who prays devotedly for "next year in Jerusalem" has a different city in mind than that experienced by the secular Israeli. But an Israeli who has acquired an alternative citizenship (or other arrangements of permanent residence in the United States) and who is ecstatically absorbed in singing "From the Summit of Mount Scopus" or "Jerusalem of Gold" is conceived by his Israeli compatriots as expressing his longing and affinity for a Jerusalem of flesh and blood. As suggested by Deshen's typology of religious symbolic changes,[28] a single symbolic action may convey different meanings to the persons involved in it, depending on the different social situations of the actors. Here too, though in a nonreligious context, the devotional singing of Israeli residents in New York was an act of profanation for those

[27]Feld (1982) analyzes the songs of the Kaluli people (of Papua, New Guinea), which echo bird sounds and bird words as expressions of social sentiments and personal emotions that evoke a desired state of identification with a particular place and geographical history. The conspicuous differences in their ecological, societal, and cultural contexts, in the patterns of song composition and performance, and in the intentional messages of the Israeli and Kaluli songs make an analogy between the sing-alongs and the "bird songs" seemingly spurious. Nevertheless, the Kaluli evidence supports my contention that an expressive modality can display and communicate a cultural ethos and a social identity.

[28]In Deshen and Shokeid 1974:151–72.

Israelis who were on an official visit (albeit of long duration) to the United States.

Though subjectively experienced, I assume I was not unique among the Israelis in associating some of these songs with, for example, the death of particular young men, as well as with the sense of danger that the return to Israel may bring to one's own children or other loved ones. This was a clear manifestation of the sentimental education embedded in a collectively sustained symbolic structure as suggested by Geertz, whereby, using a vocabulary of sentiment, singing together relates to Israeli destiny, a destiny that offers the gift of extreme happiness inseparably interwoven with deep sorrow. By attending sing-alongs, the participant "learn[s] what his culture's ethos and his private sensibility look like when spelled out externally in a collective text" (Geertz 1973:449). Singing together, the participants not only evoked their national ethos through familiar symbolic repertoire, but also updated their stock of songs and incorporated new symbolic references to present-day Israel.

The participant who commented that if we closed our eyes and listened to the singing we would have thought that we were at Tanturah Beach was indicating the potential power of communal singing to transform reality, a process pertinent to most rituals and cultural performances.[29] As already suggested, visiting Israelis were reluctant to share this transformation of reality with the permanent residents of Flushing and Forest Hills. The participants themselves were sometimes aware of this process, the spell of which they broke through the airing of comments and jokes during singing. They thus reminded themselves and their fellow participants of their paradoxical reality as Israelis in America. Through this participation and the ambivalence revealed, they supported each other by expressing the shared dual reality: an identity rooted in a country and a way of life left behind and, at the same time, a growing commitment to a new identity associated with a country and a way of life adopted through their own free choice. At these events, uninhibited by the presence of "official Israelis," they could

[29]See, e.g., Geertz 1973:112; Heilman 1983:65.

act out an existential predicament rooted in a state of social and cultural liminality in both American and Israeli societies.

The Israeli who leaves Israel for New York whether as a result of planned immigration or mere circumstance, no longer takes along the holy books his forefathers carried in earlier migrations. But he does take along the songs. However, are these songs sufficient to sustain the "vessel" of Israeli ethnic identity?[30]

I shall now turn to an examination of *yordim*'s dilemmas and their disconcerting search for Jewish roots to better support their sense of cultural integrity when confronted with the realization that their stay in the United States might extend far beyond a short adventure.

[30]In Barth's terms (1969:14). See also Shokeid and Deshen 1982:76.

[6]

The Quest for Judaism

The roots of Israeli secularism may be traced first to the Haskalah, the movement of Jewish Enlightenment that, during the early years of the nineteenth century, challenged the authority of traditional Judaism (Katz, 1961). In some parts of the European Diaspora (in Germany in particular) the movement led to cultural and political assimilation. The leading essayists, novelists, and poets of the Haskalah and their later inheritors among the Zionists[1] mercilessly depicted the shortcomings of traditional Jewish Diaspora life as embodied in the ghetto of the West and the *shtetl* of the East.

Although the Zionists rejected the aspirations of the Jewish Enlightenment and the prospects of assimilation into the European host societies, they took over its intellectual secular legacy. The growing influence of the socialists in the Zionist movement served to strengthen its secular orientation. The political dominance of the Labor parties, which lasted for three decades after the establishment of the state of Israel, further shaped the secular image of Israel.

With the rise of Zionism, the traditional concept of Jewish redemption, for many generations rooted in messianic beliefs, was transformed into political action that ridiculed the passivity of Di-

---

[1]See, e.g., Abraham Mapu, Yehuda Leib Gordon, Peretz Smolenskin, Micha Joseph Berdichevsky, Mendele, Israel Zangwill, and Chaim Brenner. See also Laqueur's (1972) description of the intellectual roots of Zionism.

aspora history. The repudiation of Diaspora existence (*shlilat hagola*) meant in particular the denial of the spiritual world, which has sustained its survival. Not surprisingly, the majority of the leading East European rabbis regarded Zionism as an "unmitigated disaster, a poisonous weed, more dangerous even than Reform Judaism, hitherto regarded as the main menace" (Laqueur, 1972: 407).

Most of those born and raised in Israel, whose education has been secular, have actually become estranged from Jewish tradition to the extent that synagogue life is as foreign as church or mosque rituals. A visit to a synagogue is usually an embarrassment experienced once in a lifetime, during the Bar-Mitzva ceremony.[2] The religious sector makes up about 15 percent of the total population of Israel.[3] The Ashkenazi population seems to be more sharply bifurcated between the Orthodox and non-Orthodox. Among the Sephardim, a more relaxed attitude toward religion prevails, as revealed in my own description of the manifestations of Sephardi *masoret* religiosity.[4]

Religious life in Israel is considerably different from that experienced by American Jews. Organized Jewish life in America is commonly focused on synagogue communities of various religious shades, from Chassidic and extreme Orthodox to modern Orthodox, Conservative, and Reform Judaism.[5] Synagogue affiliation in America does not necessarily involve deep religious convictions or the consistent observance of ritual precepts. In Israel, however, where Orthodox Judaism prevails, the Conservative and Reform movements hardly exist.[6] Synagogue affiliation among the Ash-

[2]See also Liebman and Don-Yehia (1983) as well as Elon (1971), who describe the manifestations of secular education in Israel.

[3]See, e.g., Liebman and Don-Yehia 1983:17.

[4]This mode of religiosity involves a deep attachment to a diffused concept of *masoret beit abba*—tradition of the father's home. It is characterized by spiritual and emotional involvement and a sense of belonging, rather than by the strict practice of religious observances (Shokeid 1984). For more details, see Chap. 7.

[5]See, e.g., Glazer 1957; Lazerwitz and Harrison 1979.

[6]The Israeli Orthodox establishment has continuously challenged the legitimacy of these other movements. This confrontation became particularly volatile with the demand made by the religious parties to reject conversions not carried out by Orthodox rabbis. See Tabory (1983), who discusses the Conservative and Reform movements' position in Israel.

kenazi population in particular involves the consistent observance of most precepts. Driving on the Sabbath, for example, is considered a most serious transgression, indicating a total separation from the religious community. The absence of intermediary religious streams between Orthodoxy and non-Orthodoxy has contributed to bitter confrontation between the religious and secular sectors in Israel. This conflict has gradually become one of the most serious issues in present-day Israeli society.

Alienated Religious Affections of *Yordim* of Ashkenazi Extraction

A few months after our arrival in the United States, we went to Washington to spend Yom Kippur (the Day of Atonement) in the company of an Israeli couple working at the Israeli embassy. We enjoyed the reunion with our friends, both in their mid-forties, who were born and raised in Israel. I also shared with our host a fading nostalgia for England, where we had both attended graduate school.

Although I do not follow the religious custom of fasting on Yom Kippur, I must admit to my surprise on the morning of Yom Kippur when I found our host preparing an English breakfast of bacon and eggs. I was no less surprised to discover that our hostess had lit a memorial candle to commemorate her deceased parents. She confessed that it was the first time she had ever felt the urge to light a memorial candle on this day.[7] In Israel, while the Orthodox fast and spend the day in synagogue, young secular Israelis often express their protest against the restrictions forced on them (particularly the complete halt of public and private transport) in a ritual of feasting. As odd as this might seem, the bacon and the unexpected memorial candle reminded us, in that affluent American suburb, that it was indeed a special day.

In contrast, another secular young Israeli couple from among my *yordim* acquaintances, who had been living in America for ten

---

[7]Although memorial candles are usually lit on the anniversary of an individual's death, all the dead of the family are collectively commemorated on the eve of Yom Kippur.

years, chose to fast on Yom Kippur. But apart from the fasting, they carried on their usual activities—Benny went to work and Ziva took their car to the garage for service. Only one of my younger Ashkenazi acquaintances had changed his religious views since coming to America and now went to synagogue on Yom Kippur. In his mid-thirties, Hanan had arrived in America ten years earlier. He gradually started to observe *kashrut* at home and refrained from eating at nonkosher restaurants. He occasionally visited a nearby Conservative synagogue. Although he could afford to live in a more attractive Long Island neighborhood, which his American wife would have preferred, he insisted on staying in their Jewish neighborhood in Queens. He did not tolerate mixed marriages among his friends and his American in-laws. When he finally realized that his stay in America would last indefinitely, he decided to sell his apartment in Israel and refurbish his home in Queens. It was at this point that he joined the nearby Conservative synagogue.

Although Hanan was the only one of my young Ashkenazi acquaintances who actually leaned toward Jewish tradition, others were no longer consistently contemptuous of religious life. In Israel the non-Orthodox often see themselves as confronted with the growing power of the small religious parties, which threaten their civil rights (for example, the restriction of public transport on the Sabbath, religious jurisdiction in all personal affairs, particularly marriage and divorce proceedings). In America, however, Jewish religion is mainly represented by the organized Jewish community, which has gained much prestige and influence in American society. Moreover, the mainstream of Jewish life does not have the image of unaccommodating Orthodoxy as experienced or stereotyped in Israel. The American rabbi, for example, is closer to the Israeli's image of a social worker.

Apart from the different images of Jewish Orthodoxy and its leaders, doubts among the Israelis about their former belligerent attitude toward Jewish religion stemmed from a new source: their growing quest for the roots of their cultural identity. Dani, who described himself as outspokenly anti-Orthodox and who in Israel had never hesitated to demonstrate his antipathy toward religious beliefs and customs, told me during the early stages of our acquaintance that he was considering learning about religion and possibly visiting a synagogue. He went on to explain: "In Israel there is no need for it, but here what does being an Israeli really mean? Is it enough to speak Hebrew and read *Israel Shelanu* [the Hebrew newspaper published in New York]?" On another occasion he said: "We have been misled; there is no longer anything which connects the Israeli and the Jew. I want to know about the tradition which has brought us up to this point." I asked him whether he could see himself believing in God, to which he answered: "This isn't the problem; after all, there must be something beyond our reality." During the two years that followed, however, he did not find his way back to Judaism. He was disappointed by his few encounters with Chabad (the Lubavitch Chassidic movement) teachers. While their religious confidence and satisfaction with the Orthodox life-style were appealing, Dani could not accept their spiritual and intellectual messages. The simplistic theology of Chabad, the ar-rogant dismissal of gentile society, and the aggressive nationalism they preached from the safety of their homes in New York were not the sort of Judaism Dani could contemplate. Chabad's emissaries, however, were the only representatives of Jewish religious organi-zations who cared to contact the Israelis (see Chapter 7).

Eli, who had been living in America for more than twenty years, had better experience with American Judaism. As a member of an Israeli musical group, he had met an impressive Conservative rabbi at one of his performances in Israel. Told that the group was plan-ning a visit to the United States, the rabbi suggested they contact him on their arrival and promised them his good services. They did contact him and found him to be a very different type of rabbi than they had ever met in Israel. He offered them help and became their spiritual mentor. Eli was among the few Israelis I met who had had the opportunity to become better acquainted with American Jewish community life. He could therefore better observe the hesitations and difficulties the Israelis experienced in this area. He often com-mented: "The Israelis assume that they are Jewish simply because they were born in Israel, went to school there, and served in the army. But when they come to America they discover that they don't know anything. For numerous generations we survived as Jews, but now, within one generation, nothing has been left and the Israelis don't know what to do about it."

Some of the older Israelis found their way back to the synagogue more easily. In their late fifties and early sixties, often born in Eastern Europe, they were better acquainted with their parents' Diaspora culture and could adjust more easily to the patterns of American Jewish synagogue life. Dov, the oldest Israeli immigrant with whom I was acquainted, had been in America for about twenty-five years (see Chapter 8, Profile 1) and was the president of a modern Orthodox synagogue. The synagogue was attended by a few other Israelis who had also been living in America for a long time. Another Israeli, in his late fifties, whom I met a few years after his return to Israel, told me about his gratifying experience at a synagogue he attended during his fourteen-year stay in New York. He had joined the synagogue, first, "for the sake of the children," but was able to integrate into synagogue life because he could still relate to his childhood memories in preholocaust Europe. On his return to Israel he was the only one in the family who missed the synagogue and its rabbi. The Israeli Orthodox synagogue had as little attraction for him on his return as it had before his departure.

Another Israeli in his early sixties, who had been in America for thirty years, related a similar experience. Born in central Europe, he migrated to Israel at a young age and later joined the Canaanite movement, which disassociated Israelis from Jews.[8] Now he was active in a Conservative synagogue. He explained: "At first I joined the Reform Synagogue, but it made very little impact on the children. Here, a Jew remains a Jew only if he joins a synagogue. If he is not affiliated with a synagogue he stops being Jewish." He asked me: "When was the last time you visited a synagogue?" In fact, in spite of my familiarity with Jewish Orthodoxy, I was uncomfortable on the few occasions I did go to synagogue services in New York. I often wondered about the circumstances that alienated me from the traditions I too would have embraced had my parents and grandparents gone to America instead of to Palestine.

An Israeli in his late forties, employed in the diamond industry, once commented during a discussion at the Israeli Club: "There is a basic difference in mentality between Israelis and American Jews. The Israelis are secular and the Jews are involved with synagogue

[8]See Introduction, n. 12.

life. When I went to register my son at a Jewish school I was immediately asked, 'Who is your rabbi?' When did I ever have a rabbi?" Another Israeli in his early thirties, who was completing his graduate studies, told me: "Some researchers argue that the Israelis in America return to Judaism. Assuming that I stay on here, what will happen to my son? I won't go to a synagogue! At most I'll tell him stories about my home in the country I left and take him to sing the songs we sang in our youth movements. I am an Israeli, I cannot become a Jew!"

The younger people concerned with this new problem of cultural identity who tried to join a synagogue were confronted with considerable difficulties. Joseph and Rina, born and raised on a *moshav*, had been living in New York for about twelve years. They were both employed at a prestigious Jewish organization, but insisted on preserving their national and cultural identity. They spoke only Hebrew at home and their children were bilingual. At one point they decided to join a synagogue for the sake of their children, but soon left because they felt they did not fit into the synagogue's social milieu. Instead they became involved in organizing social activities among the Israelis who they perceived as "on the whole secular and who will probably completely assimilate." Joseph was among the more active members on the short-lived Committee of Israelis in New York, which was mainly engaged in organizing celebrations at the major festivals. A successful Channukah party attracted a few hundred participants and the organizers proudly commented that at least half of the participants had never before lit a Channukah menorah. Joseph and Rina were astonished and worried by the relaxed attitude of their kibbutz relatives toward the growing trend on many kibbutzim for members to marry gentile volunteers. They could not imagine their own children marrying anyone other than their own kind. Through their own predicament they reached the conclusion: "There is a problem in Israel of which most people there are unaware." Nevertheless, they never considered the possibility of establishing an Israeli synagogue.

Other Israelis were reluctant to pay synagogue membership dues, but soon realized that unless they became full members they would be looked down on, if they were tolerated at all. Synagogues in Israel are perceived as specialized institutions for religious services, involving less social functions than those in America. It is therefore much easier in Israel to join a synagogue congregation on a casual basis without making an immediate commitment. This uncommitted association does not cause embarrassment or give rise to a sense of humiliation. In Israel, although individual participants are obliged to hold tickets for the main festival services, those who do not obtain seats can stand during the service inside or outside the synagogue. Since synagogue participation entails few social functions, those who are not ticket holders are not particularly noticeable. The Israelis in America resented the expectation that they become full members. We observed a similar reaction at the Israeli Club, where participation dropped considerably when a small entrance fee of two dollars was introduced (see Chapter 4).

Resentment toward American synagogue life was more strongly expressed by those less reconciled with their life in America. Arik, whose American wife had made him leave Israel, was contemptuous toward her parents, whose piety seemed to him phony. He often repeated how, after attending Sabbath services, they would return to work. Arik wanted to move to a Long Island neighborhood where the public schools were better and where he would not be obliged to register his children at Jewish schools. He also wanted to leave his Queens neighborhood because it was increasingly populated by Orthodox Jews. Arik sometimes expressed the opinion that many Israelis leave Israel because of the growing conflict there between the Orthodox and non-Orthodox. At the same time, he greatly resented the apparent tendency among Israelis in America to choose non-Jews for mates.

During a discussion held at the Israeli Club about the American mass media, a number of participants complained that there were not enough Jewish programs on the various television channels. Obviously amused, a young Israeli in his late twenties, who had been living in America for about seven years (engaged in business administration), commented: "The Israelis are hypochondriacs; in Israel they moan because religion is forced on them, here they moan because they are deprived of religion."

Although they did not join synagogue congregations, many of those who considered themselves non-Orthodox in Israel did send their children to private Jewish schools. Although reluctant to pay fees for synagogue affiliation and for membership in other Jewish and Israeli voluntary associations, they went to considerable expense for their children's education. The discrepancy between their own non-Orthodox life-style and their children's Jewish education was taken as part of many other alien phenomena to be adjusted to in America. However, in the many discussions on education, they insisted that if there had been an Israeli school in Queens that followed the curriculum of a secular Israeli school, most parents would have enrolled their children there.

At a meeting of the Committee of Services to Israelis in New York, set up by the Federation of Jewish Philanthropies, the participants discussed the putative cultural commitments of the Israeli local constituency. The chairman, Dr. Steven Cohen, indicated the high rate of synagogue affiliation among American Jews (40 percent in New York, 50 percent in other regions). This affiliation, he explained, is largely centered around the family cycle ceremonies (birth, Bar Mitzvah, marriage). In stark contrast, the data indicated that non-Orthodox Israelis were reluctant to affiliate themselves with organized activities. Another participant, an Israeli who had remained in America after completing graduate studies, explained the Israeli reluctance to become involved in voluntary associations by the fact that institutional affiliation may imply their stay in America was permanent. She went on to describe the goals of the now defunct Committee of Israelis in New York, of which she had been a member, emphasizing its role in organizing "collective events" during the holidays. Drora Kass, an Israeli who had also been in New York for a long time and who was engaged in a study of *yordim*,[9] ranked the Israelis on a scale of Jewish identity as compared with a scale of affiliation orientation. She found them ranking high on the scale of Jewish identity but low on the scale of affiliation. Their Jewish identity, she explained, was manifest in their attachment to the Hebrew language and to the festive traditions, in their resentment of mixed marriages, and in their commitment to Israel as expressed in frequent visits there and the reading of Hebrew newspapers. At the same time, however, she claimed that they do not join Jewish or Israeli organizations or synagogues and do not send their children to Jewish schools.

[9]See Kass and Lipset 1982.

I doubt the validity of applying the same definition of Jewish identity to both Israelis and American Jews. These reports, however, support my own observations on the reluctance or inability of Israelis to create their own organizations or join available institutions for ethnic-cultural expression. The above observers also emphasized the continuing attachment of *yordim* to collective symbols, such as the Israeli tradition of holiday celebrations. This phenomenon was particularly noticeable in the Israeli Club, where the holiday celebrations proved to be its most successful activity.

In Front of the Locked Gate to Judaism

Liebman and Don-Yehia (1983) have discussed the transformation of traditional Judaism into a civil religion, a transformation that lent support to the Israeli social order in the various phases of its development. In the formative socialist-Zionist era this process included selective recourse to traditional holidays and to the associated rituals, which were, however, transferred "from synagogue and home to more public forums" (p. 48). The authors also indicate, as a common feature of all transformed rituals, the involvement of the participants in song and dance, which became a functional equivalent of public prayer.

There is no doubt that, to the extent Israeli cultural entrepreneurs and political leaders borrowed from traditional Judaism, they emphasized and reinterpreted those elements bearing a collective nationalistic message. The full attainment of the emerging society and culture was entrusted, however, to the new generation, which was completely removed from the vestiges of Diaspora life and traditional Judaism. The Sabra generation was the fruit of the Jewish revolution in Palestine and embodied a new species of Jews, free of the supposedly crippling forces of Diaspora life.

The transformation of traditional Judaism into an epic national history linked the Sabra generation to events of two millennia ago, such as the Maccabean and Bar-Kokhba revolts and Masada's heroic resistance and fall, but alienated them from the experiences of their parents' and grandparents' generations, who epitomized Diaspora Jews. Segre (1980) has analyzed the repudiation of Jewish tradition and recent Jewish history that took place in the wake of Zionism and statehood. He quotes (p. 91) a hero in a novel by the Israeli author Chaim Hazaz, whose words sum up the Sabras' world view: "I stand in opposition to Jewish history. It is not we who have made our history, but the gentiles—they have made it for us. . . . Jewish history is boring and uninteresting. It contains no feats, no contests, no heroes, no conquerors . . . only a multitude of sighing people who weep and ask for mercy."[10] The leading poets and novelists taught at the mainstream Israeli schools are noticeably secular and often contemptuous toward Diaspora religious life. Thus, for example, an influential poem, "In the City of Carnage," by Hayim Nahman Bialik, Israel's "national poet" laments Jewish passivity during the pogroms and vividly depicts the men's reaction to the rape of their women. Lacking the courage to fight back, they instead approach their rabbis with the shameful question: "Is my wife defiled or not?" Young students perceive this poem as an indictment of Jewish traditional society, whose life rhythms, values, and modes of behavior were conditioned by their religious code.

The Zionists who came to Israel gave up the Jewish code of religious life and committed themselves and their children to the risks of physical survival and the personal sacrifices involved in living in Israel. These risks became part of the new symbolic and mythological habitat, which provided the foundations for Israeli national solidarity. The new calendar included both the historically "meaningful" holidays, celebrated in various public ceremonies and to a lesser extent at home, and the purely religious, "meaningless" holidays, mainly associated with synagogue life. The first category included those holidays that celebrate occasions when the Jews confronted political powers attempting to dominate them—Channukah, Passover, Purim, and Lag Ba'omer. This category also included holidays of the agricultural and seasonal annual cycle, such as Shavuot, which became associated with the offering of the first fruits (*bikkurim*), and Passover, the spring holiday. The second category included the major holidays of traditional Jewish life, particularly Rosh Hashanah and Yom Kippur. Removed from the Diaspora heritage, the Sabra generation was proud of its antireligious

[10]Hazaz 1954:184–202.

feelings. For the Sabras, these most solemn days of the Jewish calendar bore no relevance and could, therefore, be spent at the beach or at a feast that challenged the rules and wrath of God Almighty.

The transformation of the religio-individual and family-oriented holidays into national collective myths and festivals was a relatively easy process in a society that wished to remove itself from the Diaspora heritage. This new interpretation of traditional symbols was lent support by the Israeli system of education, as well as by the official state ceremonies and mass media. The new society and state also created additional national symbols and holidays, which offered a wide spectrum of expressive manifestations of national identity and communal participation.

But the Israelis in the ethnically mixed neighborhoods of Queens are no longer part of a larger organized community, nor are they exposed to an educational system and other state-supported institutions, ceremonies, and the mass media that continuously vivify collective symbols of national and cultural identity. The transformation of a system of collective symbols experienced in the public realm into a more individualized and family-oriented symbolic estate, such as the synagogue and home, seems much more difficult than the reverse. The reluctance to acknowledge the finality of their move to America, which inevitably implies a threat to their self-definition as non-Diaspora Jews, makes this transformation particularly difficult, if not impossible, for most secular Ashkenazi Israelis. This self-definition, which adds to their ambivalence toward American Jews, also prevents them from finding their way even into the less religiously demanding currents within American Jewry. Instead, they have been left with local Hebrew weekly newspapers, Israeli daily newspapers, and a Hebrew radio show. The holiday parties, organized by private entrepreneurs, occasional volunteers, or by public organizations, offer them a festive reminder of the Israeli national calendar. They are also able to express their Israeliness by attending performances given by visiting Israeli artists, as well as through the communal singing of Israeli folk songs. Visits to Israel, frequent phone calls, and invitations extended to Israeli relatives to visit are also effective mechanisms of preserving the integrity of their self-image as Israelis. Eli's observation, quoted earlier, succinctly illustrates a thorny new problem: "The Israelis assume that they are Jewish simply because they were born in Israel, went to school there, and served in the army. But when they come to America, they discover that they don't know anything. For numerous generations we survived as Jews, but now, within one generation, nothing has been left and the Israelis don't know what to do about it."

I have addressed myself mainly to *yordim* of Ashkenazi extraction, who have been greatly affected by the secular tradition of European Zionism. The alienation of younger Ashkenazi Israelis from Jewish Orthodoxy was manifested again during my observations of Chabad's attempts at proselytizing among the Israelis. Although representing an Ashkenazi Chassidic movement, Chabad's activities in Queens evoke more response among *yordim* of Sephardi extraction. I shall turn now to an examination of this phenomenon, which also demonstrates the growing presence of Israelis of Middle Eastern and North African extraction in New York.

[7]

The Chassidic Option

The Lubavitch Chassidic movement, also known as Chabad,[1] was established in the late eighteenth century in Russia under the leadership of Rabbi Shneur Zalman (1745–1812).[2] His eldest son, who succeeded him as "rebbe,"[3] settled in the town of Lubavitch— hence the name. The Lubavitch movement is unusual in its policy of proselytizing, which is directed to bringing unobservant Jews back into the Orthodox fold (see Shaffir 1974; Mitchell and Plotnicov 1975; Singer 1978).

My first acquaintance with Chabad's activities among the Israelis occurred when I was invited by my garage mechanic and his wife to attend the weekly evening lectures on Judaism held at their home. Shlomo and Shula were both hard workers. The garage was open every day but Saturday, and their work day often ended after 8:00 P.M. Nevertheless, they considered it essential to spare some time for spiritual and cultural activities, and to try to involve their

---

[1]Chabad—after the acronym formed from the Hebrew words for wisdom, understanding, and knowledge.

[2]The Chabad movement sprang from the fragmentation of Chassidic Judaism, founded in the mid-eighteenth century by the Baal-Shem-Tov (1700–1760). Chassidism advocated the introduction of joy and emotional fervor into traditional Judaism, which was hitherto characterized by a life of strict observance guided by a learned elite.

[3]The title "rebbe" refers specifically to the head of the movement. The Israelis and their teachers, however, pronounced his title somewhat differently, "rabee," without the Yiddish intonation. I shall therefore use the customary term "rabbi."

friends in these activities. Shlomo and Shula, both born in Israel of Yemenite extraction, were in their late twenties, intelligent, jovial, and well liked by their loyal customers. Shlomo had come to the United States with a friend ten years earlier, soon after completing his army service. He had felt an urge to leave Israel and to try whatever awaited him in a new place. Shula arrived a few years later to pursue professional studies.

At the time I met them, both were worried about the prospects of raising a family in New York and were anxious to go back to Israel. At the same time they were frustrated by the financial difficulties involved in giving up their business (on which they still owed a considerable mortgage) and starting from scratch in Israel. Shlomo's father, who had arrived in Israel at a very young age, was not Orthodox, and Shlomo, upon his arrival in America, was remote from religion. Shula's parents, who were raised in Yemen, continued to preserve an Orthodox way of life in Israel. The couple's association with Chabad and Shlomo's gradual return to Orthodoxy played an important role in easing their continuing handwringing over their return to Israel.

The participants at the gatherings in their home usually included about ten men and women in their late twenties and early thirties. About two-thirds were of Middle Eastern extraction and a third Ashkenazi. Most of the men in the group were car dealers, and the few women were mainly employed as shop assistants. Almost all the men had been living in the United States for more than five years; the women's stays were of a shorter duration.

The Chabad teacher—as in most other congregations, he was referred to in his absence as the "rav" (rabbi) and otherwise by his first name—was on close terms with Shlomo and Shula, who considered him a personal friend. He too was an Israeli who had been living in the United States for about seven years (where he also got married). He served on the Chabad Committee for Hebrew Speakers and worked among Israelis.

The teacher recommended that I attend two other similar groups in Queens. The second group was also hosted by an Israeli-born young couple in their late twenties who had come to the United States shortly after their marriage. Their parents, who immigrated to Israel in the early 1950s from Kurdistan, lived in Jerusalem. The young couple could not afford to buy an apartment in Jerusalem and had decided to try their luck in the United States. When I met them three years after their arrival in New York the host was driving a truck, of which he was part owner. They were managing nicely in a comfortable, rented two-bedroom apartment and seemed satisfied with their achievements in America. The other attendants, mostly in their twenties and early thirties, were friends of the hosts. Most were of Middle Eastern extraction and were employed in blue-collar occupations. The meetings were attended by five to ten male participants.

The third Chabad congregation, hosted by Reuben, had been meeting for the longest time. Reuben, in his late thirties, born in Israel to parents of Iranian extraction, had done extremely well in America. After seven years in the United States he owned a number of successful stores and an impressive ranch house, and he displayed other marks of affluence as well. Attendance at Reuben's home ranged from five to fifteen male and female participants. Many were recruited from among the hosts' business acquaintances, including owners, salesmen, managers, and employees in the garment industry. Most participants were of Middle Eastern extraction. Reuben's extensive economic connections and his determination to hold the meetings regularly enabled the uninterrupted life of this congregation for more than three years.

In all three cases the core of participants was based on the hosts' personal networks, of which business and friendship bonds were dominant. Other recruits were informed either by Chabad activists or by Israelis who had some experience with the movement.

For a few weeks I also attended meetings at the Piamenta family home in Crown Heights (the major neighborhood concentration of Chabad in Brooklyn, where the movement's central institutions are located). The Piamenta congregation was regularly advertised in the local Hebrew newspapers and on the Hebrew radio show. These announcements invited Israelis in New York to combine lectures in Judaism with music led by the host, whose family has a longstanding reputation in Israel for musical talent and performing skill. The members of this congregation were not part of the hosts' personal network of friends. Many were students from the nearby Lubavitch Yeshiva, which included a group of Israelis. Here again

the majority of participants were of Middle Eastern extraction. The
crowd of men and women was considerably larger and more diverse
in its occupations than at the less advertised congregations. No less
than thirty participants were present at the meetings. The women,
though seated separately, were not secluded from the men, who sat
around the main table. At the other groups the women sat with the
men around one table. Music performed by the host or visitors
added a convivial atmosphere to these gatherings.

Meetings at the home congregations started at 9:30 P.M. and
continued for about two hours. The congregants usually had some
time to socialize before the rabbi's arrival. Only a few participants
attended the weekly meetings regularly. Most others attended
once every few weeks or months. Some might come regularly for a
few weeks and then disappear for a long time.

I also spent a day at the Chabad Yeshiva in the company of a
group of Israelis undergoing training in Judaism and Chabad theology. The group included about twelve men in their twenties to
late thirties, two-thirds of whom were of Sephardi extraction and
the rest Ashkenzi. In the home congregations about 50 percent of
the participants were married and the other half single or divorced;
among the Yeshiva participants most were single or divorced. On
the whole, many of the participants at Chabad activities were recent arrivals in the United States, although there were also some
who had been there for more than five years.

Chabad teachers never declined an invitation to address a group
of Israelis, and they also lectured at the Israeli Club in Forest Hills
at two Wednesday meetings during Channukah 1982 and 1983. The
teacher-rabbis at the home congregations were assigned to specific
groups, with which they met every week for as long as the group
survived or as long as the teacher remained in New York. The same
teacher, for example, was associated with Reuben's group for more
than three years. When a teacher could not attend a meeting,
another teacher was immediately assigned to replace him. The
temporary assistants were either from the Chabad Brooklyn community or newcomers from Israel who had come for a short visit to
the headquarters. In most cases the permanent teachers were former residents of Israel who had been summoned by the rabbi for an
unspecified period in order to work in New York. They all spoke

the modern Hebrew used by most Israelis without an accent that could be associated with American English, Yiddish, or Arabic. Most of them, if not all, could speak Yiddish fluently. Attired in a somber outfit (dark suit and hat) and with a command of Yiddish, they looked like Orthodox Ashkenazim, although a few of them were of Sephardi extraction. They rarely used Yiddish idioms at their lectures, but often switched to Yiddish with their colleagues.

None of the participants was Orthodox prior to association with Chabad. One participant told me that although his parents were very religious, he himself had given up Orthodoxy during his army service and since then paid an annual visit to the synagogue on Yom Kippur only. Although he had recently discovered the importance of Judaism, he still did not consider himself Orthodox. He thought that many other participants also felt that they missed Judaism since coming to the United States. He argued, however, that some participants came to the meetings at Reuben's home in order to please the host, with whom they did business. He also claimed that the host himself used Chabad for his business interests: "In order to do well in business here you need to master Yiddish or wear a skullcap. The Jews control the textile business in New York and it's enough that they extend their credit to you for a longer period in order to succeed. Chabad is Reuben's alibi in business. If they see you from time to time at the rabbi's *hitvadeu't*,[4] or if you get the rabbi's recommendation, then you'll get special treatment." Reuben, who indeed may have profited from his relationship with Chabad, also reciprocated with generous financial contributions. In addition, he provided employment in his stores for Chabad's new recruits.

This instrumental reciprocity between the Chassidic movement and its new disciples was less noticeable at the other home congregations although the teachers offered help and support to whomever seemed to be in need. Chabad's worldwide organization, its local connections, and its abundant resources appeared to be able to provide easy solutions to most problems.

The participants showed great differences in their commitment

---

[4]*Hitvadeu't*—the rabbi's periodic appearance in front of his disciples. These appearances are usually associated with the major holidays.

to religious observances. Shlomo, for example, closed his garage on Saturdays and on all Jewish holidays (he stayed open on Sundays and other American secular holidays). The teacher at Shlomo's congregation must have had this increasingly observant attitude in mind when he commented: "You need patience, after all they come from an Orthodox background." When I asked the teacher if Reuben was strictly observant, he answered: "No, but he is making good progress."

Chabad's efforts at proselytizing did not seem very successful among *yordim* of Ashkenazi extraction. Most puzzling was the particular appeal of Chabad's activities to Sephardi *yordim*, whose religious experience and cultural traditions were remote from those represented by Ashkenazi Chassidim. The male Sephardi participants, most of whom were born in Israel, had not been observant prior to their involvement with Chabad, although their parents were often observant. Most of them had been through junior high school in Israel[5] and were employed there in small business and in technical and blue-collar occupations. In New York they were mainly employed in business or had become independent craftsmen.

The association of the few Ashkenazi male participants with Chabad seemed to be more often related to a turbulent personal history of soul-searching and disappointing experiences. In most cases, this was their first encounter with the Jewish religion, which had not been practiced by their parents. The women, both of Ashkenazi and Shepardi extraction, were in most cases single and their participation also entailed the expectation of meeting a male companion.

The following discussion of the major themes raised by the teachers and a consideration of some other characteristics of Chabad may offer an explanation for the particular appeal of an Ashkenazi Chassidic movement among Sephardi *yordim*.

---

[5]Korazim's survey of *yordim* in Queens and Brooklyn (1983) revealed that the educational level of families of Sephardi origin was significantly lower than that of Ashkenazi families (pp. 84–85).

The Message

The Unity of the Jewish People

The lectures at the home congregations usually began with a reading from the two-page Hebrew weekly pamphlet. The pamphlet, based on the rabbi's Sabbath afternoon *drasha* (rabbinical lecture), was often related to the portion from the Torah (Pentateuch) read in the synagogue during the morning service (*parashat hashavua'*). Other texts often used were *Pirkei Avot* (Ethics of the Fathers) and, for the more advanced, the *Tanya*, the major book of Chabad scholarship and beliefs.

Although the texts or the context of the lecture and its subject matter might differ at the various types of Chabad meetings, in all settings the teachers consistently conveyed the same specific messages. I once recorded two lectures by different teachers on the same cassette. When I transcribed them, I could hardly differentiate between the two, since both teachers used a similar style and structure of presentation, as well as similar intonations. At all meetings and with all audiences the lectures clearly led to the same ideological and practical conclusions.

Most lectures touched upon the revelation of the divine ingredients of the Jewish soul. This interpretation was new to me, as well as to most other participants. We were all well aware of the special position supposedly bestowed upon the Jews as the "chosen people" (*am segula*), but not as being "next to God" in their personal substance. The idea of the divine quality of each and every Jew thus shifted from the tradition of a collective attribute into the domain of personal properties.

At a meeting during Channukah at Reuben's home, the teacher argued that every Jew has two souls: the natural, animalistic soul (composed of fire, wind, water, and soil) and the divine soul (the container of pure oil). The gentile lacks this divine substance, and even his animalistic soul is of an inferior quality. While a gentile can be taught to be good, a Jew is inherently good. The teacher used as evidence the Germans, who, although famous for their good manners and civility, and their celebration of philosophers and sociologists—the reference to sociologists was made by the speaker while looking pointedly at me—succumbed to the leadership of a madman. The teacher went on to claim that the Jewish soul is part of God. As it is written in the Torah: "Israel, you are my first-born child," and "You have blown life into me." God blows life from his own soul into every Jew, thereby adding the special quality to the Jewish soul.

At a lecture on Chassidic theory presented one Sunday morning at the Chabad Yeshiva, an Israeli in his mid-twenties of Ashkenazi extraction, who prior to his involvement with Chabad, had been far removed from Jewish religious life, asked: "Why were the laws of the Torah given only to the people of Israel?" He got an immediate answer: "If you are an engineer, you don't ask, 'Why aren't I a janitor?' Don't ask why you aren't a slave and don't ask 'Why am I not as base as others?' We have a mechanism which ignites immediately. Every action you take transforms you into a divine creature. I may go hungry for two days and then come upon a nice piece of meat. But I will not eat it because it has not been ritually cleaned and prepared according to Jewish custom." He went on in a conciliatory mood to explain that we should differentiate between Jews, gentiles, and pious gentiles (a select category of gentiles whose noble character has been proved through their humane actions). The Jews receive directly from the source of holiness, the pious gentiles receive something from the same source, but the ordinary gentiles are completely removed from holiness. This special substance[6] was also used to explain why the Jews do better than others in so many spheres. Even a Jew who does not fulfill God's commandments is superior to the ordinary gentile. This conclusion, as evidenced more clearly in the following observations, ultimately leads to an eradication of the separation between religious and secular Jews.

---

[6]The substance of holiness embedded in each individual was often phrased in terms of vessels such as the container of oil associated with the miracle of Channukah (when the menorah at the Temple was kept alight for eight days by the oil provided from one small container) or Noah's Ark. These containers and their contents were at the same time associated with the essence of Judaism as a system of belief and a way of life. The divine soul, as well as the substance of holiness, were described as aspiring to infinity.

A major theme in Chabad's teachings stressed that, since all Jews are part of the same entity, they are mutually responsible and accountable. As expressed by one teacher: "From the point of view of the rabbi there are no secular Jews and Orthodox Jews. All Jews perform *mitzvot* [precepts], some do more and some do less." As evidence, he quoted the rabbi's letters, which are always addressed to "All the sons and daughters of Israel" and not to particular Jews. This concept of the unity of the Jewish nation and the indispensability of every individual was symbolically expressed through the rabbi's project of inscribing every Jew on a list, since it is believed that every letter in the Holy Scripture stands for a living Jew. At all Chabad meetings the participants were encouraged to inscribe themselves and their relatives on this list, which, it was claimed, already included six million names.

The message conveyed by Chabad's teaching was flattering indeed. It endowed every participant, including those whose material or intellectual achievements and social or moral standing were less than satisfactory in their own eyes, with an undeniable innate value and status. The rabbi's representatives, who were themselves successful in many ways, were most sincere in their offer of this new sense of self-esteem. I never saw a Chabad teacher falter in his expression of respect toward anybody, even when provoked by obscene or offensive behavior, by conspicuous ignorance of Judaism, or by irritating demands. The lectures at Shlomo and Shula's home, for example, were often interrupted by jokes and obscene sexual references to the participants and their past experiences. At one meeting a young car dealer of Moroccan extraction seemed to be trying to test the teacher's patience. He continuously made bodily gestures toward a good-looking female participant, focusing attention on her breasts. Moreover, he made frequent jokes about the teacher's moral and sexual life. For a long hour the teacher made only feeble smiles of protest at this continuing offense, which gradually made it impossible for him to teach. At last he could no longer restrain himself and asked the troublemaker whether he had nothing on his mind except cars and girls. Seemingly offended, the young man retorted: "So it seems you think me no good and wish me to leave." The teacher immediately apologized—"No, you are a saint [*tzadik*]"—and brought as proof an ancient saying that claims all children of Israel are *tzadikim* even when they do not seem to be so. Moreover, if the young man promised to put on phylacteries,[7] he would present him with a one-dollar bill that he had carried in his inside pocket as an amulet ever since the rabbi had given it to him. The young man, though touched by the offer, refused politely. He promised to let the teacher know when he felt ready to put on phylacteries. At a later meeting the teacher told me that he had a lot of patience in dealing with his audience and added: "You need to get close to them; they come from a religious background [implying their parents' generation] and can be recruited back to Orthodoxy."

The differences between Chabad's Ashkenazi Chassidic tradition and the Middle Eastern religious traditions, the background of many if not the majority of the Israeli participants, were never referred to. The teachers addressed the participants in the neutral Israeli Hebrew dialect and emphasized the intrinsic importance of every Jewish individual regardless of his religious status and cultural background. They were never carried away into a discussion about the differences between Ashkenazim and Sephardim, even when provoked. Once during an intermission, for example, Reuben seized the opportunity to share an idea that had occurred to him during the previous Sabbath service in synagogue and which he thought "might explain the ethnic disparities [*pa'ar adati*] in Israel." "I go to an Ashkenazi synagogue," he began. "While the congregants gossip (since they know each other well and possibly speak to each other in Yiddish), I read. I was reading in Genesis how Canaan, the son of Cham, and his descendants were cursed by God to be slaves forever. It suddenly struck me that since Oriental Jews have been dispersed for many generations in the lands of the children of Canaan, they must have been infected by their hosts' impurity and therefore arrived in Israel disadvantaged in comparison with Ashkenazim." As proof of his hypothesis Reuben quoted a verse from the Book of Genesis and went on with his argument: "If you look around [in Israel] you always see the Sephardim in manual

[7]Phylacteries (*tefillin*)—two black leather boxes containing scriptural passages, which are bound by black leather strips round the left hand and on the head and worn during the morning services on all days of the year except the Sabbath and scriptural holy days (see *Encyclopaedia Judaica* 15:898–904).

jobs while the Ashkenazim do office jobs. It is a fact that the Sephardim arrived in Israel disadvantaged, but not because of a lower IQ." The teacher reacted to Reuben's insight briefly and in an unimpressed tone: "I have never thought about it—we always think about what unites the Israeli nation rather than about what divides it." The host retorted: "I agree with you, but if everything is written in the Torah, then this too is written there. This chapter shows the destiny of the Jews in the lands of Canaan." At that the lecturer resumed the theme he had been discussing before the interruption.

Our host, Reuben, had not been satisfied in Israel with his economic and social standing and, according to a close family member, was bitter about the ethnic prejudice he thought had adversely affected his achievements there. He now seemed greatly reconciled to his existential position. Economically successful and enthusiastically embraced by an Ashkenazi establishment, he looked back without bitterness at the Israeli ethnic reality, which in the past must have caused him considerable pain.

The only reference made by the teacher to the ethnic divisions in Israel was intended to demonstrate how alien any such divisions are to Chabad. Answering a question about the rabbi's opinion on Israeli politics, the teacher mentioned that while Prime Minister Golda Meir held office, she was reported to have expressed resentment about the rabbi's intervention in Israel's internal affairs. The rabbi reacted to her complaints by relating a parable: "Imagine, had a simple Jew from Brooklyn . . . " At this point the teacher interrupted his own narrative and said: "But let me add, 'and one who doesn't speak Yiddish,' since according to Golda those who can't speak Yiddish are not Jews!" He then continued with the parable: "This Jew from Brooklyn phoned her up and told her about a bomb due to explode in her Jerusalem office. Wouldn't she accept his call?" Thus the secular Israeli prime minister had apparently used Yiddish as a criterion for distinguishing between Jews. But although Chabad people used Yiddish for many purposes (including the rabbi's periodical appearances in front of his disciples, which were also broadcast on radio and television), it did not serve as a barrier between Jews, who were all considered equal.

The notion of embracement by Chabad once led Reuben to relate in an amused mood an early life experience. While still a teen-ager employed in Tel Aviv at a workshop owned by Ashkenazim, he overheard somebody saying he had a *goyishe kop* ("a gentile head," a Yiddish term for incompetence). Yiddish, although largely alien to most Sephardim, did not seem to deter them from joining a movement noticeably Ashkenazi in its symbolic expressions.

The Essence of Judaism and Its Transmission

At one session at Reuben's home, after reading from the weekly Torah portion (which dealt with Noah's Ark), the teacher argued that it is commonly assumed that a person who lives in Israel, speaks Hebrew, and serves in the army is Jewish. But if this is the case, then the Israeli Druse citizens are also Jewish, since they too fulfill the same three criteria. And what about Russian Jews, who do not live in Israel, do not serve in the army, and cannot speak Hebrew? Would we not consider them Jews? The teacher went on to reassure his listeners that Jewish identity cannot be defined as evenings of folk singing or dancing, thus alluding to a major manifestation of secular Israeli culture. Jewish identity is what we call "Judaism," it is the "ark" that reappears every generation. Otherwise, he explained, there would be no reason to retell the story of Noah's Ark and the flood. Judaism is the "ark" that survives the continuing deluge of foreign cultures and senseless pursuits.

A similar theme was repeated by another teacher, whose lectures I attended at both the Chabad Yeshiva and at the Israeli Club and who used the image of *pakh hashemen* (the container of oil) which kept the menorah lit at the temple in Jerusalem and which is symbolized every year by the Channukah candles. The oil represents the substance of Judaism. He said that the Torah holds everything, including the technical inventions and scientific theoretical revelations of which the modern world is so proud. He promised his audience that learning the Torah was not the study of the irrelevant past, but a way of improving their general education in fields about which most of them were uninformed. He also reassured his listeners that the practice of Judaism would not interfere with their individual professional lives.

[150]

The teacher, who revealed that a few years ago he too had been "anti-Torah," related his recent experience in the army, where he witnessed highly educated men "go nuts" from boredom. They could not concentrate on books related to their professional work and absorbed themselves in pornography. They phoned their wives and complained as if they had been away from home for a few years. Yet, once home, they immediately rushed out to see friends and find entertainment. The speaker himself had had no problems whatsoever during his seven weeks of army service because, as he said: "The Torah is with you everywhere and it answers all problems. It is a way of life. Without the Torah people escape from themselves. They search for entertainment, which is no more than a method of escape. Judaism calls you to come and learn about yourself, which is a world in itself!"

The teacher thus invited his listeners to share his recent Israeli experiences. He was also associating Chabad with major issues of Israeli life, army reserve duty in particular, and at the same time raising doubts about the strength of Israeli Ashkenazi secular culture, often associated with higher education and professional skills (of which most participants of Sephardi extraction were deprived). Pinpointing the weakness of secular education, the teacher presented Chabad's education as a modern system capable of solving problems inherent in contemporary life.

Israelis of secular background commonly perceive Judaism as a body of archaic and demanding precepts as well as a corpus of complicated texts which requires many years of learning. The Chabad messages, however, presented Judaism as a goal easily attainable by all Jews regardless of their religious status. To be Jewish by birth was already halfway toward the attainment of this goal, and the rest of the way was not burdensome. Participation in Chabad's relaxed meetings was an important step in this direction. The participants were not questioned about their practice of religious observances. It was assumed that they would gradually, at their own pace, commit themselves to an increasing load of daily observances.

One of the regular participants at Reuben's congregation told me that he had transferred his seven-year-old son from a Jewish school to a public school, an action he knew would greatly displease the

Chabad teacher. He explained that he was not satisfied with the standard of teaching at the Jewish school. This action might also have been influenced by financial considerations (in 1982–83 the annual fees of Jewish schools in Queens, unless subsidized, ranged from $1,250 to $2,700). He also worked on the Sabbath, since he might otherwise have lost his job as store manager. He went on to point out that Reuben himself, who appeared to be a pillar of Orthodoxy in Chabad circles, kept his stores open on the Sabbath. The teachers, however, did not criticize their recruits' behavior and treated the participants and the hosts in particular with much respect.

A Saint in the House

The Chabad teachings also stressed the importance of the association of its disciples with the leader of the movement, the venerated Lubavitch rabbi, Menachem Mendel Schneerson, who at the time was over eighty years old. The involvement of Reuben's family with Chabad was most noticeable upon entrance into their spacious home, which was like a shrine to the Lubavitch leader. The walls were decorated with photographs of the rabbi, one of which showed Reuben in his company.

A young Israeli of Middle Eastern extraction who lived in the Chabad Yeshiva compound and knew the rabbi's daily schedule, took me along to see the rabbi when he arrived at his office for the morning session. At 10:00 A.M. the rabbi's limousine stopped in front of Chabad headquarters. I remained in the small corridor leading to his office with an Israeli friend and a few women who were waiting for the opportunity to be blessed by the rabbi's presence. All other local attendants disappeared into the adjacent corridors and rooms. Suddenly a dead silence fell upon the busy place. The rabbi marched alone along the path leading to the building and into his office. I was impressed by his firm walk and authoritative expression. Our guide, who reappeared after the door closed behind the rabbi, told us he felt very small in the presence of the rabbi. An Israeli of Ashkenazi extraction who was visiting the Chabad center for a few weeks appeared on the scene and explained that the women waiting for the rabbi had already sent him a letter requesting his help. He also told us that a relative of his, a thirty-eight-year-old woman of many talents who could not find a suitable spouse, sent a letter to the rabbi and came to see him from Israel. "It is enough that the rabbi looks at you," he explained. She returned home after seeing the rabbi in this corridor and soon was happily married.

The reverence and adulation the Chassidic leader is held in, as expressed in his presence as well as in the stories relating his mystical powers, resemble that of religious leaders of many groups of Middle Eastern Jews, particularly in North Africa. As I have described elsewhere (Shokeid 1979), these leaders were scholars whose authority was invested with charismatic traits demonstrated by the individual, as well as by the family patrimony, best expressed in *zekhut avot* (merit of the fathers). The leaders, who were not formally appointed and who did not receive a regular salary, were known for their extraordinary deeds and the power of their blessing. In Israel this type of leadership could not easily accommodate itself to the religious bureaucratic system (based on, among other things, formal appointments to various offices). Consequently, the authentic leadership of many Middle Eastern communities lost its position among its constituencies. The sense of loss and the yearning of Middle Eastern Jews for their traditional leaders manifest themselves in Israel particularly in the popularity of pilgrimages to the tombs of scholars and saints (Shokeid 1974; Ben-Ami 1977) and the *hilulot*, the commemorative celebrations dedicated to sages from earlier times (Deshen 1974:95–121).

In Israel, the Ashkenazi Chassidic movements led by charismatic families (which remain unaffected by the religious bureaucratic establishment) are on the whole removed from the Sephardi community. In New York, however, the Sephardim are enthusiastically encouraged to join the flock of Chabad and share with its disciples the power and blessing of the illustrious Lubavitch leader.

Once, during a home congregation meeting, the participants were discussing the rabbi's good health and youthful appearance, as well as the enigma of his childless marriage. A participant of Moroccan extraction suggested that the rabbi would one day reveal himself as the Messiah for whom the Jews have waited so long.

Chabad and Israel

Although Chabad teachers were mainly involved in the revival of Judaism and the redemption of individual Jews, Israeli affairs were constantly brought up during the sessions, often by the teachers themselves. Moreover, they mentioned Israel mainly in reference to controversial political issues, seemingly far removed from the goals of religious teaching. These references repeatedly attacked Israeli groups and individuals who expressed opposition toward the Likud government. The teachers manifested an unreserved nationalistic orientation. Thus for example, when discussing the continuing dangers of the "flood" from which the Jews can find refuge in the "ark," the teacher added sarcastically: "But instead of searching for the Torah, people look for Peace Now or for a guru." Peace Now, an Israeli political movement associated with leftist parties, represents the strongest ideological opposition to the Likud and its political partners. In the same breath, the teacher was also alluding to the various Eastern religions that have reached Israel. A similar reference was made while reading from the weekly Chabad Hebrew flier related to Channukah: ". . . the Hellenistic and liberal party which emerged among the Jewish people and wished to integrate Judea within the Greek world of cultural normality." The teacher added by way of explanation: "As is the case with Peace Now . . . while the Greek empire, its culture, and way of life are now the subject of historical research, the Jewish people and its Torah are eternal!"

On another occasion the teacher explained the rabbi's support of the occupation of the West Bank as based on the biblical promise to Abraham. He quoted the rabbi, who argued that had Israel shown to the nations God's written promise and particularly the contract detailed in Genesis of the sale of the Patriarchs' Cave in Hebron to Abraham (who first bought it as a graveyard for his wife, Sarah), international pressure would quickly have subsided. The rabbi was reported as supporting the Lebanon war, which, in his view, would have attained its goals had the Israeli government not been inhibited by various cabinet members and by the opposition parties.

The rabbi's political stand, enthusiastically presented by the teacher, suited the political attitudes of most if not all regular participants. The opposition parties in Israel and particularly the Labor alignment (which ruled the country until 1977) and its present-day leaders seemed to be resented for more complicated reasons than their political stand over the West Bank. An opportunity for airing these opinions was offered before the start of meetings, when the participants usually listened to the news on the Israeli radio program "Kan Israel" at 9:30 P.M. It often mentioned the latest debates in the Israeli parliament and quoted the arguments and mutual accusations made by the leaders of the coalition and the opposition parties. On hearing these announcements the participants added their own offensive ridicule and evaluations about the personal characteristics and the policies proposed by the opposition leaders. Support of the Likud government and its nationalistic policies was prevalent also in other segments of *yordim* population. But the unanimous consensus in support of the Likud and the vehement resentment of the opposition parties was particularly overwhelming among Chabad's congregations.

On various occasions participants asked why the rabbi never visited Israel. On one such occasion the teacher reacted with emotion: "There isn't a more dedicated Zionist than the rabbi. In recent years no other movement or organization, the Jewish Agency included, has recruited more immigrants to Israel than Chabad. Go and see how many neighborhoods in Israel have been built by Chabad. Chabad started its settlements in Israel before Hashomer Hatzair [a kibbutz movement associated with a more extremist socialist ideology] and it is now planning a settlement on the West Bank." He went on: "If the rabbi stays in America it is because it is better for the Jewish people, most of whom are still in the Diaspora and shouldn't be left alone. The rabbi can better support both Israel and the Jews from here. The time is not yet ripe for the rabbi to leave America. Furthermore, he cannot visit Israel because he wouldn't be allowed to leave again [as prescribed by the *Shulhan Aruch,* a guide to rules of conduct in daily life]." But although the rabbi had never been to Israel, the teacher insisted, he knows it as intimately as if he had walked throughout the land. Alluding to the imminence of the rabbi's arrival in Israel, he ended his defense by informing the group that a fully equipped apartment is ready and waiting for the rabbi in the Old City of Jerusalem.

[155]

When the teacher was challenged by a newcomer of Ashkenazi extraction that the survival of Zionism necessitates living in Israel, the teacher stingingly retorted: "Is Udi Adiv a Zionist? He lives in Israel!" Udi Adiv is a young kibbutz member who was convicted for espionage and whose trial and verdict shocked the Israeli public. He went on to explain: "Wherever they are the people of Israel are attracted to Judaism. There are many important values in Judaism and one of them, though not the most important, is Zionism. The fact is that the young people brought up on the values of Zionism, including those raised in the kibbutz, have left Israel or even cooperated with the PLO. It is Judaism which is at our roots, it is Judaism which carries the true promise for the return to Israel, for the return to values, and for health."

Chabad's position was positively committed to Israel. It presented a clear nationalistic viewpoint associated with the Israeli right wing's wishes for a "greater Israel." It supported Israel's government and its policies at a time when these were less than popular with the American government and the American mass media. At the same time, however, Chabad's position toward immigration to Israel was ambiguous. While assuming it to be an important religious duty, residence in the United States was not stigmatized, since the battle for the survival of Judaism was more important. Chabad Chassidim were called upon by the rabbi to leave Israel for America or vice versa, according to the tasks he considered vital at a specific time. As one of the teachers exclaimed: "We have a task and it doesn't matter whether it is to be carried out in Israel or in New York." The trouble, he pointed out, is that "in Israel, too, the Jews are in exile—spiritual exile [*galut ruchanit*]." This attitude was often adopted by participants who interpreted their own stay in America in mystical terms.

When Shlomo confessed that living in the Diaspora was a source of pain to him, the teacher insisted that although he was residing outside of Israel he was not in exile. He thus differentiated between territorial exile and spiritual exile (*gola* versus *galut*). Shlomo often argued that exile was most probably forced upon "us," implying the other participants as well. He attributed the responsibility for his departure from Israel and his prolonged stay in New York to an external force. He thus assumed circumstances similar to those of

Chabad missionaries summoned to the United States by the rabbi's command. Although the teacher gave no support to this interpretation, Shlomo did not give it up. Reuben once aired a similar idea. When the teacher expressed the wish that Reuben might go back to Israel next year, Reuben reacted in a wishful tone: "I hope he [God] who took me out of there will also take me back." The teacher made no comment at this transfer of responsibility to the Almightly. Another participant once commented: "We don't know why we are here, but I believe we are serving as delegates for some good reason. God must know why we are here."

Compatability between Chabad and
Its Sephardi Constituency

The data available on Chabad's achievements in its proselytization activities among Jews seem to indicate that Chabad's missionaries are satisfied with much less than full "conversion" and with modest numbers of converts. As reported by Mitchell and Plotnicov (1975), in over forty-five years of work among Pittsburgh's Jews, the Lubavitchers have succeeded in attracting only six new recruits. However, within four years of missionary work at centers situated near colleges and universities of Los Angeles, Singer (1978) reported forty-five converts to Chabad.[8] Among the Israelis I observed, the impact of Chabad activities was varied. Without taking into account the Chabad Yeshiva students, whose social characteristics were possibly similar to the Los Angeles recruits, the hosts of the home congregations seemed closest to the status of converts. Most other participants developed a positive attitude toward Chabad teaching, but their life-style was otherwise very little affected. Although they did not become either synagogue congregants or observant, their participation produced a new awareness of their Jewish identity and provided them with an experience of social and cultural belonging in an alien environment. The teachers, for their part, seemed gratified by any act that involved their

[8]One should probably compare Chabad's achievements in Los Angeles with those of other proselytizing movements active among university students.

audience in Jewish activities. This tolerant approach was remarkably different from the image of Ashkenazi Orthodoxy as most participants had experienced it in Israel.

Although the Chabad movement is rooted in a Chassidic Eastern European tradition, whose major features have been remarkably preserved in its voyage from the *shtetl* to New York, the majority of Chabad's new recruits from among the Israeli *yordim* were of Middle Eastern extraction. Three elements of compatability seem to have given rise to Chabad's particular appeal among this segment of Israeli immigration: that between the religious demands made by Chabad and its pattern of religious leadership with the religious tradition of Middle Eastern Jews, that between Chabad's ethos and its strategy of relating to the existential experience of Sephardi Jews in Israeli society, and that between Chabad's nationalism and the "rightist" tendencies among Sephardim in Israel.

In a study of contemporary trends in the religiosity of Middle Eastern Jews in Israel, I observed the development of a particular style of religious behavior which I called *"masoret* religiosity" (Shokeid 1984). This mode of religiosity involves a deep attachment to a diffused conception of *masoret beit abba* (tradition of the father's home), which is usually connected with synagogue life, but more specifically entails an attachment to the religious details of family ceremonial life on the Sabbath and the festivals. This type of attachment is remarkably tolerant toward partial participation in synagogue life, as well as toward the selective preservation of religious observances in public and at home. The ethos distinguishing this pattern of behavior suggests a scale of religiosity which ranks and rewards each believer according to his particular existential circumstances. The believers perceive this scale as the natural order of religious life, which endows contemporary leaders, as well as scholars and saints of the past, with the spiritual power to supplement their own religious deficiencies. The leaders of past and present provide seasonal opportunities for religious elevation, as for example during the pilgrimages to the saints' tombs and other celebrations. This mode of religiosity is characterized by spiritual and emotional involvement and the notion of belonging, rather than by the strict practice of religious observances.

Chabad's particular ethnocentric religious theory, which attributes a special religious status to all Jews, regardless of their religious comportment, and which accommodates a relaxed attitude toward religious observance among the new recruits, is remote from the severe attitude toward partial observance held by Israeli Orthodoxy. Thus Chabad's position was compatible with the religious experience and affective modalities that characterize Israeli Sephardim. Chabad's anchoring in the rabbi's charismatic leadership added a further element to the compatability between the seemingly distinct Ashkenazi and Sephardi cultural traditions. Further evidence for religious attitudes among Sephardi versus Ashkenazi *yordim* may be found in Korazim (1983:104), who reported that among his sample of Israeli families in New York the majority of Sephardim (60 percent) defined themselves as "traditional," whereas the majority of Ashkenazim (58 percent) defined themselves as "secular." This information supports our observation that the Sephardim were more receptive to Chabad's proselytizing activities.

Sephardi immigrants in New York include some, if not many, who harbor bitterness about their disadvantaged position in Israeli society, where the Ashkenazim still control important resources of power and prestige. Chabad, however, represented Ashkenazim who seemed to be openhearted and anxious to absorb them as equals among their ranks. Chabad's theological message, as well as its missionaires' behavior, placed great emphasis on the indispensability of every individual to the welfare of the Jewish people. In contrast, both the secular and the Orthodox establishments in Israel had looked down at their brethren arriving from the Middle East, who were expected to strip off their cultural and behavioral traditions as soon as possible. The saga of Middle Eastern Jews' journey to a new country was now being repeated, but this time for the better. The Ashkenazi Jews they met at the other end, as represented by Chabad, exhibited the hospitality, love and understanding that had been missing at the earlier encounter.

Chabad's position on Israeli politics also seemed compatible with dominant attitudes among Israeli Sephardim. Chabad's support of the Likud was mainly related to its interest in annexing the West Bank. Chabad's political sympathies coincided with the popularity of the Likud among the Sephardi constituency (see, e.g., Arian

1981), which was influenced by additional motivational factors. Although the Likud was headed by an Ashkenazi leadership, it was nevertheless able to contain a Sephardi protest against the veteran Ashkenazi establishment. This veteran establishment, mainly associated with the Labor party, had ruled the country since the attainment of statehood. The Labor governments were responsible for the absorption of all immigrants and were therefore accountable for the failures in the integration of the newcomers and the gaps that continue to divide the Sephardim and the Ashkenazim in Israel.[9] Last, Chabad's nationalism, combined with a relaxed attitude toward residence outside Israel, helped relieve the dilemmas with which most *yordim* were besieged. Its message offered an alternative version of identity, which, while preserving Israeli loyalties, also incorporated a newly acquired American component. That part, however, was not associated with the dominant American Jewish self-presentation and institutions, which lay beyond the reach or aspiration of many Israelis.

[9]In addition, the Sephardi support of the nationalistic policies of the Likud seems to me to represent a latent protest against the old style Zionism, which did not greatly involve the Sephardim. Today Ashkenazi Zionism is represented by the kibbutz movement and the new "leftist" avant-garde such as Peace Now, all of which advocate the end of territorial expansion and a search for accommodation with the Palestinians. In contrast, Sephardi Jews join forces with the advocates of a militant ideology, which does not carry the vestiges of intellectual and political traditions originating in the socialist and liberal European schools.

[8]

Twelve Profiles of Immigrant Careers

Yordim have usually been stigmatized by the Israeli media and by popular opinion as an undifferentiated group. The Israelis in the United States remain extremely sensitive to the assessments made by their compatriots in Israel concerning their material achievements and moral standing. In a recent interview published in an Israeli newspaper (*Maariv*, March 20, 1985), an Israeli from New York, a successful heart specialist who had left Israel fifteen years earlier, made the following statement: "*Yerida* is indeed antithetical to everything we were brought up on. We, the *yordim*, may be in the wrong party [*miflagah*] when considered in national terms, but this doesn't necessarily make us bad people. All Israeli *yordim* have been labeled with the image of taxicab drivers, idiots who live dishonestly and who are too ashamed to go back. This is, of course, completely distorted."

In Chapter 1, I presented some general features of the research population, including a distribution of major and secondary motives affecting their immigration. In other chapters I described their collective presentation as related to various issues. I will now present twelve profiles of individual *yordim*, each of which summarizes their particular "immigration career" and offers a deeper insight into the life experiences underlying the transformation of their status from that of Israelis to that of *yordim*.

Much of my work leading up to the writing of this book involved the unfolding and reconstruction of the life histories of many of the

Israelis I met. I rarely interviewed my acquaintances about their past. My knowledge was accumulated through the information they volunteered on various occasions and through the observation of their routine activities in daily life. Some information was volunteered by others as part of the natural flow of discussion and gossip between friends and acquaintances.

Some were extremely open, even at our first meeting, about their life history in Israel and America. Others were more hesitant to allow a stranger into the details of their life. It was only after a stronger bond had developed that I learned of crucial details and painful memories that either affected the first stage of immigration or later fortunes in America. If, however, an Israeli preferred to avoid sharing information about himself, he could remain to some extent anonymous even among Israelis he saw often. The absence of close networks of kin or friends facilitated such reserved behavior.

Any selection of twelve cases cannot but be arbitrary. My original plan was to write up only eight profiles, but this did not satisfy my sense of an adequate portrayal of the world I witnessed. And twelve profiles seemed to be the most I could expect the reader to be willing and able to comprehend without getting lost in a welter of life histories. I have selected those individuals who, most of all, seemed to epitomize and display the inner world of experiences I observed during my stay in Queens and whose life histories exhibited a transparency and inner consistency that could be easily conveyed.[1] Moreover, in order to preserve a notion of continuity and to familiarize the reader with the people studied, I included some of the people quoted in earlier chapters. I also tried to introduce a variety of cases representing the major characteristics of our population. Thus they include six Israeli couples, four men married to American women, one woman married to an American, and one single man. Eight profiles introduce Israelis of Ashkenazi extraction, three of Sephardi extraction, and one mixed couple. They also represent a variety of occupations, as well as motives and

---

[1] I do not consider my presentation of profiles as strictly representing the life history method (see, e.g., Langness and Frank 1981). Thus, for example, the selection of events is guided by the main topic of our discussion.

factors that affected their immigration. The order of presentation indicates the length of stay in America, which reflects, among other things, the changing patterns of Israeli immigration and particularly the growing numbers of men married to American spouses (see Table 9, which represents the list of profiles and their major characteristics).

Is there a lesson to be learned from the collective experience of these individual life histories? Do they communicate a reality or a myth particular to the group with which they are voluntarily or arbitrarily identified? We shall return to this question in the summary that follows the profiles.

*Table 9.*Profiled persons: nationality and ethnic extraction, length of stay, and reasons for emigrating

	Nationality of spouse and ethnic extraction	Length of stay in U.S. (years)	Circumstances of emigration
1. Dov and Lea	Israeli couple, Ashkenazi	30	Relatives' invitation (economic enticement)
2. Eli and Yaffa	Israeli couple, Ashkenazi	20	Professional engagement
3. Jacob and Rachel	Israeli couple, Sephardi	18	Financial difficulties
4. Joseph and Rina	Israeli couple, Ashkenazi	12	*Shlichim* (emissaries) who stayed on
5. Benny and Ziva	Israeli couple, Ashkenazi	10	Professional studies
6. Yehuda and Naomi	Israeli couple, mixed	3	Relatives' invitation (economic enticement)
7. Alex and Claire	American spouse, Ashkenazi	15	Parental pressure
8. Nira	American spouse, Ashkenazi	10	Discontent
9. Nathan and Ellen	American spouse, Sephardi	8	Discontent
10. Arik and Carol	American spouse, Ashkenazi	7	American spouse's pressure
11. Saul and Jean	American spouse, Sephardi	6	Financial difficulties and American spouse's pressure
12. Dani	Single, Ashkenazi	3	Matrimonial crisis and economic enticement

Profile 1: Dov and Lea

Dov and Lea, in their early sixties, were the oldest *yordim* I met. They lived on our block and were very friendly toward the Israelis in the neighborhood, particularly those with young children, for whom they tried to act as substitute grandparent figures. They originally arrived in New York "for a short visit" (*banu lezman katzar bilvad*), which had lasted for nearly thirty years. Dov had come to Israel from Eastern Europe in the 1920s as a young child. Lea had come for a visit in the late 1930s and thus escaped the war in Europe, which eventually trapped her family. She met Dov and they were soon happily married and living close to Dov's family in a small town. Dov was employed as a mechanic in a successful cooperative. Lea's father and sister escaped from Hungary with the help of her father's brothers, who had immigrated to the United States a few years earlier. Her mother and brothers all perished in the holocaust. Lea was anxious to see her father and sister after many years of separation and in 1950 was delighted to get an invitation and tickets offered by her uncles to come and visit them with the children. She received a warm welcome and was encouraged to come again. Her relatives suggested that they all come over for some time and make some money. To her hesitant response, they added: "You can always go back to Israel." With the mass influx of immigrants during the early 1950s, Israel was going through severe economic difficulties. Lea's family, who knew that the situation in Israel was difficult, did everything necessary to bring her over to the United States. They arranged visas for Dov and Lea and their three children and paid their travel expenses. Dov could neither resist the generosity of his wife's family nor the temptation they presented. His family tried to persuade them to give up their plans, but Lea and Dov believed that after a short stay in the United States they would be able to return and open a business. In the words of a common Hebrew expression: "We thought we would do a little better for ourselves and then go back" (*Hashavnu she nistader ketzat venahzor*).

In 1953 they sold their apartment and Dov's share in the cooperative and sailed to the promised shores, where they expected a smooth arrival. Their hopes were soon shattered. Their relatives obviously thought they had done enough by providing them with entry visas and tickets. They assumed that Lea and Dov would settle down and adapt through their own efforts, as had millions of earlier refugees and newcomers to America. Dov told me: "They promised us hills and mountains, which turned out to be dark pits."

Dov was left alone to find his new fortune in various low-paying and degrading blue-collar jobs. At first he was ashamed to go back to Israel without achievements to show after having given up everything he had owned there. When they eventually did decide to go back, they could not afford the fare and this time Lea's family was not ready to pay the expenses. They were stuck. Lea went through a difficult period of adjustment: "I cried every day, longing for Israel. My little daughter used to ask me: 'Mummy, why are you crying?'" Dov often asked himself how it had all happened. He would blame Lea for their misfortunes but knew how unhappy she was. Eventually he got a job for which he was qualified.

During the first years Dov toiled very hard for a living. Even on Fridays and holidays he used to work until late at night. Lea started to work as a teaching assistant in a kindergarten and together they managed to make a better living. When I met them Dov was retired. They were now economically comfortable and owned some property. Their children were raised as Americans—they did not speak Hebrew and had never visited Israel. In later years, Dov, who came from an Orthodox family, became active in a synagogue frequented by other veteran *yordim*. He told me that in America the synagogue offered the only opportunity to meet with Jews. He was very pleased that his grandchildren were enrolled in a Jewish school.

Dov and Lea made their first visit to Israel many years after they had departed. As much as they were reconciled to their life in America, were proud of their children's achievements, and had long ago stopped considering returning to Israel, they still felt a sense of bewilderment and uprootedness. Dov once commented: "I often ask myself, has it been a story of good or bad luck?" To which Lea responded: "I don't want to think about what would have happened had we returned to Israel soon after our arrival here. Our children have been successful here and are happy. That is what matters most." Dov quoted his brother, who had visited him recently, and said: "I prefer my one-room apartment in the kibbutz to your American home full of appliances." It was an echo of Dov's own questions concerning the consequences of his immigration. Another Israeli on a short stay in New York who met Dov told me in a less charitable tone: "That man who was a mechanic in Israel came over to be a mechanic in America! Had he at least become a millionaire!"

Profile 2: Eli and Yaffa

When Eli and Yaffa left Israel twenty years earlier, they were in their early thirties, their children not yet of school age. Eli was a part-time musician and his wife a teacher. Eli, who was born in Israel, had no intention whatsoever of emigrating. He and Yaffa were satisfied with their life-style. They lived modestly in Jerusalem surrounded by family and friends, enjoying the touch of bohemian life through their association with musicians and other artists. When I met the now retired Eli in his comfortable apartment in Kew Gardens he told me that he had not yet mentally grasped that he was a resident of the United States. He often used to tell his acquaintances: "I didn't wait in line at the American consulate in Tel Aviv in order to get an immigrant visa. When I left I didn't think for a minute that I would stay here. One thing just followed another. So I don't see myself cut off from Israel and I don't consider myself American."

A summer adventure of a few weeks in early 1960, prolonged for twenty years, was over. It had remained an adventure for so long partly because up until retirement Eli had never considered his departure from Israel as other than a temporary arrangement. He applied for a Green Card and later for American citizenship as a mere matter of convenience for work and traveling. The Hebrew he spoke was meticulous without the slightest blending of English words or an American accent. He was fully informed about political, cultural, and musical life in Israel. In addition to the Israeli newspapers, the local Hebrew radio station, letters, visiting friends and relatives, and occasional trips to Israel, he often listened to Israeli radio programs, which he managed to receive on short wave.

He was proud to be as informed about daily life in Israel as Israelis who live in Israel. He also thought that the geographical distance granted him a "tension-free" perspective, clearer than that of Israeli residents. His descriptions of scenes of life in Israel were as vivid as that of a sensitive photographer. Although he was well integrated into the surrounding culture, the literature, music, politics, geography, and friends most meaningful to him were those related with Israel.

Eli had originally come to the United States as a member of a troupe of five young musicians invited by an American Jewish promoter for a short visit. The group, warmly received by Jewish audiences, was tempted to stay on for a few more months. At that stage the members of the troupe brought along their families to share the new experience. The challenge of performing before a growing audience and of adapting their repertoire to the American audience's musical preferences was very rewarding. What started in Israel as a semiprofessional, part-time occupation, turned out to be a full-time job in the competitive American world of show business. Survival itself was a sign of tremendous success. The troupe preserved its Israeli identity, although they soon gave up the original Israeli folklore content. The Israeli origin and symbols and a short presentation of Israeli popular music offered the troupe an exotic attraction in a field crowded with professional talent. Surprised and excited by their first success, the prospects of further achievements were infatuating. They stayed on, rented apartments, and later became homeowners. Their wives looked for work and their young children quickly adjusted to American schools and youth culture. The longer they stayed the more difficult it was to go back. They had no chance of making a comeback in the Israeli entertainment world—they had become too Americanized. They were neither young enough to start new professions, nor did they earn enough to allow them to open businesses or to retire early. But when they reached the age of retirement and were ready to go home, their wives and children refused to go along. Only one of the five troupe members went back with his wife to make their permanent home in Israel. Another couple who went back returned after a short while to rejoin their children, who had remained in America.

Yaffa, who had to bring up the children while Eli was on tour and had managed to secure an influential position in a Jewish school, was unwilling to give up her job and start all over again in Israel. Moreover, their son and daughter, both of whom had married American spouses, had no plans to join their homesick father, whose American engagement had come to an end. Eli's children had not gone to Jewish schools, but nevertheless were fairly competent in Hebrew; otherwise, however, they did not share any of their father's Israeli cultural and social experiences.

Yaffa was less attached to Israeli life than her husband. She had immigrated to Israel from Germany in her teens and had already lived for more years in America than she had in Israel. Yaffa once jokingly remarked that when she died, Eli, rather than look for another woman, would pack immediately and go back to Israel. She thus demonstrated her decisive role in making her family's stay in America permanent.

Thus, twenty years after the move he had made so enthusiastically and that had changed the life of his family, Eli discovered he was stuck in a country he had always considered a temporary host. Eli and Yaffa had never sold their apartment in Jerusalem, although doing so might have eased their financial situation. Eli explained: "It is a psychological matter. If I sell our apartment, it would imply the burning of all bridges. It makes me feel good that I still own this apartment. As long as my name appears in the telephone directory of Jerusalem it means I am still there!"[2]

Eli never interpreted his stay in the United States as related to his past experiences in Israel or present developments in Israel. He often said: "Everything changes the minute you leave." Although some of our common acquaintances suggested the rising cost of living or the changing ideological atmosphere in Israel as an explanation for Eli's continued stay in the United States, Eli himself never used these arguments. He did, however, mention that had he and his wife gone back, it would have been too expensive to travel regularly in order to visit their children.

Retirement made separation from Israel more painful. With no

[2]Telephone lines in Israel are allocated (often after a long wait) to individual renters of lines who retain the line and its number as long as they carry the title to the apartment (or other location) in which the telephone was first installed.

more performances and trips to prepare for, he missed the Israeli routine of life. Friday, for example, was a constant reminder of a lost rhythm. On this day, he once told me, his memories took him back to past Friday afternoons, which he used to spend in a coffee shop in the center of Jerusalem, meeting friends, watching the young soldiers arriving for the weekend furlough and older people busy with last-minute shopping for sunflower seeds, peanuts, and flowers in the bright afternoon sunshine. He went on: "In Israel you sense and smell Friday. Everybody is Jewish, public transport comes to a halt. The weekend is short and you have to do everything in one day. But here, whatever you don't do on Saturday you can do on Sunday. Transport goes on and your neighbors—one is gentile and the other is something else. Everyone is locked in his home and carries on his separate way of life."

When Eli met a young Israeli musician who had recently arrived in America he was happy to part with the equipment and clothing he had used in his own performances. He could now clearly observe the temptation that had driven this young man from what seemed to be his natural milieu into the difficult beginning of an artist's career. The young man made a living as a cabdriver during the day and performed occasionally in Israeli and Jewish restaurants. Eli was also well aware of the almost unavoidable process through which successful Israeli artists are gradually cut off from the particular cultural sources that endowed them with an authentic individuality. He considered the pieces he had first performed in Israel the best part of his troupe's repertoire.

Eli relieved his nostalgia through a growing interest in Israeli culture and artists. He had a remarkable collection of Israeli records of music and songs and he made his own recordings of music, songs, and speeches. He initiated correspondence with Israeli authors, musicians, and other performers. His friends were almost exclusively Israeli, but meetings with Israeli friends were less frequent and regular than in Israel. Eli explained this different pattern of sociability as a consequence of the shorter distances in Israel and the urge to share experiences arising from the various continuing pressures, such as service in the reserve forces, as well as the desire to compare newly purchased home commodities. In spite of the availability of Israeli friends in New York, the sense of intimacy was considerably less. Eli was among the few active participants in the Israeli Club, and even he did not attend regularly. Although he was critical of its management and doubted the Israelis' interest in communal activity, he was nevertheless always ready to offer advice and make his collection of Israeli records available to the club.

At a club party held on one of the festivals, Eli expressed the irony of Israeli life in New York, the club included, when he read a comic description of an Israeli who arrives in New York and immediately feels very much at home. There are old friends everywhere, Israeli newspapers at every newsstand, Israeli performers, falafel, humus, the familiar noise and dirt, and even Israeli nightclubs. So why waste time in Israel? The cynical description ended, however, with an unrestrained emotional exclamation that nowhere is there such a warm place as home, such a beautiful port as Haifa, such a lively place as Tel Aviv and such a home as Jerusalem. He concluded by wishing his audience every success in their enterprises, but "with God's help we'll all meet again in Israel." Eli's longing for Jerusalem and Tel Aviv was not very different from an Orthodox Jew's prayer "Next year in Jerusalem"—a compelling desire that circumstances prevented one from realizing. It never lost its authenticity and vitality, with one continuously anticipating a sudden dramatic development to come along and change the course of events.

Profile 3: Jacob and Rachel

Jacob and Rachel came to New York with their three young children in the mid-1960s. They were both born in Haifa into old Sephardi families. Jacob was a skilled glassblower who, in spite of his expertise, could not offer his family a comfortable living. His frustration became intolerable when, already in his mid-thirties, he could not afford to buy a work space in a new small-industry center in Haifa. Some of his admiring clients, who had lived for a while in America, said he could make a fortune in America. At this moment of deep disappointment, he decided to give it a try. His decision was further encouraged by an old friend who had left Israel a few years earlier to establish a business in New York. His friend promised to help him upon his arrival and indeed offered him hospitality for a few weeks and helped him find his first job (by answering advertisements in the *New York Times*). Jacob soon applied for a Green Card, rented an apartment, and sent for his family. Two years later he invested in his own workshop. He gained a considerable reputation and an appreciative clientele, but chose not to expand the workshop, which provided him with a comfortable living and some savings. The couple soon became homeowners and later invested in property, which secured them additional income. Jacob and Rachel both became remarkably attuned to the complexities of American bureaucratic, legal, and financial arrangements and were an invaluable source of information and advice, which they gladly offered to old-timers and newcomers from Israel.

Jacob never regretted his move to America, which offered him financial security and self-assurance. He often argued that he had not gone to America for the sake of money: "I came, not for the dollars, but in order to further myself in my work. Had it been only for money I would have started up another sort of business, such as a lamp store in the Bowery" (where a close friend of his had been very successful).

Jacob's and Rachel's sense of achievement and satisfaction was not affected by the brutal killing of one of their sons, an innocent bystander at a fight between two youth gangs at school. They could not adjust to the Orthodoxy prevailing in the Jewish schools and sent their children to public schools. Their children could speak Hebrew, but otherwise were completely removed from Israel and Israeli culture. Moreover, most of their friends were not Jewish.

Although Jacob and Rachel were satisfied with their life in America, there was a dimension lacking in their life—family ties. They had left behind a wide network of close relatives who they missed very much. More than anything else, Israel was, in their lived experience, the embodiment of "family." Jacob once told me that if they ever went back to Israel "it would not be because of patriotism—I haven't been a patriot for a long time now—but because of our family there." He insisted that he felt no guilt for leaving Israel and added: "In Israel I felt I couldn't further myself, but here I advanced immediately on arrival. Here my profession has enabled me to improve myself."

With the improvement of their economic situation, Jacob and

Rachel traveled to Israel every year for long vacations. When Rachel underwent an operation in 1977 and again when Jacob fell ill in 1981, events that magnified their sense of loss at not having close relatives nearby, they considered partial retirement and the purchase of an apartment in Israel, where they would stay for a few months during the winter season. But they were soon discouraged by the soaring prices of apartments in Israel and the realization that their sons would never join them. They did not pursue that possibility again, although Jacob finally retired in 1983.

Jacob and Rachel had many friends, mainly Israelis, but some Americans as well. In contrast to many other Israelis I met, they did not read Israeli newspapers and were not well informed about social and political developments in Israel. At the same time, they were proud of their Israeli identity and did not hide their commitment to Israel. On Israel's Independence Day they hung the Israeli flag at the entrance to their home. They inscribed their names in Hebrew on the front door and displayed a large collection of popular Israeli books, records, and decorations. Aware that they would not return to Israel, Rachel confessed at one of our last meetings, when an Israeli visitor probed into the dilemma of Israeli identity in America: "I am not a *yoredet,* I love Israel, but neither am I an Israeli, since I am not there when the Israelis fight and suffer. I consider myself a New Yorker. I am now reconciled with this definition after many years of resentment." Residence in New York thus granted Rachel a "no-man's-land" identity that accommodated her continuing loyalty to Israel. Assuming that identity, however, Rachel acknowledged the termination of her active Israeli citizenship.

Profile 4: Joseph and Rina

Joseph arrived in New York twelve years earlier as a *shaliach* of a national fund-raising organization. He and his wife, Rina, were born in a veteran *moshav* and had many relatives in *moshav* and kibbutz settlements. They were in their early thirties when they arrived in the United States with four young children, two of whom were not yet of school age. Joseph was very successful at his job and was asked to stay on when the first two years of his engagement were over. His contract was extended for another year and then again for two more years.

Joseph's growing independence at his job provoked resentment among his colleagues at the organization's headquarters in Israel. He was asked to change his style of work and leave most decisions to the office in Israel. Joseph, who considered these requests expressions of pettiness and jealousy, refused to accept orders. He thought he had convinced a visiting senior member of the organization's board of trustees to take his side in the conflict with the executives in Tel Aviv. He was, however, taken by surprise and utterly shattered when a few months before the end of his five-year assignment, he was fired from his job in the organization and his contract was terminated. Joseph and Rina were in a state of chaos. He had no job and their apartment in Israel was rented until the end of their intended stay. Had they decided to move back immediately, they would have disrupted their children' schooling in the middle of the term. Moreover, the harsh communication from Israel did not include return tickets or any financial compensation. They experienced an acute sense of humiliation and defeat. The least they could do in order to prove they were not completely powerless was to demonstrate that they could survive on their own in America. Instead of going back immediately with the reputation of a *shaliach* forced to return because of failure at his task, Joseph was determined to find a temporary job that would carry them along until they could return on more congenial terms.

Joseph's reaction was similar to that of a university academic I met whose promotion was delayed as a result of what he considered the instigation of less talented and jealous colleagues. He was on sabbatical when the news reached him. Under the circumstances he was easily persuaded to accept a high-paying, prestigious position at an American research institute. In both cases a deep sense of degradation, of not having been appreciated, stimulated Israelis who were economically comfortable and socially integrated into elite segments of Israeli society to extend their stay in the United States beyond the point of return.

Joseph found employment with a prestigious Jewish organization, where he was gradually promoted to a senior position. During the first years he and Rina believed they would soon return to Israel. But the executive jobs in Israel to which Joseph aspired could not be secured from abroad by an individual who lacked political or organizational support. He continued, however, to keep a close eye on possible positions and was registered with the Israeli consulate for professional placement.

Joseph and Rina did not sell their apartment in Israel, although its sale would have greatly eased their adjustment in New York. After a few years they became homeowners, but had they sold their apartment in Israel they could have bought a bigger house or refurbished and modernized the house they did buy. Moreover, although the renting of their apartment in Israel was a continuing source of trouble, they did not consider its sale. Holding onto an apartment in Israel symbolized an unbroken commitment to their Israeli citizenship. They still retained an Israeli home address and their names continued to appear in the Israeli telephone directory.

Joseph and Rina were extremely well informed about Israeli affairs and continued to read Israeli newspapers. Although their children went to public schools (due to financial constraints), they insisted on speaking Hebrew at home and cherished Israeli culture. They attended performances of Israeli artists and entertainers and continued to pay regular visits to Israel. The older children were contemplating serving in the Israeli army after graduating from college.

Although the prospects of Joseph and Rina's return to Israel faded as the job opportunities in Israel decreased with the passing of time, they never admitted the finality of their departure. The attachment of the older children to Israel was proof of their success in adhering to a viable Israeli commitment. At a meeting of Israelis Rina once stated: "We all got stuck [*nitka'nu*] here, but Israel is our home and we consider ourselves different from Americans." Joseph was also among the few Israelis who actively wished, albeit unsuccessfully, to organize the population of *yordim*. They had a wide though not close-knit network of Israeli acquaintances and friends. Rina once told me: "In Israel everyone has his close circle of friends who meet every Friday, but here you are linked to many circles which only rarely come together, perhaps for a family celebration." Joseph and Rina continued to entertain in a fashion similar to the pattern of Friday-evening meetings in Israel, with the same food, atmosphere, and topics of discussion.

Although they lamented the circumstances that had made them stay in America, there was nothing pathetic about their life. They did not regret their decision to stay on, were economically comfortable, and were well integrated into the American environment. At the same time, they continued to regard themselves as Israelis in America, as if they were still *shlichim* whose job was not yet complete. Discussing the case of a friend who made an unsuccessful attempt to return to Israel, I once asked them what drove a person to return to Israel after many years in America. Rina answered me in a surprised tone: "What's unusual about that? We would also have returned had it been possible!" The viable Israeli identity they managed to communicate to their children (particularly noticeable with the older son and daughter) made their self-perception as Israelis who had not severed ties with Israel most convincing. To the extent that they gradually became reconciled to their own departure, they continued to entertain the belief that their children, or at least one of them, would one day return to Israel.

The *shlichim* who stay on are diverse in their life histories and characteristics. There is, however, one feature common to most of them: their discovery of options and opportunities in the United States. Most *shlichim* who possess professional skills or other personal talents and who through their work develop professional and personal links with local Jewish and non-Jewish organizations, industries, and their representatives are able to stay on if other factors arise that encourage such a decision.

Profile 5: Benny and Ziva

Benny had arrived in the United States ten years earlier, after completing his army service and a course in industrial management. Then in his early twenties, he was not yet ready to settle down and take a "boring" job. Instead, he decided to carry on with his studies in the United States, which he had visited as part of his training program. He contacted some people who he had met during this visit and through them found a job doing maintenance work in an office building. He enrolled at a local university, where he earned an engineering degree. In the meantime his Israeli girl friend also arrived in New York to work as a secretary with the overseas branch of her Israeli firm. They got married and started to raise a family. Benny moved from one job to another, each move entailing a raise in salary.

Benny and Ziva were granted American citizenship and looked forward to a comfortable life in New York. Ziva was flattered by Americans' surprise when they discovered she was an immigrant. Her command of English was excellent. At home they spoke Hebrew with the children (who went to a Jewish school), but in public they spoke only English. Ziva sometimes quoted her previous employer, who encouraged her to stay on in America because, he claimed, she could easily assimilate and pass as a third-generation American.

During his first years in New York, Benny did not read Israeli newspapers. According to Ziva: "He couldn't care less about Israel—as if it were another planet." But Ziva missed her parents and sister in Israel and could not reconcile herself to the prospect of a permanent separation. She often told of her experience on a trip back from Israel. At takeoff she could not hold back a terrible sob, to which an American passenger in the next seat commented sympathetically: "You must have left behind a terrible tragedy."

Benny was increasingly annoyed by his children's life-style and physical development in New York. They seemed to him "too Americanized," too "soft," addicted to television and overprotected. He often compared this with the freedom children enjoy in Israel, where they play unchaperoned in the streets, parks, and with youth groups. When professionally ready, he was determined to leave New York for a warmer place, close to the sea. The West Coast, as well as Israel, suited these needs.

The absence of close relatives was felt most urgently when the children were ill and Ziva was stuck at home. When Benny was hospitalized for a few days for minor surgery, Ziva could not be at the hospital during the operation and could not visit him regularly because she had no one with whom to leave the children. They did not feel friendly toward the Israelis they met in their neighborhood, and they were not otherwise involved with Israeli company. Referring to the lack of close Israeli friends even after their long stay in New York, Ziva told me: "We never considered ourselves *yordim* and we haven't sought out their company. We were always Zionists." The idea of "singing in New York about the Israeli desert" amused Benny. He preferred American entertainment: "I understand English and don't need to listen to an Israeli singer in New York." At the same time, Benny started to read *Israel Shelanu* and adopted its Likud nationalist attitudes.

Benny and Ziva grew increasingly convinced that they would return to Israel in the near future. Rather than buying a house in New York, they started to save money in order to buy one in Israel. They could not rely on their parents' financial support and had to amass the enormous sum necessary to buy a modest apartment in a neighborhood close to Tel Aviv. They refrained from any spending that might delay reaching this goal; for example, they never took long family trips in America. Ziva commented: "One day I'll visit California as an Israeli tourist." In 1980 they finally purchased an apartment close to Ziva's sister, due to be ready in 1982.

I first met Benny and Ziva at a time when they were planning to leave within a year. When I asked Benny why he was going back, he answered abruptly: "I don't belong here." He thought that most Israelis who come to the United States leave Israel "not because they don't love Israel, but because of an economic problem." Since buying the apartment, Ziva's long-felt sense of "sitting on our suitcases" (*yoshvim al hamizvadot*) became a reality for them. Nevertheless, both Benny and Ziva participated in the 1982 elections of governors, senators, congressmen, and other public officials in the United States.

Among my Israeli acquaintances a few others had purchased apartments in Israel, but most of them did not have a specific date of return. For a long time I was not certain Benny and Ziva would actually make the move. In February 1983 Benny, together with Hanan (another of my close acquaintances, who was married to an American), went to Israel in search of jobs (supported by the Israeli consulate in New York). Although both had similar skills and apartments in Israel, their conclusions were quite different. Hanan was finally convinced that he could not make it on an Israeli salary, but

[177]

Benny thought he could. While Hanan considered his wife's loss of her teaching job at a prestigious local school, Ziva was looking forward to the opportunity of working in Israel. Hanan put his apartment in Israel up for sale, while Benny and Ziva started to purchase the electric appliances and furniture they were allowed to bring back to Israel tax-free.

When Benny informed his employers about his plans to leave New York for Israel, they suggested he take a job with an Israeli company with which they had business connections. On his research trip to Israel, Benny compared this offer with other jobs available. Hanan, however, declined a number of propositions because they could not compare with his present salary. Hanan's American wife was far less enthusiastic than Ziva about moving to Israel. Hanan's wife reacted not much differently from another Israeli acquaintance whose Israeli wife, Dina, was hesitant about returning. Her husband had actually signed a contract with an Israeli company during a similar research trip, but was persuaded by Dina to delay departure for more than a year. In the meantime he was promoted to a senior engineering position at his firm and his Israeli contract expired.

In all these cases, the attitude of the female spouse was most influential. Had it not been for Ziva's unwavering wish to return to Israel, Benny might have settled for a new job and a permanent home in California or Florida. Their young children were also at an age where a change would not harm them. In contrast, Dina's children were in junior high school and one daughter was already thinking about college. Soon after their return to Israel, Ziva found a job as a manager's assistant and was able to start work after a period of several years at home. Although she could rely on her parents' or sister's help in an emergency, she usually employed a reliable baby-sitter, who collected the younger children from kindergarten and waited for the oldest children on their return from school. Two years after their return, Ziva did not regret their departure from the United States. Benny, however, was increasingly concerned about the continuing inflation and depreciation of his salary. Again, had it not been for Ziva, he might have considered returning to America.

Profile 6: Yehuda and Naomi

Yehuda and Naomi arrived in New York in 1980 when they were in their early thirties and their two boys not yet ten years old. Yehuda came to join his two brothers, who had arrived seven and ten years earlier. The three brothers were born in Morocco and had immigrated to Israel with their parents and younger siblings in 1956. In Israel they were all successfully employed in crafts and business. The oldest brother, who left first with considerable funds, had done well in the boutique business and urged his brothers to join him.

In 1979 Yehuda went for a short trip to visit his brothers in New York and was greatly impressed with their achievements. On his return he told his wife that he was ready to leave immediately. Naomi was not enthusiastic and was worried about the occupational prospects, but Yehuda had no doubt about the opportunities awaiting them. They soon sold their apartment and the restaurant they owned in Bat Yam (a town close to Tel Aviv), which left them with sufficient capital to join or to start an enterprise with Yehuda's brothers. Upon arrival, however, Yehuda discovered that neither of his brothers, who owned separate businesses, was willing to take on a new partner. They suggested that he try his luck independently. He invested a major part of his assets in a business that failed abysmally.

When I met Yehuda and Naomi three years after their arrival in New York, they were both working in a boutique, where Yehuda held the position of salaried manager and Naomi was paid an hourly rate. Yehuda worked until late at night six days a week, while Naomi worked seven hours a day six days a week. They had only one free evening and as a result their social ties were restricted (in stark contrast to their Israeli experience of close-knit networks of relatives and friends). The children also spent most of their free time in the boutique. After the failure of the first investment, they could no longer afford a Jewish school and enrolled the boys at the nearby public school, which was attended mostly by minority and black children.

Yehuda and Naomi were greatly disappointed with the lack of

family support, and their children were very unhappy. They lived in a rented apartment isolated from relatives and friends and other Israelis and admitted they worked "like donkeys." Nevertheless, they did not admit failure or regret. They were anxiously waiting for the Green Card sponsored by Yehuda's brothers and hoped that once they got it they would be able to start afresh. When I met Yehuda's brother he told me a similar story of his own arrival: "When I arrived I discovered that you can't rely on your family here. In America everyone lives his own life. True, your family has a lot of influence on you and you try to follow the same path. I soon discovered I was stuck. At first I was a salaried employee, a situation I was not accustomed to. But after some time I opened my own business." He was obviously pleased with his financial achievements, which seemed to compensate for the absence of the expected family cooperation and the loss of close friends. Their story is similar to that of Dov and Lea (see Profile 1), who had been tempted by promises made by Lea's uncles. In their case too, it soon became clear that these relatives were not willing to share their fortunes with the newcomers.

Although close relatives instigated the decision to move and the legal sponsorship of immigration in a number of cases I observed, they did not always provide a permanent source of economic and social support. Thus, Yehuda and Naomi celebrated the Passover seder (festive meal) of 1984 in the company of a few friends they had met in New York. Another couple at the same seder had arrived in New York in similar fashion and also were not celebrating the holiday with their relatives. At the same time, however, the relatives left behind constituted a major continuing link with Israel. Yehuda told me once that on sleepless nights he often saw before his eyes his parents and brothers in Israel.

In 1984 Yehuda and Naomi at last received their Green Cards. They could now apply for a bank loan and make other legal arrangements under their own names. Yehuda considered taking over the boutique of which he was manager, a goal he accomplished a few months later. Naomi, who was never enthusiastic about the move to New York and was often disappointed by their misfortune and difficulties, felt relieved at last. On the day they received their Green Cards she told me: "For three years I had guilt feelings.

Now suddenly I have decided that I am going to stay here. It suddenly occurred to me that it is comfortable here—there is no army service, no frequent changes in prices, none of the tensions which always accompanied us in Israel."

Yehuda did not harbor any bitterness about his life in Israel. His family there was doing well and a few of his brothers and sisters had married Ashkenazi spouses. He did, however, harbor deep resentment toward the Labor party and strongly supported the Likud government. He never suggested specific causes for his immigration, but emphasized: "Here a man who has some knowhow can succeed. Here you have peace. In Israel you are always in the midst of turmoil." At this point in his life Yehuda could no longer go back to Israel, even if he so desired. He had lost most of the money he brought over from Israel on his first abortive venture. He had a long way to go before achieving a comfortable life in America. But he could see the first glimpse of success coming his way to compensate for his immense efforts and losses. One day he might encourage a younger brother to join him in the "Land of Promise."

Profile 7: Alex and Claire

Alex was ten years old when his parents immigrated to Israel from Rumania. Ten years later, after completing his army service, his parents, holocaust survivors, were ready to leave Israel for a safer place. Supported by their relatives in America, they applied for immigrant visas and Alex, loyal to his parents, agreed to accompany them to New York. When I met him fifteen years later, he was married to an American and was a taxicab medallion owner. He was very different from the Israeli stereotype of the uneducated, robust, low-status cabdriver. I later met a few other Israeli cabdrivers of Ashkenazi and Sephardi extraction, most of whom also did not fit that stereotype.

Explaining to me his preference for cabdriving, Alex emphasized that it allowed him freedom. He could stay at home whenever he wished or could employ a driver. He was never short of money, since whenever he needed extra funds he could easily get credit at his bank (as a medallion owner he was considered a reliable customer). He had started in the taxi business through the advice of a family friend he had met in New York. His in-laws helped him get the bank loan with which to purchase the medallion, and he repaid it within a few years. Alex interpreted the attraction of Israelis to this occupation in an analytical fashion: "The ownership of a taxi is similar to other businesses that have always attracted Jews in America. You are your own boss when you need to deal with one *item* only [Alex's own term]." He knew other Israeli cabdrivers who gradually expanded their fleet and owned a few medallions, but he himself preferred a "peaceful life."

An Israeli friend once suggested to Alex that they invest together in a few medallions. Alex could get a loan from the bank to cover his share in the project and could thus stop driving his own car and deal mainly with the administration of the fleet of cars. But Alex backed out of the plan. He explained his retreat from the enterprise: "You feel that you have reached some comfort, so why look for trouble?" Instead he started to lend his taxi to a driver who used it on night shifts and over the weekends. This new arrangement offered him considerable extra income. He used to work for ten to twelve hours five days a week, bringing in a minimum of a hundred dollars a day (after deducting expenses for gas and breaks for food and drink). And he was considering the possibility of joining a new radio-call network that would further increase his income.

Alex and Claire lived in comfort as homeowners and their children attended a Jewish school. Alex was aware of the low status attributed to cabdrivers in Israel, which he ironically compared with the higher status attributed there to bus drivers, who are organized into large cooperatives. He also enjoyed telling his friends about the surprised reaction of both Jewish and non-Jewish passengers when they discovered he was Jewish. They tended to assume that Jews are involved in more lucrative occupations and refrain from providing personal services.

Alex, who left Israel because of his parents, was ambivalent toward Israel. He felt that he was "becoming Americanized in the material dimension, but not socially and spiritually." He was critical of the political situation in Israel, which he thought encouraged the continuing state of war that had driven his parents away. He had a small circle of Israeli acquaintances, most of whom were also married to American women and whom he met sometimes on Saturday nights. Since his parents and younger brother also resided in New York, his longing for Israel was not as painful as that of other Israelis. Having been in America for a longer period than in Rumania or Israel, and being married to an American spouse, he was not anxious to go back, but would have been pleased had one of his children chosen to settle there. He told me that he might then consider joining him.

Most of my cabdriver—medallion owner acquaintances were equally satisfied with their standard of living and social position. The more enterprising among them joined radio-call networks or invested in another medallion. There were other Israelis who were not engaged in actual cabdriving but who owned medallions as investments that carried a permanent income considerably higher than the banks' interest rate and were safer than investment in the stock exchange or other business partnerships. Most of the cabdrivers had originally come to the United States after completing army service. They could start driving a taxi immediately, since this work did not require any professional training or technical skills. Others transferred to this occupation after facing difficulties elsewhere. Only one of the cabdrivers I met had been similarly employed in Israel. He left Israel after many years of futile hopes of getting a "green number," which is the Israeli equivalent of a medallion.[3] In New York it is easy to purchase a medallion: you give a broker a modest downpayment and repay the rest of the loan by regular deduction from the earnings of the medallion[4] or from the taxi's earnings (in 1982–84 the market value of a medallion was $50,000–$60,000).

Profile 8: Nira

Nira left Israel in 1972 because she was "fed up with the lack of privacy and the continuing competition for material achievements." She believed that the atmosphere of conspicuous consumption

[3]Green numbers are strictly allocated by government agencies, which consider them a sort of social benefit reserved for crippled army veterans and the like.
[4]Medallion owners can sometimes rent their medallion without owning a taxicab.

started with the reparation money from Germany, which had completely changed the pioneering spirit in Israel. She claimed: "Since that time everybody in Israel is mainly concerned with buying furniture, curtains, and cars. They watch each other and then rush out to purchase the latest item seen at their friends' homes. Now everybody is buying a color television and soon they'll be running after video sets." She said that Israelis who visit her in New York are astonished to discover that she owns neither a car, an apartment, nor fashionable furniture.

Nira was born in Ramat-Gan to a veteran Ashkenazi family. She had a wide network of relatives in kibbutz and *moshav* settlements. Intelligent, strong-willed, and good-looking, she was usually at the center of social occasions. After completing her army service, she received a B.A. at the Hebrew University. She did well as a mathematics teacher at the high school level and also tutored students at home. Most of her friends were getting married, but Nira was not yet ready for domestic life. At the age of twenty-five she was beginning to feel out of tune with the Israeli style of early marriage and child rearing. In 1971 she left Israel for a summer vacation spent with relatives in Belgium and France. She was excited by the new freedom and the wide horizons she discovered. She told me that on her return home "I went into the teachers' lounge and was disgusted to listen to my colleagues' discussions about their salaries. I went to the bank and met a neighbor who didn't hesitate to look into my balance sheet and question me about my earnings!" She could not stand it any longer and left within a few months.

During the first three months she lived with relatives in Washington, D.C., and then moved to New York, where she got a teaching position in a Jewish school. She married an American Jew, but did not contemplate returning to Israel, although she was soon widowed and was raising her daughter alone. She had no doubts about her preferred citizenship: "I no longer have a common language with my friends in Israel, whose lives focus around their apartments and curtains. In America people get divorced and change their apartments whenever they feel like it."

Nira was also convinced that it was much easier to make a living and to get ahead in America: the income tax authorities treat citizens in a civil manner and it is relatively simple to be admitted to a university. When Nira had wanted to change her concentration for her M.A. studies at the Hebrew University she was burdened by the requirements of a complicated bureaucracy. In New York, not only was she admitted to a Ph.D. program, but she also received a generous scholarship. Moreover: "Here I get mostly A marks while in an Israeli university I had to be grateful for the mere permission to enroll for an M.A. program." She ended the conversation by telling me: "Had you and I met at a public place in Tel Aviv as we are now no doubt some old *yenta* would have spread ugly gossip about us, but here who cares about what you do? You can do whatever you want here—there are so many opportunities!"

After her husband's death in a car accident, Nira started to work as an editor of manuscripts and correspondence. This enabled her to stay at home and raise her child. In her new career she turned to the official Israeli representatives. The consulate and other Israeli agencies refused to use or recommend her services as part of their policy of not employing *yordim*. Her resentment of Israeli society was now directed toward the *shlichim*—"*yordim* in disguise"— who, she claimed, prove their moral superiority at the expense of Israelis at home and abroad. But in spite of these obstacles, she gained a reputation among Israeli students who needed her help with their manuscripts and who also sought her advice on other subjects. As much as she was critical of Israeli society at large and resented the character of the "typical Israeli," she was in fact surrounded by Israelis.

Nira did not speak Hebrew with her daughter, who, however, had a Hebrew name that was difficult to render in English. She wanted to raise her free of the commitment to Israel, free of the "brainwashing which we went through in Israel when told so many times 'It is good to die for our country.'" She went on, alluding to her first trip abroad (in 1971): "Once you get out, you discover there is more somewhere else." Nevertheless, she visited the Israeli Club during the festivals and the monthly sing-alongs. She also often brought her daughter along and tried to inculcate her with her own enthusiasm for the singing. I once made an attempt to understand this paradoxical behavior and commented jokingly on the involvement of her daughter in Israeli culture. She was obviously annoyed and told me she was tired of the issue and would discuss it with me another time. I felt that she had become suspicious of my apparent neutrality on the subject of *yordim* society and at a later meeting I refrained from any personal questions.

Later, on a short visit to New York, I bumped into Nira, who was accompanying her daughter to Manhattan. She said that she had noticed my absence and was surprised to discover that I had returned to Israel. She went on to tell me about her recent visit to Israel to attend her father's funeral. During this visit her bitterness toward Israel had suddenly vanished—for the first time since her departure she had enjoyed walking around and traveling in the country. She thought that it might have been her father's death that released her from the compelling bonds and the pressing obligations that had encouraged her escape from Israel in the first place. Accompanying her daughter on a cold day, forced to spend a Sunday aimlessly in the department stores waiting for their return home to Queens, made her appear less enthusiastic about the freedom she had sought in America.

Profile 9: Nathan and Ellen

Nathan arrived in America in 1974 a few months after completing his army service. He was born in Israel to a family that had originally come from Iraq. His parents were economically comfortable and resided in Haifa. Nathan left Israel in order to meet his American girl friend, whom he had met during his army service. Although he had relatives in New York who had moved to the United States many years before, he had no specific plans for a permanent move. Although he soon separated from his girl friend, he stayed on with the support of his relatives. He took on various unskilled jobs and started university studies in business administration. He went through a few difficult years, combining studies with poorly paid jobs. He later married Ellen, an American Jew, and was employed in a managerial position in the pharmaceutics industry. As it turned out, Ellen, who was not enchanted with American life, was willing to go to Israel, but Nathan appeared ambivalent about the prospects of returning.

More than most other Israelis I met, Nathan seemed to be

pleased not only with his economic and professional accomplishments, but also with his social achievements. He was the only Israeli I met who took an active part in a Jewish organization. Gentle, handsome, soft-spoken, and eager to listen and learn, he was good at making American friends. He even seemed to be more at ease speaking English than he was speaking Hebrew. After eight years in America he confessed that he sometimes found himself unable to come up with an appropriate Hebrew term. He made many efforts to recruit other Israelis into Jewish organizations, but not one of our common acquaintances seemed interested. One of them explained his reluctance by defining the activities at these organizations as "too Americanized." Nathan was also a regular participant at the Israeli Club, which he wished to transform into an association with a stable membership.

He often aired his plans to return to Israel within two years. He offered a few related explanations for his reluctance to make the move sooner. First, he felt he had at last made a professional breakthrough. He was successful at his job, which seemed to be a first step on the career ladder in larger industry. He assumed that with his growing experience he would be better able to adjust at a later stage in Israel. He once told me: "Now I am at a stage of growth. If we stay here for another two years I shall be able to reap the harvest. If I leave now I shall lose everything."

His worries about occupational prospects in Israel were not groundless. Without an engineering degree, prospects in the much smaller Israeli industry would have been very limited had he looked for a position equivalent to his job in New York. He thought that Ellen would soon be disappointed with what would probably be a lower standard of living. "I am not rich, but some of my dreams have come true. If I go back when I am ready, things could turn out quite different."

Nathan increasingly emphasized another reason for his hesitation to return to Israel, which also seemed to offer an alternative motive for his original departure. He revealed a painful aspect of his life in Israel related to his ethnic background. His comfortably situated family resided in a neighborhood mainly populated by Ashkenazi residents. His sense of alienation was even greater, since he went to a religious school some distance away from home and was there-

[187]

fore isolated from the company of neighborhood children. His first full comprehension of ethnic discrimination occurred when, at the age of seventeen, he came to call on an Ashkenazi girl he was dating. Her parents answered the door and told him she could not go out. The girl later sneaked out and apologized. "But here in America," he went on, "American Jews accept everybody as Jewish whether he is Moroccan or Yemenite."

Nathan's sense of ethnic discrimination in Israel was reinforced by the growing influx of literature dealing with the subject, such as the series of articles in the *New York Times* written by its correspondent in Israel, David Shipler (April 6–8, 1983). He thought highly of the articles, which seemed to offer an impartial description of the Israeli situation. Most other Israeli readers of the *New York Times* I met were less enthusiastic and thought they were not fully representative and injured the image of Israel in America. Nathan argued that in Israel he had always felt that a Sephardi youth had no chance of mobility. He himself experienced it in the army and felt that it was the same in party politics, the university, and all other spheres of life. His growing conviction about ethnic discrimination in Israel led him to conclude that he had no chance of an attractive job there because he was not Ashkenazi.

After a few years of hesitation, Nathan and Ellen bought a house in Queens. Nathan argued that it was a good investment and would facilitate his eventual return to Israel. But after having a third child, his wife was less enthusiastic about an immediate move to Israel. In 1985 they returned to visit Nathan's family and were astonished to see the high standard of living enjoyed by many Israelis. "Am I just envious?" he asked. "Or do I resent the fact that this is where the income tax I pay in America is ending up?" [by way of U.S. government financial aid to Israel]. Nathan thus found a new reason for moral indignation and resentment, which appeared to be increasingly separating him from Israeli society. He did not mention any plans for returning to Israel in the foreseeable future.

Profile 10: Arik and Carol

Arik arrived in New York in 1974 with his American wife after five years of married life in Israel. He had met Carol in Israel when he was still serving in the army. He had been much impressed by the pretty, intelligent, lively American girl, and they'd gotten married a year later. Arik had never wished to leave Israel. He had a wide network of friends and relatives and a good job as a computer technician. Carol also seemed to love Israel. They bought a nice apartment in Ramat-Gan and purchased electric appliances and a car, which Carol was entitled to import tax-free. Carol seemed satisfied with her job as an editor at a leading publishing house, but sometime later became increasingly unhappy and refused to stay on. Arik eventually succumbed to her pressure and decided to see what awaited them in Carol's country. Arik looked at his departure in terms similar to those of the Israeli student who goes abroad in order to complete a professional degree. Although he was leaving because of his wife, he looked forward to enrolling in an engineering school in New York, an opportunity he did not have in Israel. He assumed they would come back after a few years.

When I met them seven years later, Carol emphasized two major reasons for her desire to go back to America. First, she missed her parents and two sisters. Second, she could not tolerate the Israeli system of public health. She was humiliated by the crowds and lack of privacy at clinics and hospitals. The frequent visits to the clinic with their baby daughter was an ordeal she could no longer bear.

On arrival in New York, Arik completed engineering studies and began to make professional advancements. They bought an apartment and lived in middle-class style. Arik's main satisfaction was with his work. He easily adjusted to the American system of mobility and competition for better jobs and told me proudly: "Here everybody takes care of himself. It is not like in Israel, where everybody looks for a cousin or friend to support his application for a position. Here you undergo an examination and an interview and they evaluate exactly how much you know."

But as much as Arik enjoyed his professional achievements, he painfully missed Israeli sociability, his friends, the army service, and comradeship. He regretted the day he had agreed to leave Israel and had made the mistake of selling their apartment there. He felt trapped in a life-style he bitterly depicted this way: "In America you live in order to work, eat, and sleep." He often commented that Israeli men should rather marry Israeli girls who are better attuned to their preferences and would not force them to leave Israel. He also related jokes about JAPs (Jewish American princesses), for example: "Have you seen the latest advertisement for condominiums especially built for JAPs? No kitchen, no bedroom!" Carol once commented on his unrestrained enthusiasm for Israeli life: "You can take a man away from a country, but you can't take a country away from a man." He sought out Israeli company but was often disappointed. Most of their friends were mixed couples. Arik was also among the most dedicated participants at the Israeli Club.

Although Arik had a well-paid job, he lived modestly. With three young children, two of whom were registered at Jewish schools, Arik was anxious to increase his income. He refused the help of his in-laws, yet hesitated to start a business. Instead, he took on freelance jobs after work and on weekends. He saved this additional income for a family trip to Israel every year. His main ambition was to move to Long Island, where the public schools were considered better and where he would therefore not be obliged to enroll his children at Orthodox Jewish schools. He was caught in a conflict. Although he wanted his children to preserve an Israeli-Jewish identity, he deeply resented American Jewish communal life, which was largely centered around the synagogue. He was aware, however, that he was unsuccessful in transmitting Israeli culture to his children, and Hebrew in particular. With the birth of his third child, he made a decision to speak only Hebrew.

Arik often reminisced nostalgically about his army experiences, including the feeling of freedom when sweeping through the desert in tanks, the fun of flirting with women soldiers and of outsmarting stupid sergeant-majors. During his frequent visits to Israel he observed his friends, whose standard of living was continually improving. He knew well that had he stayed on in Israel his own standard of living would also have improved. When he came back from one such visit to Israel, he told the Israeli Club participants that the men there look much healthier and in better shape than their counterparts in New York. He went on to comment on American youth: "They hang out on street corners and eventually get into trouble and end up with drugs. We had the army service instead and the swims at night in the Kinneret [the lake of Galilee, a popular resort for young people]." He said seriously: "One day I shall take the kids and go back to Israel," and then added with bitter humor: "But she [Carol] would never let me do that!"

He demonstrated his loyalty to Israel as best he could. He regularly read Israeli newspapers and rarely missed the evening news on the Hebrew radio station. He was much concerned about political and economic developments in Israel. On celebrations and holidays he used to present his friends, colleagues, and secretaries with gifts of Israeli products, such as wines and chocolates. He regularly attended the Israeli parade on Fifth Avenue. On one such occasion, in 1983, I saw him buying a T-shirt with the slogan "I love New York, but Israel is Home," which he immediately put on. He told me a few days later that when the Israeli army orchestra participating in the parade played a popular tune, he felt his heart beating faster, and added with emotion: "You should know that everyone feels the same. An Israeli remains an Israeli, whether he has a full or an empty bucket of dollars."

At one of our last meetings, another acquaintance told us that he wanted to go back to Israel, but on hearing the news of the growing economic difficulties in Israel, he had decided to delay his return for another two years. Arik reacted angrily: "I can't stand these excuses. Those who want to stay here should admit it without looking for excuses." Another listener came to the defense of the first speaker, telling Arik: "People are not looking for excuses, they honestly want to go back. Don't you?" Arik, however, was not ready for compromises: "I admit that I am here and that I have no intention of going back. But when I do decide to go back I won't make a fuss about it."

Arik was not ambivalent about having acquired U.S. citizenship, which he considered a matter of convenience. At our last talk he told me that he had accepted an invitation to participate at a reception convened by a Republican congressman whom he had met at his job. Arik supported the Republican attitudes toward Israel and considered it worthwhile to establish friendly relations with influential Americans. Arik thus accepted as rationally as possible the fact of his departure from the country and people he preferred above his newly acquired home.

Profile 11: Saul and Jean

Saul and Jean arrived in the United States in 1976. They had met in Israel a few years earlier and decided to leave to the States because both had lost hope for a better future in Israel. Saul was born in North Africa, from which he emigrated in 1956 at the age of five. In Morocco his father owned a shop and was considered affluent. But upon arriving in Israel Saul's parents settled in a poor development town where they earned a meager living. His father learned carpentry in Israel, a trade Saul adopted after he completed elementary school. During his army service, Saul enrolled in a training program for technical education which enabled him to take a job in a nearby kibbutz industry. Saul liked the kibbutz environment, where he met female volunteers from Europe and America and from whom he learned some English. He eventually decided to go back to carpentry, which afforded him more freedom to take on jobs in changing projects and to move from place to place. In this way he met Jean, who was a hotel receptionist at a tourist resort where Saul was working on a building project.

Jean was born in Philadelphia to holocaust survivors. She completed college, married a childhood sweetheart, and was soon divorced. After that shattering experience she decided to take a break somewhere else. She went to Europe and stayed with relatives in London for a few months and then went on to Israel. She immediately felt at home and applied for immigrant status. Things went well at the start. She got a small apartment and a job at a tourist resort in Tiberias. She fell in love with an Israeli academic, but unfortunately this turned into another matrimonial disaster and she got another divorce. She was also soon dissatisfied with her job, for which she was overqualified. At this stage of dispair she met Saul, who offered her warmth and stability. But Saul's economic situation was somewhat precarious. The freedom of movement and changing income that suited the life of a young bachelor was no longer compatible with the prospects of family life with Jean. As Saul himself put it: "In Israel you can't really be a carpenter; if you are steadily employed by a building contractor your salary can't support a family. But if you are self-employed, then you are often short of cash in order to pay your assistants in time. You have to wait for a long time until you get the money owing you from other contractors."

Jean was ready to leave Israel and start again in the United States. Saul was somewhat hesitant. He was anxious about the separation from his parents and other relatives and was also worried about occupational and social prospects in the United States. However, with Jean's growing unhappiness and with the continuing economic difficulties during the two years of their marriage, he decided to try his luck in America. The couple lived for some time with Jean's parents in Philadelphia. Jean advertised Saul's skills in a local Jewish newspaper and thus initiated Saul's adjustment to American life. Because he could not find a permanent job, they decided to move to New York. He applied for a position advertised in the *New York Times* which suited his qualifications. For the first time in his career, Saul found security and satisfaction as the resident carpenter of a large hotel. He was left alone to carry out his work and felt that he was independent and respected, although modestly paid. He was also satisfied with the company of the other maintenance workers, who came mostly from other ethnic minorities. He was an alien in the company of other aliens among whom his professional, linguistic, and cultural skills were compared positively. Jean found a job in a bank. Together they could earn a secure though modest living (by now they had three children). They could not afford to buy a house and often considered moving to a smaller place close to Philadelphia, where living expenses would be considerably lower.

Jean never considered returning to Israel. Saul, who missed his family, mentioned the possibility of returning sometime in the future. They were both realistic about the difficulties awaiting them in Israel, where they lacked both the means and the qualifications (in Saul's case in particular) necessary for a sufficient income to support their growing family. They were no less realistic about the limited prospects awaiting them in America. Neither could expect the high salaries of professionals, but they could always find employment sufficient to get along at some level of lower-middle-class income and life-style. Saul once commented: "The Moroccans in Israel assume that everyone in America is a millionaire. To the fools there I say that I am rich, but to the wise I say that Jean and I work hard to make a living. We don't lack any necessities, but we are not rich." Saul did not encourage his relatives to join him. On the contrary, when attending his brother's wedding, he was approached by a cousin who requested that Saul help him to come over and start a joint business. Saul, amused, answered: "I shall be glad to offer you hospitality if you come to visit us in New York, but don't fool yourself with dreams of making a lot of money in America. I won't get involved in these dreams. Take my advice, you can do better in Israel, so stay where you are right now."

In spite of their modest income, they enrolled their children at a Jewish school. They were not Orthodox in any way, but assumed that there the children would be better protected from violence and drugs (Saul himself was twice mugged during the time I knew him in New York).

Saul did not harbor bitter memories of his life in Israel. He considered his move to New York an inevitable development of his marriage and professional situation. He interpreted his own parents' poor conditions mainly as a consequence of his father's miscalculation. His father had not invested the assets he brought over from Morocco in a business, and they were subsequently wasted before he could adjust to a better occupation. He never complained of ethnic discrimination in Israel and was not impressed by the ethnic agitation that followed the 1981 elections. On the contrary, he was critical of the continuing support given by many Moroccans to Aharon Abu Hatzeira, the minister of Religious Affairs (who was of Moroccan extraction), in spite of the fact that he was taken to court and accused of mismanagement of public funds. Saul showed me a homemade bottle of arak, a strong Oriental alcoholic beverage, brought by his parents on their last visit and added: "Once the Moroccans drank for pleasure, today they drink in order to escape reality."

Saul and Jean had no relatives or close friends in New York. They were busy all week with work and caring for their children. On vacations they often went to visit Jean's parents and sister in Philadelphia. The occasional visits of Saul's Israeli relatives caused a major change in their routine. Saul did not socialize with Israelis, nor did he look for the company of Americans. His life was dedicated to his work and family, with which he was content.

Profile 12: Dani

When I first met Dani in October 1982, he was going through the most difficult period of his life since his arrival in the United States.

After three years in New York the American dream of this enthusiastic man in his early thirties was completely shattered. He had unceremoniously been fired by the employers who had sponsored his application for a Green Card.

In Israel, Dani was a blacksmith employed in the decorative industries, but the generous terms he agreed to upon his divorce compelled him to give up most of his assets. Even before his divorce he had felt that his work did not compensate him adequately when compared with friends who were successfully engaged in professional, managerial, and army positions. With the failure of his marriage, which also broke up long-established relationships with relatives and friends, he was engulfed by a diffuse feeling of inadequacy and failure. He left Israel to look for a new start somewhere else, so he could eventually return in better emotional and economic shape.

Dani had never before wished to leave Israel. On the contrary, since his arrival from Yugoslavia as a young boy, he had successfully integrated into the mainstream of Israeli society. He enjoyed the solidarity of men in the army and became a popular figure among his friends in Tel Aviv. He loved the Israeli social informality, the warm weather, the scenery, and the sense of historical continuity. He also remained deeply attached to his two sons. But now he wished to move out for a while to a place "where a man who is ready to work hard will be compensated immediately, accomplish his aims, and then live peacefully." While searching for possibilities in Canada and Australia he met a friend who was living in New York and who offered his help during Dani's initial period in America. Dani accepted his suggestion and went to New York on a tourist visa.

He had only two thousand dollars with him and the friend was less helpful than expected. He had to start immediately with the first job he found through a newspaper advertisement. It was a simple job at low pay in the company of other minority workers, who were not friendly to the white, Jewish, ambitious newcomer. But gradually he impressed his employers with his professional skills and reliable character. They supported his application for a Green Card, raised his salary, and gave him more responsibility. His sudden layoff at the worst state of the 1982 U.S. unemployment crisis was a brutal blow to Dani's plans, as well as to his self-image.

He told me at the time: "I thought that if I worked hard enough I would succeed. I thought I would soon be able to start my own small business. I really nourished the American dream." He went on: "It may be stupid, but I thought that had I been able to make a lot of money I would have proved to myself and others that I am able to beat my bad luck and shortcomings and do the things I really like doing. I have no passion for money; quite the contrary. But without it there is no way of going back. I am worried! What does the future hold for me!"

He now had to start all over again, insecure in a game whose rules, he discovered, were beyond his control. Dani was also bitterly disappointed by his failure to integrate into American society. Although good-looking, outgoing, and ready to help, his efforts to make American friends (Jewish and non-Jewish) were far from successful. He realized he had to fall back almost exclusively on Israeli company, if he was lucky enough to find it. I was among the first Israelis with whom he started to communicate.

After a few weeks' unemployment, Dani believed that he had reached rock bottom. He was afraid he was losing the will to go on fighting. He told me: "Sometimes I feel I should give up the futile race." In his panic he went to see a doctor, who suggested antidepressants, but Dani was not ready for that. Instead, he decided to go back to his former employers and ask them to take him back at whatever pay they could afford. He preferred humiliation to uncertainty and to the anticipated conflict with minority employees awaiting him in a new place. As it turned out, his employers were ready to take him back at drastically reduced pay. He was at least relieved of the immediate need to live on the modest savings he had earned during the last three years. He also now had some time to rethink his options. He thought he might try his luck in California, but was soon informed that the prospects of employment were no better there.

In the meantime Dani began to satisfy his hunger for Israeli company. He stopped reading the *New York Times* and read only Hebrew newspapers. He became deeply involved with the Israeli Club, where he soon became a popular figure and was usually among the main speakers in discussions and debates concerning Israel. He was particularly concerned with the ideological changes and the moral position of Israeli society and lamented the rise of materialistic ideals and increased acquisitiveness, which were diminishing the pioneering spirit that made it worth living there. He expressed his convictions emphatically: "I don't need a second car, a bungalow in a new Tel Aviv suburb, and investments in the Israeli stock exchange. I want to get back the self-assurance that justice is on our side." He often claimed that Israel could offer the thousands of American Jewish youth the values they lacked in the United States and looked for instead in drugs. He had no doubt that the Israelis in New York could convince them that their right place was in Israel.

Dani gradually became used to the drawbacks of fortune and decided to take a constructive step; with a friend, a recent immigrant from Europe, he started to look for work they could do in their spare time. Dani knew that as long as he was a salaried employee he had no chance of returning to Israel. He and his friend were able to compete for small projects because, with lower expenses, they could afford to charge lower prices. They soon decided to make arrangements for the establishment of their own plant. Dani decided to risk most of his savings to rent an industrial worksite and bought secondhand machinery and tools for their venture.

Six months after the shock of being laid off, Dani signed the contracts that would transform his fortune in America. His friend resigned from his job, but Dani, who could not expect his employers to take him back again if their venture failed, continued with his job. He shared his salary with his partner and worked with him in the evenings and weekends. He worked twelve hours a day for six and often seven days a week. Now that they had the space and tools, they could compete for larger projects. Dani invested in advertising, contacted numerous engineering firms, did everything possible to satisfy his new clients, and succeeded in getting their recommendations when contracting for new work. After a few months he felt secure enough to give up his former job. He regretted that he had not started this venture much earlier: "I would have now been much closer to my goal of returning to Israel."

By December 1984, the volume of work and the growing number of employees forced the partners to move to a much bigger worksite. Dani moved to a bigger apartment and bought new furniture and new cars for himself and the business. He made frequent enjoyable trips to Israel to visit his family and friends. He was now planning to start a new business in a different field. He hoped to establish business projects and make investments that would enable him to return to Israel free of economic pressures and free to pursue his desires. He was contemplating investment in real estate in New York areas that he believed would soon become the new locus of industrial and residential expansion. At last he could see the American dream coming true.

When we met in Israel in 1985 Dani told me that he could not see himself reaching these goals in Israel. He offered both figurative and substantial explanations: "In Israel I couldn't fly. There is more air for me to expand in New York. In Israel you need higher education and degrees in order to get into academic and managerial positions. If you don't have these, you need to lie and cheat continuously in order to do business. I am unsuitable for that." He thought he should stay in New York for another few years (three to five at most), until he could move back to Israel permanently. He felt strongly that he had to live close to his sons. He could not let them down and stay away indefinitely.

In the meantime Dani lost interest in the Israeli Club. He organized a few successful sing-along parties and thus satisfied some of his hunger for Israeli company, as well as the conviction that he had not disassociated himself from Israel. He assumed that most of those invited to his parties were seriously thinking about returning to Israel. Dani could not believe that the Israelis of whom he was fond would not go back. On my last visit to New York I was in a car with Dani when, to my surprise, he threw the remains of an apple he had been eating out of the window. I commented hesitantly that I would not have done that as a tourist in Europe. He answered laughingly: "I wouldn't have done it in Israel either, but this isn't my home."

What Do the Profiles Tell Us?

In search of both the unique and the shared elements among the twelve profiles, we should first look at the circumstances that made

the people portrayed leave Israel in the first place. Only one-third seems to have been pushed out by pressing economic or personal difficulties (Profiles 3, 10, 11, 12). About two-thirds were directly or indirectly attracted by professional and economic opportunities. This factor seems to be particularly dominant among the migrant Israeli couples. Another structural element is most significant: the migration of couples and individual Israelis was not part of an inter-related wave of relatives, friends, or community members.[5] Only one case clearly indicates a pattern of a chain migration of a group of brothers (Profile 6). It is evident, however, that almost all arrivals had somebody waiting for them on the American shore, although in most cases these bonds did not entail a binding commitment. Usually even those who received some support from relatives and friends did not settle down close to them. Emigration, as presented by our profiles, was mainly an independent action taken by individual couples or single persons regardless of the experience of the majority among their relatives, friends, or neighbors.

Although some were encouraged at the first stage by relatives and friends, none was employed for either a short or long period in the businesses of other Israelis. Even those who came to join their relatives and expected to be engaged in the latters' enterprises (Profiles 1, 6) were soon obliged to manage independently. Although some received reliable information and advice from Israelis, no one had made a "breakthrough" with the active support of other Israelis. No doubt this pattern does not apply to those of my acquaintances who arrived unskilled and with no capital, for example, some of the employees in Reuben's boutiques. But these formed a minority among the Israelis in Queens.

Most of our profiles could be roughly defined as belonging to a middle-class income category and standard of living, but the range of their occupations was very wide. There are no signs of their continuing concentration in specific types of trades and professions or in particular commercial and business undertakings. The more Israelis I met the more diverse their occupational distribution and the proliferation of their "commercial imagination." Although Israelis did sometimes penetrate into a particular business such as the

[5]For a comparative perspective see, for example, the Dominican case of family chain migration (Garrison and Weiss 1979).

cabdriving and ownership, garment boutiques, and lamp shops, these occupations did not become their ethnic monopoly.

Most of the people profiled related their economic success to the structure of the American economic system—its wide range of opportunities, the negligible extent of interference by bureaucratic agencies, the lack of ascriptive obstacles and the paramount position of personal merit, and the flexible definition of success, which does not stigmatize economic achievements unrelated to traditional symbols of status (such as the stigmatized image of the cabdriver in Israel).

About half of the people introduced in our profiles left Israel with the clear intention of remaining abroad for a long time, if not indefinitely (Profiles 3, 6, 7, 8, 9, 11). The other half did not wish to stay away beyond a limited period of a few years at most, during which time they expected to accomplish their goals (Profiles 1, 2, 4, 5, 10, 12). But whether they left Israel with the clear intention of staying away or with the strong conviction of returning, in most cases there was no way back. It was still too early to see what would happen to Dani, who appeared to be highly committed to Israel (Profile 12). Nevertheless, there were already some signs that his return would not take place as early as he expected. Moreover, he had realized that his return would require separation from the newly experienced sources of achievement and success: "In Israel I couldn't fly; there is more air for me to expand in New York." The trials and personal transformation Dani went through offer a dramatic exposition of the forces that work against the termination of *yerida*.

Only three of those profiled left Israel because of financial difficulties (3, 11, 12). The latter, and most if not all the others, managed, though sometimes after severe difficulties and disappointments, to improve their professional and economic situation. Although most of the people discussed were economically comfortable, the balance of their achievements, as materially considered and subjectively experienced, was not in all cases superior to that which they might have attained in Israel. (These doubts were noticeable in Profiles 1, 2, 4, 6, 10.) It thus appears that the "price" of immigration was somewhat higher among the immigrating Israeli couples than among those who arrived single.

The only case of returners (Profile 5) demonstrates the crucial role of the female partner in the decision to return to Israel. While the men usually initiated the first stage of emigration from Israel, it was often the women who had a major influence on whether they stayed in the States (see Profile 2) or returned to Israel. The return of Israeli men married to American spouses seemed most unlikely, the positive attitude of Nathan's wife (Profile 9) was very unusual.

Our profiles seem to demonstrate that Israeli immigrants did not represent an occupational-economic ethnic enclave, nor did they develop a cultural enclave that generated the continuity of an ethnic tradition. Many of those described here were dedicated to some form of Israeli culture, such as the Hebrew language or Israeli songs of past and present. Most of them (excluding those in Profiles 8, 9) were not critical of Israel. Almost all were continuously nostalgic and some (particularly those in Profiles 1, 2, 4, 5, 10, 12) experienced acute anguish at the separation. The separation from close relatives was a specific, permanent source of pain and generated a sense of loss even among those who left Israel willingly and were satisfied with their achievements (for example, Jacob and Rachel, Profile 3). They yearned for Israeli patterns of informal relationships and sought agreeable Israeli company. Nevertheless, they did very little to perpetuate their cultural heritage and to support the organizations that could offer them the tools for developing ethnic institutions.

The great majority of children born to Israelis in the United States, and many of those who came to the United States at an early age, could not speak Hebrew and had no commitment to Israeli society and culture. Excluding Benny and Ziva, who went back (Profile 5), only Joseph and Rina (Profile 4) made serious efforts to inculcate their children with Israeli culture. The children of Israeli couples could sometimes speak Hebrew (particularly those who arrived at school age or as teen-agers). Some of these children developed a degree of attachment to Israel and their parents sometimes considered a return to Israel. But children with only one Israeli parent (usually the father) were not at all exposed to Hebrew. Furthermore, they had more limited contact with Israeli relatives and their parents very rarely considered plans to settle in Israel.

Among the ten participants who had children of school age, five sent them to Jewish schools. Four of them were married to American spouses and only one was involved with synagogue life (Profile 1). Arik in particular was painfully aware of the estrangement of his children from Israeli culture and society (Profile 10). The enrollment of his children at Jewish schools was no consolation; on the contrary, it further intensified his frustration.

While the majority of those profiled were not involved with organized Jewish life, their "Israeli connection" was personally centered and often anonymous. Some regularly read the weekend issue of such Israeli newspapers as *Maariv* and *Yedioth,* or the local weekly, *Yisrael Shelanu.* Others regularly listened to the Hebrew radio program "Kan Yisrael" and attended the infrequent concerts and performances by Israeli artists. They telephoned and visited Israel frequently, maintained a small network of close Israeli friends, and irregularly attended the Israeli Club in Forest Hills or other Israeli events in Queens and Manhattan. Even Dani, who for nearly a year was among the most committed of club participants, lost interest in the club's activities once he became successful in his business. Instead, he became increasingly involved in a close circle of Israeli friends. Eli, although he often advised David on the management of the club, did not attend regularly, and his wife, Yaffa, attended the club only once in two years. Benny and Ziva, who returned to Israel after ten years in New York, had little contact with Israelis and refrained from attending Israeli social and cultural activities. Joseph, who was active in Israeli affairs, assumed that there was no need for and no prospect of success with regular organized activities. Instead, he was active in organizing parties at the festivals planned to draw a large audience. However, although most Israelis I met had some Israeli acquaintances in their immediate neighborhood or in other parts of Queens, in many cases this did not constitute a viable social network of close friends. In fact, half of those profiled did not have a stable circle of Israeli friends (1, 5, 6, 7, 9, 11).

Those who appeared to be strongly committed to Israeli society and culture were more seriously troubled by the problem of national identity (Profiles 2, 4, 5, 10, 12) and continuously stressed their separation from American society, as well as from the company of *yordim.* They often emphasized that they had not intended to remain away from Israel for a long time; for example: "I did not wait in line at the American consulate in Tel Aviv in order to get an immigrant visa. . . . I don't see myself cut off from Israel and I don't consider myself American" (Eli, Profile 2). Or Rina, who stated at a meeting of Israelis: "We all got stuck [*nitka'nu*] here, but Israel is our home and we consider ourselves different from Americans" (Profile 4). In addition, they did not challenge the stigma attributed to *yordim*, but disassociated themselves from those who apparently deserved that designation; for example: "We never considered ourselves *yordim*, we were always Zionists" (Ziva, Profile 5). Dani could not perceive that "nice Israelis" would consider staying in New York indefinitely (Profile 12). In order to separate himself from *yordim* he often differentiated between "those from our forces" and all others "who are not of our forces," thus using an army metaphor designating Israeli units versus enemy units.

Rachel's position, however, was more complicated (Profile 3). She left with her husband well aware that they might stay in the United States for a long period. Eighteen years after they left, she knew there was little chance that they would ever return to Israel. She expressed the complexity of their situation and self-image as compared to that of American, Israeli, and *yordim* identities when she exclaimed: "I am not a *yoredet*, I love Israel. But neither am I an Israeli, since I am not there when the Israelis fight and suffer. I consider myself a New Yorker!" But Nira, who was much more critical of Israeli society, which she was apparently glad to leave behind, wished to restrict the intrusion of Israeli sentimental education into her own life and to raise her child free of the "brainwashing which we went through in Israel when told so often, 'It is good to die for our country'"(Profile 8). Nathan's strategy of disassociating himself from Israeli society was more subtle (Profile 9). After eight years in the United States, he felt more comfortable speaking English than Hebrew. He also joined an American Jewish organization, consequently converting his Israeli loyalties into the American Jews' diffused responsibility toward Israel's survival. He was among the very few who sometimes made direct positive references to his acquired American citizenship.

The perception of national identity, the loyalties and commitment to Israel, as well as the evaluation of the American experience, were also not equally shared by the Israeli spouses. Thus, while Eli instigated his family's immigration, his wife became more immersed in American identity and removed from Israeli loyalties (Profile 2). Benny and Ziva returned to Israel mainly because of Ziva's unwavering desire to go back (Profile 5). Joseph and Rina's success in preserving an Israeli atmosphere at home was the consequence of their shared commitment to an Israeli culture and identity (Profile 4).

We are accustomed to conceiving of ethnic minorities and groups of immigrants as carrying an immutable collective identity. Our discussion indicates, however, the changing attitudes and positions adopted by Israeli immigrants on their commitment to Israeli society and culture a few years after immigration. The outside observer may conclude that the Israelis manifest a viable ethnic identity that could potentially be mobilized for corporate ethnic action, a conclusion based, for example, on observation of shared behavioral traits. But this did not seem to be the case in the eyes of the Israelis themselves. This perception of an individualized ethnic personality fits the observations revealed in previous chapters. There we indicated the lack of organized support in the process of immigration, the dispersion of occupations, the lack of ethnic organizations and associations, the frailty of social networks, and the discontinuity of cultural traditions in socializing the younger generation.

In spite of the continuing expansion of Israeli immigration, its growing presence in specific neighborhoods, and the attention it raises in the Israeli media, Israeli immigration is still a private matter. The management of national identity and the negotiation of the immigrants' reality is carried out independently by individual Israelis regardless of the waxing presence of a "society of *yordim.*"

[9]

Conclusions:
Yordim's Affective Ethnicity

The presence of the "new ethnics" in America appears compatible with the general acknowledgment of ethnicity as intrinsic to the human condition. This acknowledgment has sometimes been expressed in poetic terminology, such as "primordial sentiments," "ethnic symbolic estates," "ethnic cultural paradigms."[1] The Israeli immigration, however, seems to represent a "deviant" case on the American scene of recent immigration, as well as within contemporary ethnicity.

The numbers of Israeli immigrants are considerable and equal those of other "new ethnics," such as the Asian Indians, Koreans, Dominicans. Although they too tend to concentrate in particular sections of New York City, they remain quite invisible. Not only have they been neglected by the experts on immigration and by the mass media, but they themselves have avoided the public display of an ethnic presence. While various types of voluntary associations, religious institutions, and shared economic enterprises flourish among other groups of newcomers, the Israelis, who are also unaffiliated to the American Jewish community and its institutions, remain almost anonymous.

The Israelis are remarkably different from earlier major waves of Jewish immigration to the United States (as well as from the recent immigration of Russian Jews). The early waves of Jews left an "old

[1]See Greeley 1974:14; Shokeid and Deshen 1982:45.

[205]

country," where for many generations they retained the status of sojourners and to which they had no wish to return. Upon arrival in the United States they were almost unique among immigrants in the nonsojournment of their position.[2] Although they might have missed some elements of the culture of the *shtetl,* they did not yearn to go back "home." Nevertheless, they established many *landsmanshaften* to commemorate the society and heritage of their *shtetls* and soon founded the influential and continuously viable national and communal Jewish organizations. The Israelis, in contrast, are expatriates from an "old country" that they continue to regard as their homeland.

Sojourners, as commonly described since Siu's (1952) seminal portrayal of the homesick Chinese, express their longing and loss by establishing an American reproduction of their native society. The homesick Israelis, however, refrain from recreating a substitute Israeli environment, although this does not imply that the prospects of the Israelis staying or returning home are different from those of the more visibly organized societies of sojourners in the various "ethnic towns."

The Israelis are relatively successful in America. Most, if not all, are employed, and only a minority in low-status and poorly paid occupations. Furthermore, they are not obliged to support their relatives left behind in the old country, which was often the case in the early waves of Jewish immigration, as well as in most other contemporary immigrations. On the contrary, they often take along (and actually smuggle out)[3] considerable personal wealth. From the point of view of their home society they represent an egoistic type of behavior. This egoistic behavior has a particularly strong impact on a society that still considers its citizenship fundamentally altruistic. Most Israelis perceive themselves as called upon to sacrifice their material resources, daily comfort, and sometimes even their lives for the sake of national survival.

The Israelis who remain abroad cannot escape being penalized by their compatriots in the old country and their representatives in the United States. Furthermore, the *yordim* are suspiciously and

[2]See, e.g., Howe 1976:58.
[3]Because of the restrictions imposed in Israel on transactions of foreign currency.

unsympathetically observed by American Jews. The stigmatized *yordim* respond to this designation by their home society and by American Jews, as well as to their own sense of inadequacy, by a behavioral style not dissimilar from that of other stigmatized groups. They perceive other *yordim* as morally inferior and unworthy of their company.

The Israelis, by refraining from investing in the establishment of institutions and associations to support their stay in a new environment,[4] appear to be denying their new status. The Asian Indians present a pertinent counterexample. Although they represent a successful immigrant group (many of them are engaged in the professions and business) and in spite of the serious religious, geographical, and linguistic divisions that characterize their community, they have evolved a national ethnic organization and founded numerous local associations. Their national organization successfully campaigned, for example, against the categorization of the Asian Indians as whites, which deprived them of the special rights assigned to "minorities" (Fisher 1978). Of course, the emergence of ethnic organizations does not involve all those who could be classified as members of these groups. However, contemporary studies are usually based on the actual participants and tend to ignore those who remain unaffiliated. But neither success nor failure has stimulated enough *yordim* to initiate communal or national organizations.

Although *yordim* refrain from acting out and advertising their Israeliness in formally established ethnic institutions, they do participate, on the basis of a "one-night-stand" relationship, in expressive activities that display Israeli culture and sentiments. They flock to concerts and performances by Israeli artists, attend the Israeli annual parade on Fifth Avenue, visit (albeit infrequently) the Israeli Club, express deep emotions at the communal singing of Israeli folk songs, and read *Israel Shelanu* or listen to "Kan Israel."

Emigration has primarily been considered a consequence of social, economic, or political deprivation in certain societies. Such emigrants often form ethnic concentrations in their new country of

---

[4]I accept Schmalenbach's (1961:333) assertion that the individual can directly contribute to the evolvement of a community.

residence. Alternatively, emigration has been considered an action initiated by adventurous, highly mobile, and sometimes exceptionally talented individuals. These latter are less prone to join an ethnic constituency. The majority of Israeli emigrants were not pushed out by pressing conditions. It must be emphasized that most Israelis I observed did not perceive those threatening factors in Israeli existence which impress outside observers, such as the political and economic hazards, as responsible for their emigration. The *yordim* thus represent a particular type, though possibly not a unique case, of an immigrant community. They may be considered by some as a group of energetic, risk-taking, mobile, and adjustable people, representatives of the process of self-selection of the "fittest" among their ranks. Others, however, may perceive their emigration as the incarnation of a deeply embedded cultural trait (or neurosis, as A. B. Yehoshua calls it) among Jews who have been conditioned for millennia to remain in exile or to move on whenever a better opportunity for survival and achievement becomes available. The latter interpretation can be substantiated by the British example. In spite of the continuing economic decline and its damaging effects on British society, emigration has not yet emerged as a major phenomenon in Britain.[5]

[5]The data available supports this assessment. The number of immigrants from Britain seems to have remained unchanged during the last decade.

Migration from the United Kingdom (in thousands)

Immigrants	Total persons	Males	Females
1973	196	105	91
1974	184	104	80
1975	197	102	95
1976	191	100	91
1977	163	88	75
1978	187	96	91
1979	195	103	92
1980	174	92	82
1981	153	82	71
1982	202	101	101
1983	202	107	95

From Table 2.10 in *Annual Abstract of Statistics*, 121(1985):20, a publication of the Government Statistical Service, London.

I have neither the necessary data nor the ideological conviction to assess and reliably compare the motivational sources that stimulate the emigration of Israelis as compared to other groups of immigrants. Neither can I assess the factors that influence behavior of "nonimmigrants" (in Israel or Britain). Israeli "sojourners," however, are different from the Chinese prototype and from many other other groups of sojourners in their comprehension of the circumstances of their departure. Chinese immigrants would not describe themselves as getting "stuck" in the United States as a result of an unplanned turn of events. They left China purposefully, with a clear economic goal they assumed they would achieve within a given period and then return home. But the Israelis' first step in America is perceived by many *yordim* as unrelated to a premeditated plan. Most of them started out as tourists visiting relatives, a friend, or a girl friend; others were induced by relatives and friends to "taste" America; some arrived as students or *shlichim;* some married an American Jewish girl who originally intended to live in Israel; others escaped a temporary personal entanglement or came over for a short, prearranged professional engagement. Only a minority considered their prolonged stay an inevitable development of their first step in America. They also rarely reconciled themselves to the initial events that ultimately became a permanent move.

This presentation of self and mythmaking may be part of the *yordim's* reaction to a situation of acute ambivalence arising from a stigmatic designation. Whatever the source and validity of this interpretation, the perception of the impromptu circumstances of their departure produces the sense of a forced separation intermingled with acknowledgment of the repercussions of the original move and, therefore, a self-designation closer to that of an expatriate than that of an emigrant.[6]

The Israeli emigrants who acknowledge the stigma of *yordim* consider themselves to be victims of circumstance, either of a pragmatic nature (easily identifiable) or of involuntary, mental, and other less identifiable processes and conditions. Therefore they

[6]See E. Cohen's (1977) survey of expatriate communities.

conceive of themselves as only partially responsible for their continued stay away. Those *yordim* who retain their apartments in Israel are symbolically expressing a personal sense of a forced or unplanned emigration and a profound claim for separation from the community of other *yordim*.

Most immigrations in world history have offered a unique strategy for human beings to change or escape their previous social and ethnic identity. This transformation, though not always experienced in full by the immigrants, often promised a complete change of identity for their children and grandchildren. America has been unique in evolving the immigrant society par excellence as often expressed in the vocabulary of the "melting pot" society. The American melting pot, however, has gradually granted the privilege of preserving some elements of separate ethnic identities that do not necessarily conflict with the supra-embracing American identity. This ethnic status quo was well suited to the Jews, the archetypal Diaspora people, the classic strangers and sojourners. For the first time in their history, Jews could legitimately claim equal citizenship while continuing to retain a separate ethnoreligious identity.

But although Israeli immigrants are the flesh and blood of American Jews, whose fathers and grandparents came from the same *shtetls* in Eastern Europe, they cannot easily share the American Jews' satisfaction with the attainment of civil equality while preserving a separate identity. To be born or raised in Israel is an irrevocable act of transformation. The Israeli experience represents a dramatic turn in Jewish history, as well as in the components of personal Jewish identity which sharply separate Israelis and other Jews. Nevertheless, the *yordim* are the first generation of Jews in thousands of years who have voluntarily chosen to leave the land of Israel for life in the Diaspora. The solution offered by Chabad's missionaries, who encourage *yordim* to join a particular segment of American Jewry is, however, congenial only to some Sephardi Israelis among whom Ashkenazi Orthodoxy does not evoke the antinomy and antagonism it does among secular Israelis of Ashkenazi extraction. On the other hand, the creation of a semi-Israeli environment in America is indeed antithetical and paradoxical to the essence of Israeli identity rooted in a revolutionary denial of Diaspora existence.

The pattern of *yordim's* accommodation with the conflicts and the stigma related to their position may prove, however, conducive to the acculturation of the younger generation into the American mainstream. Most noticeable is the rapid loss of Hebrew among the younger generation, particularly among those born in America. Although Hebrew is the major vehicle of identity and cultural and sentimental expression, the majority of Israeli parents do not insist on speaking Hebrew to their children. Educated in public schools, unbound by close-knit networks of relatives and friends and lacking an Israeli (or Jewish) communal organization that would support and display an Israeli ambience, the Israeli children grow up under little pressure to conform to their parents' social commitments and cultural heritage.

The effect of communal organizations on the survival of ethnicity has been observed in the case of the Asian Indians. The development of ethnic associations was seen as an obstacle to the Asian Indians' expectations for assimilation in American society (Varma 1980:34). Although I have emphasized the Israelis' lack of ethnic organizations, I do not advocate a "functionalist" assumption about an intrinsic value concerning the presence or absence of ethnocommunal institutions. But whatever the instrumental, cultural, or emotional losses incurred by Israelis who refrain from associational activity, it seems that this abstention does not handicap their entry into American society. It may even be argued that it frees them from the physical and symbolic barriers of an ethnic town, its institutions, and agents who volunteer to intermediate between the newcomers and the receiving society.

The Israelis would not be the first group to have disappeared into the American scene without having developed their own particular ethnic patterns and institutions. The Germans are a similar case. Glazer and Moynihan (1963:311–12) suggest a number of factors— religion, education, and professional skills—which hampered the development of a German ethnicity, particularly the heterogeneity that characterized this immigrant group as compared to the relative homogeneity of other groups. The German immigrants "reflected, as it were, an entire modern society, not simply an element of one.

The only things all had in common were the outward manifestations of German culture: language for a generation or two, and after that a fondness for certain types of food and drink and a consciousness of the German fatherland" (p. 312). While the Israelis, too, reflect an "entire modern society," this alone cannot explain a process that may lead to disappearance of Israeli ethnicity. The case of the Asian Indian puts in question the validity of the conclusion suggested by Glazer and Moynihan. Although they are a highly heterogeneous group, they soon evolved a strong ethnic presence.

Glazer and Moynihan go on to emphasize the religious aspect that "serves as the basis of a subcommunity and a subculture" (p. 313). This theme also serves as a major explanation in Glazer's earlier analysis (1957) of the expansion of communal Jewish organizations in the United States. He interprets that development as part of the accommodation of Jews to the religious forms of mainstream Christian culture which they encountered as they moved into the affluent suburbs. If this observation is valid, we may expect the eventual integration of some of the Israelis into the Jewish constituency. This possible development may form part of the processes of economic and social mobility which could remove them from their present concentrations in Queens and Brooklyn.

It is already noticeable that although Israeli immigrants have not yet joined American Jewish institutions, they seem to prefer Jewish neighborhoods. At a later stage some may indeed enter into more active patterns of mutual relationships with American Jews. For their part, American Jews may reconcile themselves to the presence of these unwelcome newcomers, who can both compensate for the demographic shrinkage of American Jewry and offer a soothing answer to a conflict that many American Jews experience over their unfulfilled commitment to the Zionist calling: if the Israelis themselves prefer to live in America, why on earth should American Jews move to Israel?

The major phenomenon observed in our research is that Israeli immigrants tend to disassociate themselves from the social groupings and organizations that could offer the basis for an Israeli "institutionalized" ethnicity. Not only are they alienated from American Jewry, but also from the Jewish religion and its association with Diaspora tradition. Furthermore, they reject the community of *yordim* and are estranged from the company of Israeli official representatives. The Israeli environment of *yordim* is voluntarily and sporadically organized: they sustain loosely knit networks of Israeli friends and participate occasionally at Israeli "happenings," while Israeli newspapers, Hebrew radio programs, frequent telephone calls, and visits to Israel add to the repertoire of ethnic activities. In other words, their Israeli ethnicity is mainly sustained as an affective modality.

Affective ethnicity is far less demanding than other forms of ethnic expression, which manifest and make claims for social, cultural, political, and economic interests. The latter are also usually supported by organized action through communal or national associations and institutions. I am not underplaying the importance of the affective roots of ethnicity. They are indeed, as suggested by Epstein (1978:104), "the foundations on which other forms of organization and association can be built." In the Israeli case, however (as well as in the German precedent), these affective roots are not employed in order to expand informal personal relationships and regulate them into more solid bases of ethnic action and as a vehicle for cultural continuity.

I suggest that ethnic behavior is one component in the repertoire of affective mechanisms which regulate both social sentiments and the individual's ongoing negotiation of his or her social position, particularly in a changing environment. Affective ethnicity may serve as a convenient definition and as a tool of observation for the manifestations of other, less visible ethnic groups. It also relates certain forms of ethnicity to a broader phenomenon of minorities and groups whose public display is largely affective. I compared, for example, the *yordim's* performance and display of "Israeliness" with "soul" and "camp."

Yordim represent a most astonishing phenomenon in modern Jewish history. At the turn of the century and to a large extent during the first decades of the twentieth century, the majority of Jews in Europe, the Middle East, and North Africa experienced precarious political and economic conditions. The hazardous position of Jews in gentile society reached unprecedented extremes with the European holocaust. The subsequent founding of the state of Israel seemed to provide the solution that would at last eradicate the sources of Jewish vulnerability and would transform the existential position of Jews wherever they were. The emergence of Israeli expatriates who have given up the haven of Jewish independence has caused a reaction somewhat reminiscent of the response toward conversion to Christianity in earlier centuries. In both cases it seems to represent a bold act of breaking away from the internal and external constraints set up by the Jewish community and its surrounding environment.

The Israelis do, however, often reside in close proximity to other *yordim,* thus sustaining what may be considered a symbolic community.[7] They know that they are not alone in this breaking away from their ethnic and national commitments. Disassociating themselves from an organized Jewish or Israeli community demonstrates that act of secession. At the same time, however, affective ethnicity endows the often disparaged and unwelcome *yordim* a satisfactory self-perception of personal integrity. Unlike the apostates of earlier generations, they acknowledge and on occasion even noursih their ethnic and cultural identity. On a cold night, the songs will carry them back home: "Go, go to the desert, the roads will lead you. . . . Oh, my land, we have returned to you."

[7]See Ginsberg 1975.

References

Achiram, E., N. Danziger, and J. Liebman. 1984. *The Development of High-Tech Industries and the Return of Scientists*. Ministry of Science and Development, National Council for Science and Development (in Hebrew).

Arian, Asher. 1981. "Elections 1981: Competitiveness and Polarization." *Jerusalem Quarterly* 21:3–27.

Armstrong, John A. 1976. "Mobilized and Proletarian Diasporas." *American Political Science Review* 70:393–408.

Avineri, Shlomo. 1976. "The Yerida." *Maariv* (January 30):17 (in Hebrew).

Barth, Fredrik. 1969. *Ethnic Groups and Boundaries*. Boston: Little, Brown.

Bar-Yosef, Yehoshua. 1976. "Yordim Bekhoach Vebefoal" [Actual and Potential Yordim]. *Moznaim* 42:83–86 (in Hebrew).

Bell, Daniel. 1975. "Ethnicity and Social Change." In *Ethnicity: Theory and Experience*, ed. N. Glazer and P. Moynihan, pp. 141–74. Cambridge, Mass.: Harvard University Press.

Ben-Ami, Issachar. 1977. "The Folklore of War: The Motif of Saints." In *Dov Sadan*, ed. S. Verssess et al., pp. 87–104. Tel Aviv: Hakibutz Hameuhad (in Hebrew).

Ben-Gurion, David. 1953. *Chazon Vederekh*, 2d ed. Vol. 3. Tel Aviv: Israel's Workers Party (in Hebrew).

Bonachich, Edna, and John Modell. 1980. *The Economic Basis of Ethnic Solidarity: Small Business in the Japanese American Community*. Berkeley: University of California Press.

Bryce-Laporte, Roy Simon. 1979. "New York City and the New Caribbean Immigration: A Contextual Statement." *International Migration Review* 13:214–54.

——, ed. 1980. *Sourcebook on the New Immigration*. New Brunswick, N.J.: Transaction Books.

[215]

References

Caroli Boyd, Betty. 1982. "Recent Immigration to the United States." *Trends in History* 2:49–69.

Cohen, Erik. 1959. "A Study on the Causes of Immigration from Israel." Stencil, Department of Sociology, Hebrew University (in Hebrew).

——. 1977. "Expatriate Communities." *Current Sociology* 24:5–91.

Cohen, Steven M. 1986. "Israeli Emigres and the New York Federation: A Case Study in Ambivalent Policymaking for 'Jewish Communal Deviants.'" *Contemporary Jewry* 7:155–65.

Cohen, Steven M., and G. Linda Levi. 1983. "Sub-Committee on Services to Israelis in New York: Final Report to the Communal Planning Committee." Stencil, Federation of Jewish Philanthropies of New York.

Cohen, Yinon. [1986; n.d.] War and Social Integration: The Effects of the Israeli-Arab Conflict on Jewish Emigration from Israel. Stencil, Department of Sociology and Anthropology, Tel Aviv University.

Dahbany Miraglia, Dina. 1983. "An Analysis of Ethnic Identity among Yemenite Jews in the Greater New York Area." Ph.D. diss., Columbia University.

Davis, Fred. 1979. *Yearning for Yesterday: A Sociology of Nostalgia*. New York: Free Press.

Deshen, Shlomo. 1974. "The Situational Analysis of Symbolic Action and Change." In Deshen and Shokeid, *The Predicament of Homecoming*, pp. 151–172. Ithaca, N.Y.: Cornell University Press.

——. 1980. "Religion among Middle Eastern Immigrants in Israel." In *Israel—a Developing Society*, ed. A. Arian, pp. 235–46. Assen, Netherlands: Van Gorcum.

Deshen, Shlomo, and Moshe Shokeid. 1974. *The Predicament of Homecoming: Cultural and Social Life of North African Immigrants in Israel*. Ithaca, N.Y.: Cornell University Press.

Douglas, Mary. 1966. *Purity and Danger*. London: Routledge and Kegan Paul.

Eisenstadt, Shmuel N. 1954. *The Absorption of Immigrants*. London: Routledge and Kegan Paul.

——. 1956. "The Social Conditions of Voluntary Associations." *Scripta Hierosolymitana* 3:104–25.

——. 1985. *The Transformation of Israeli Society: An Essay in Interpretation*. London: Weidenfeld and Nicolson.

Elizur, Dov. 1980. "Israelis in the United States: Motives, Attitudes, and Intentions." *American Jewish Yearbook*, pp. 53–67. American Jewish Committee and Jewish Publication Society of America.

Elizur, Dov, and Mickey Elizur. 1974. "The Long Way Back: Attitudes of Israelis Residing in the United States and in France toward Returning to Israel." Stencil, Jerusalem: Israel Institute of Applied Social Research (in Hebrew; summary in English).

Elon, Amos. 1971. *The Israelis: Founders and Sons*. London: Weidenfeld and Nicolson.

Encyclopedia Judaica. 1971. Jerusalem: Keter Publishing House.

Epstein, Arnold L. 1978. *Ethos and Identity*. London: Tavistock.

———. 1981. *Urbanization and Kinship*. New York: Academic Press.

Fein, Aharon. 1978. "The Process of Migration: Israeli Emigration to the United States." Ph.D. diss., Case Western Reserve University.

Feld, Steven. 1982. *Sound and Sentiment: Birds, Weeping, Poetics, and Song in Kaluli Expression*. Philadelphia: University of Pennsylvania Press.

Fisher, Maxine P. 1978. "Creating Ethnic Identity: Asian Indians in the New York City Area." *Urban Anthropology* 7:271–85.

———. 1980. "Indian Ethnic Identity: The Role of Associations in the New York Indian Population." In *The New Ethnics: Asian Indians in the United States*, ed. P. Saran and E. Eames, pp. 177–92. New York: Praeger.

Freedman, Marcia, and Joseph Korazim. 1986. "Israelis in the New York Area Labor Market." *Contemporary Jewry* 7:141–54.

Freedman, William. 1983. "Israel: The New Diaspora." In *Diaspora: Exile and the Jewish Condition*, ed. E. Levine, pp. 229–46. New York: Jason Aronson.

Gaber, Lee Bennet. 1983. "The Psychological Phenomenology of Exile." In *Diaspora: Exile and the Jewish Condition*, ed. E. Levine, pp. 63–65. New York and London: Jason Aronson.

Garrison, Vivian, and Carol Weiss. 1979. "Dominican Family Networks and United States Immigration Policy: A Case Study." *International Migration Review* 13:264-83.

Geertz, Clifford. 1973. *The Interpretation of Cultures*. New York: Basic Books.

Ginsberg, Yona. 1975. *Jews in a Changing Neighborhood: The Study of Mattapan*. New York: Free Press.

Glazer, Nathan. 1957; reprinted 1972. *American Judaism*. Chicago: University of Chicago Press.

Glazer, Nathan, and Daniel P. Moynihan. 1963; reprinted 1970. *Beyond the Melting Pot: The Negroes, Puerto Ricans, Jews, Italians and Irish of New York City*. Cambridge, Mass.: MIT Press.

Glazer, Nathan, and Daniel P. Moynihan, eds. 1975. *Ethnicity: Theory and Experience*. Cambridge, Mass.: Harvard University Press.

Gleason, Philip. 1982. "American Identity and Americanization." In *Concepts of Ethnicity*, ed. W. Peterson, M. Novak, and P. Gleason, pp. 57–143. Cambridge, Mass.: Belknap Harvard University Press.

Goffman, Erving. 1961. *Encounters*. New York: Bobbs-Merrill.

———. 1963; reprinted 1968. *Stigma*. Harmondsworth, Middlesex: Penguin Books.

Gothalf, Yehuda. 1976. "Hayordim Lechaiey Ha'am Vearetz" (The Yordim Who Torment Nation and Land). *Davar* (January 16):11, 19 (in Hebrew).

Grant, Geraldine S. 1981. "New Immigrants and Ethnicity: A Preliminary Research Report on Immigrants in Queens." Stencil, Ethnic Studies Project, Queens College, CUNY.

References

Greeley, Andrew M. 1974. *Ethnicity in the United States: A Preliminary Reconnaissance.* New York: John Wiley.

Hannerz, Ulf. 1969. *Soulside: Inquiries into Ghetto Culture and Community.* New York: Columbia University Press.

Harvard Encyclopedia of American Ethnic Groups. 1980. Ed. Stephan Thernstrom. Cambridge, Mass.: Harvard University Press.

Hazaz, Chaim. 1954. "Hadrasha." In *Selected Stories*, pp. 184–202. Tel Aviv: Dvir (in Hebrew).

Heilman, Samuel C. 1983. *The People of the Book.* Chicago: University of Chicago Press.

Howe, Irving. 1976. *World of Our Fathers.* New York: Harcourt Brace Jovanovich.

Humphreys, Laud. 1970; reprinted 1975. *Tearoom Trade: Impersonal Sex in Public Places.* Chicago: Aldine.

Isaacs, Harold R. 1975. "Basic Group Identity: The Idols of the Tribe." In *Ethnicity: Theory and Experience*, ed. N. Glazer and D. P. Moynihan, pp. 29–52. Cambridge, Mass.: Harvard University Press.

Kass, Drora, and Seymour Martin Lipset. 1979. "Israelis in Exile." *Commentary* 68(5):68–72.

———. 1982. "Jewish Immigration to the United States from 1967 to the Present: Israelis and Others." In *Understanding American Jewry*, ed. M. Sklare, pp. 272–94. New Brunswick, N.J.: Transaction Books.

Katz, Jacob. 1961. *Tradition and Crisis: Jewish Society at the End of the Middle Ages.* New York: Free Press.

Keil, Charles. 1966. *Urban Blues.* Chicago: University of Chicago Press.

Keinan, Amos. 1976. "A Letter to a Yored." *Yedioth Ahronoth* (April 4, Passover issue supplement):5 (also published in *The Emigration from Israel.* Jerusalem: Prime Minister's Office, 1982, pp. 25–26 (in Hebrew).

Kessner, Thomas, and Betty Caroli Boyd. 1981. *Today's Immigrants, Their Stories: A New Look at the Newest Americans.* New York: Oxford University Press.

Korazim, Joseph. 1983. "Israeli Families in New York City: Utilization of Social Services, Unmet Needs and Policy Implications." Ph.D. diss., Columbia University, School of Social Work.

Lahis, Shmuel. 1980. "Israelis in the United States—a Report." Stencil, Jerusalem: Jewish Agency (in Hebrew).

Lamdani, Reuven. 1983. "Emigration from Israel." *Economic Quarterly* 30:462–78 (in Hebrew).

Langer, Susanne K. 1953. *Feeling and Form.* New York: Scribner's.

Langness, L. L., and Gelya Frank. 1981. *Lives: An Anthropological Approach to Biography.* Novato, Calif.: Chandler and Sharp.

Laqueur, Walter. 1972. *A History of Zionism.* New York: Holt, Rinehart and Winston.

Lazerwitz, Bernard, and Michael Harrison. 1979. "American Jewish Denominations: A Social and Religious Profile," *American Sociological Review* 44:656–66.

Levi, G. Linda. 1986. "Israelis in New York and the Federation of Jewish Philanthropies: A Study of Anomie and Reconnection." *Contemporary Jewry* 7:167–80.

Liebman, Charles, and Eliezer Don-Yehia. 1983. *Civil Religion in Israel.* Berkeley: University of California Press.

Liebow, Elliot. 1967. *Tally's Corner.* Boston: Little, Brown.

Lyman, Stanford M., and Marvin B. Scott. 1975. *The Drama of Social Reality.* New York: Oxford University Press.

Meyer, Leonard B. 1956. *Emotion and Meaning in Music.* Chicago: University of Chicago Press.

Mitchell, Douglas, and Leonard Plotnicov. 1975. "The Lubavitch Movement: A Study in Contexts." *Urban Anthropology* 4:303–15.

Nahshon, Gad. 1976. "Israelis in America—Moral Lepers." *Midstream* 22(8):46–48.

Netzer, Ephi. 1983. *To Sing with Ephi Netzer.* Tel Aviv: Histadruth (in Hebrew).

Newton, Esther. 1972; reprinted 1979. *Mother Camp: Female Impersonators in America.* Chicago: University of Chicago Press.

Paltiel, Ari M. 1986. "Migration of Israelis Abroad: A Survey of Official Data from Selected Countries." Supplement to the *Monthly Bulletin of Statistics* 37(6):43–80. Jerusalem: Central Bureau of Statistics.

Paz, Octavio. 1981. *The Labyrinth of Solitude.* New York: Grove Press.

Peacock, James L. 1968. *Rites of Modernization.* Chicago: University of Chicago Press.

Pesachzon, Raphi, and Thelma Eligon. 1981, 1983, 1984. *The Israeli Sing-Along: 200 Best Loved Israeli Songs.* Vols. 1, 2, 3. Tel Aviv: Kinneret (in Hebrew).

Rabi, Zion. 1976. "Emigration from Israel." Supplement to the *Monthly Bulletin of Statistics*, no. 10. Jerusalem: Central Bureau of Statistics.

———. 1978. "Emigration from Israel, 1948–1977." *Economic Quarterly* 25:348–58 (in Hebrew).

———. 1986. "The Emigration from Israel, 1948–1984." *Haaretz* (January 5):9 (in Hebrew).

Ratosh, Yonathan. 1974. "The New Hebrew Nation." In *Unease in Zion,* ed. E. Ben Ezer. New York: Quadrangle Books.

Rischin, Moses. 1962. *The Promised City: New York's Jews, 1870–1914.* Cambridge, Mass.: Harvard University Press.

Ritterband, Paul. 1969. "The Determinants of Motives of Israeli Students Studying in the United States." *Sociology of Education* 42:330–49.

———. 1986. "Israelis in New York." *Contemporary Jewry* 7:113–26.

Ritterband, Paul, and Steven M. Cohen. 1984. "Sample Design and Population Estimation: The Experience of the New York Jewish Population Study (1981–1984)." In *Perspectives in Jewish Population Research,* ed. S. M. Cohen, J. S. Woocher, and B. A. Phillips, pp. 81–96. Boulder, Colo.: Westview Press.

Sabatello, P. Etan. 1978. "The Emigration from Israel and Its Characteristics." *Betfuzot Hagola* 19:63–76.

References

Sanjek, Roger. 1978. "A Network Method and Its Uses in Urban Anthropology." *Urban Anthropology* 37:257–68.

Saran, Permatma, and Edwin Eames, eds., 1980. *The New Ethnics: Asian Indians in the United States.* New York: Praeger.

Saran, Permatma, and J. Leonhard-Spark. 1980. "Attitudinal and Behavioral Profile." In *The New Ethnics: Asian Indians in the United States,* ed. P. Saran and E. Eames, pp. 163–76. New York: Praeger.

Schmalenbach, Herman. 1961. "The Sociological Category of Communion." In *Theories of Society,* ed., T. Parsons, pp. 331–47. New York: Free Press.

Segre, Dan V. 1980. *A Crisis of Identity: Israel and Zionism.* Oxford: Oxford University Press.

Shaffir, William. 1974. *Life in a Religious Community.* Toronto: Holt, Rinehart and Winston.

Shapiro, Daniel. 1978. "Services to Jews from Israel—a Memorandum." Stencil, Federation of Jewish Philanthropies of New York.

Shapiro, Yonathan. 1980. "The End of a Dominant Party System." In *The Elections in Israel—1977,* ed. A. Arian, pp. 23–38.

Shemer, Naomi. 1967, 1975, 1982. *All My Songs.* Vols. 1, 2, 3. Tel Aviv: Yedioth Ahronoth (in Hebrew).

Shokeid, Moshe. 1971. *The Dual Heritage: Immigrants from the Atlas Mountains in an Israeli Village.* Manchester: Manchester University Press (augmented ed., 1985. New Brunswick, N.J.: Transaction Books).

———. 1974. "An Anthropological Perspective on Ascetic Behavior and Religious Change." In Deshen and Shokeid, *The Predicament of Homecoming: Cultural and Social Life of North African Immigrants in Israel,* pp. 64–94. Ithaca, N.Y.: Cornell University Press.

———. 1979. "The Decline of Personal Endowment of Atlas Mountains Religious Leaders in Israel." *Anthropological Quarterly* 52:186–97.

———. 1982. "The Regulation of Aggression in Daily Life: Aggressive Relationships among Moroccan Immigrants in Israel." *Ethnology* 21:271–81.

———. 1984. "Cultural Ethnicity in Israel: The Case of Middle Eastern Jews' Religiosity." *Association for Jewish Studies Review* 9:249–72.

Shokeid, Moshe, and Shlomo Deshen. 1982. *Distant Relations: Ethnicity and Politics among Arabs and North African Jews in Israel.* New York: Praeger Publishers and J. F. Bergin Publishers.

Simmel, George. 1950. *The Sociology of George Simmel.* Trans. and ed. Kurt H. Wolf. New York: Free Press.

Singer, Merril. 1978. "Chassidic Recruitment and the Local Context." *Urban Anthropology* 7:373–83.

Singer, Milton. 1955. "The Cultural Patterns of Indian Civilization." *Far Eastern Quarterly* 15:23–36.

Siu, Paul C. P. 1952. "The Sojourner." *American Journal of Sociology* 58:34–44.

Smooha, Sammy. 1978. *Israel: Pluralism and Conflict.* Berkeley: University of California Press.

Sobel, B. Zvi. 1983. "Unease in Zion: The New Israeli Exile." In *Diaspora: Exile and the Jewish Condition*, ed. E. Levine, pp. 247–57. New York: Jason Aronson.

———. 1986. *Migrants from the Promised Land*. New Brunswick, N.J.: Transaction Books.

Stark, Tadeusz. 1967. "The Economic Desirability of Migration." *International Migration Review* 1:3–22.

Statistical Abstract of Israel 1985 (no. 36). Jerusalem: Central Bureau of Statistics.

Styles, Joseph. 1979. "Outsider/Insider: Researching Gay Baths." *Urban Life* 8:135–52.

Tabory, Ephraim. 1983. "Reform and Conservative Judaism in Israel: A Social and Religious Profile." *American Jewish Year Book*, 83:41–61.

Toren, Nina. 1976. "Return to Zion: Characteristics and Motivations of Returning Emigrants." *Social Forces* 54:546–58.

Turner, Victor. 1967. "Betwixt and Between: The Liminal Period in *Rites de Passage*." In Turner, *The Forest of Symbols*, pp. 93–111. Ithaca, N.Y.: Cornell University Press.

Ugalde, Antonio, Frank D. Bean, and Gilbert Cardenas. 1979. "International Migration from the Dominican Republic: Findings from a National Survey." *International Migration Review* 13:235–54.

van den Berghe, Pierre L. 1981. *The Ethnic Phenomenon*. New York: Elsevier.

van Gennep, Arnold. 1960. *The Rites of Passage*. Trans. Monika B. Vizedom and Gabrielle L. Caffee. Chicago: University of Chicago Press.

Varma, Baidya Nath. 1980. "Indians as New Ethnics: A Theoretical Note." In *The New Ethnics: Asian Indians in the United States*, ed. P. Sarna and E. Eames, pp. 29–41. New York: Praeger.

Waxman, Chaim I. 1976. "The Centrality of Israel in American Jewish Life: A Sociological Analysis." *Judaism* 25:175–87.

Whyte, William F. 1955. *Street Corner Society*, 2d ed. Chicago: University of Chicago Press.

Yehoshua, A. B. 1981. *Between Right and Right*. Garden City, N.Y.: Doubleday (first published in Hebrew, 1980. *Bezekhut Hanormaliyut* [For the Sake of Normality]. Tel Aviv: Schoken).

Zerubavel, Yael. 1986. "The 'Wandering Israeli' in Contemporary Israeli Literature." *Contemporary Jewry* 7:127–40.

Index

Index

Waxman, C. I., 4
Weiss, Carol, 199
Whyte, W. F., 16

Yehoshua, A. B., 7, 50, 208
Yerida, definition of, 3, 20. *See* also
   Stigma attached to *yordim*

Yordim. See Yerida

Zerubavel, Yael, 6
Zionism, 4, 126, 135, 160

Library of Congress Cataloging-in-Publication Data

Shokeid, Moshe.
    Children of circumstances: Israeli emigrants in New York/Moshe
Shokeid.
        p.   cm.—(Anthropology of contemporary issues)
    Bibliography: p.
    Includes index.
    ISBN 0-8014-2078-4.   ISBN 0-8014-9489-3 (pbk.)
    1. Israelis—New York (N.Y.) 2. Jews—New York (N.Y.) 3. Immigrants—
New York (N.Y.) 4. Queens (New York, N.Y.)—Emigration and
immigration. 5. New York (N.Y.)—Emigration and immigration. 6. Israel—
Emigration and immigration. I. Title. II. Series.
F128.68.Q4S56   1988   306'.08992707472—dc19   87-23934